HRAC2

# Mac® Computer Basics

Lisa Lee

# Contents

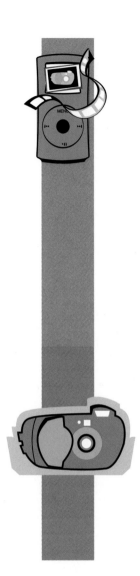

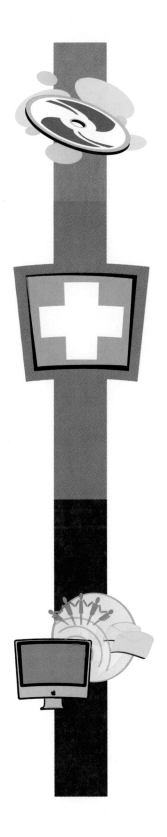

# EASY MAC® COMPUTER BASICS

ISBN-13: 978-0-789-73808-0
ISBN-10: 0-7897-3808-2

*Library of Congress Cataloging-in-Publication data is on file.*

Printed in the United States of America

First Printing: August 2008

## TRADEMARKS

All terms mentioned in this book that are known to be trademarks or service marks have been appropriately capitalized. Que Publishing cannot attest to the accuracy of this information. Use of a term in this book should not be regarded as affecting the validity of any trademark or service mark.

## WARNING AND DISCLAIMER

Every effort has been made to make this book as complete and as accurate as possible, but no warranty or fitness is implied. The information provided is on an "as is" basis. The author and the publisher shall have neither liability nor responsibility to any person or entity with respect to any loss or damages arising from the information contained in this book.

## BULK SALES

Que Publishing offers excellent discounts on this book when ordered in quantity for bulk purchases or special sales. For more information, please contact

**U.S. Corporate and Government Sales**
**1-800-382-3419**
**corpsales@pearsontechgroup.com**

For sales outside of the U.S., please contact

**International Sales**
**international@pearson.com**

**Associate Publisher**
Greg Wiegand

**Acquisitions Editor**
Laura Norman

**Managing Editor**
Patrick Kanouse

**Project Editor**
Seth Kerney

**Copy Editor**
Keith Cline

**Indexer**
Ken Johnson

**Proofreader**
Arle Writing and Editing

**Technical Editor**
Paul Sihvonen-Binder

**Publishing Coordinator**
Cindy Teeters

**Book Designer**
Anne Jones

# ABOUT THE AUTHOR

**Lisa Lee** is an avid Mac user. She works at Apple and is the author of several best-selling Mac books, including *Easy iMac, Easy iBook, Introducing Adobe Photoshop Elements,* and *Upgrading and Repairing Your Mac.* She has also written about digital photography, networks, and operating systems. Lisa has also worked at Microsoft, where she worked on WebTV, MSNTV, UltimateTV, and Windows Media Center. When she's not writing, she enjoys painting, drawing, digital photography, and an occasional babysitting gig.

# DEDICATION

*This book is dedicated to Annika Brown, who loves dragging and clicking in Mac OS X Leopard, iTunes, Safari, and who likes watching Pixar movies.*

# ACKNOWLEDGMENTS

A big thank you to Laura Norman for all her expertise and help putting this book together. Thanks to the many, many wonderful folks at Pearson Education for bringing this book to you. Naturally, thanks to Apple for making so many cool products: Macs, iPods, iPhones, Mac OS X, Safari, iTunes, iPhoto, and Pages.

Thanks to all my friends and family, and especially to all the folks at Apple, Microsoft, and Google for being so supportive and passionate about technology. Also, special thanks to Mike, Mom and Dad, and the Brown family for all your support and love. A special thank you to Anne Clarke for helping many, many folks learn how to use Macs. This book is for you!

# WE WANT TO HEAR FROM YOU!

As the reader of this book, *you* are our most important critic and commentator. We value your opinion and want to know what we're doing right, what we could do better, what areas you'd like to see us publish in, and any other words of wisdom you're willing to pass our way.

As an associate publisher for Que Publishing, I welcome your comments. You can email or write me directly to let me know what you did or didn't like about this book—as well as what we can do to make our books better.

*Please note that I cannot help you with technical problems related to the topic of this book. We do have a User Services group, however, where I will forward specific technical questions related to the book.*

When you write, please be sure to include this book's title and author as well as your name, email address, and phone number. I will carefully review your comments and share them with the author and editors who worked on the book.

Email:    feedback@quepublishing.com

Mail:     Greg Wiegand
          Associate Publisher
          Que Publishing
          800 East 96th Street
          Indianapolis, IN 46240 USA

# READER SERVICES

Visit our website and register this book at informit.com/register for convenient access to any updates, downloads, or errata that might be available for this book.

# IT'S AS EASY AS 1-2-3

Each part of this book is made up of a series of short, instructional lessons, designed to help you understand basic information.

**1** Each step is fully illustrated to show you how it looks onscreen.

**2** Each task includes a series of quick, easy steps designed to guide you through the procedure.

**3** Items that you select or click in menus, dialog boxes, tabs, and windows are shown in **bold**.

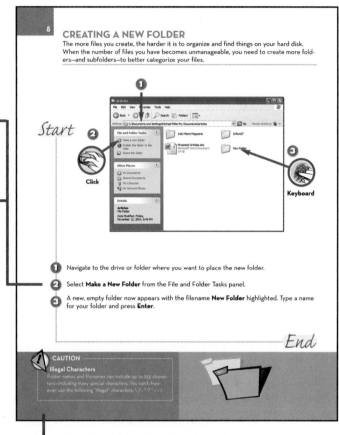

### 8 CREATING A NEW FOLDER

The more files you create, the harder it is to organize and find things on your hard disk. When the number of files you have becomes unmanageable, you need to create more folders—and subfolders—to better categorize your files.

*Start*

**Click**

**Keyboard**

**1** Navigate to the drive or folder where you want to place the new folder.

**2** Select **Make a New Folder** from the File and Folder Tasks panel.

**3** A new, empty folder now appears with the filename **New Folder** highlighted. Type a name for your folder and press **Enter**.

*End*

**CAUTION**
**Illegal Characters**
Folder names and filenames can include up to 255 characters—including many special characters. You can't, however, use the following "illegal" characters: \ / : * ? " < > |

**Drag**

**How to Drag:**
Point to the starting place or object. Hold down the mouse button, move the mouse to the new location, then release the button.

**Click**

**Tips, notes and cautions** give you a heads-up for any extra information you may need while working through the task.

**Click:**
Click the mouse button once.

**Double-click:**
Click the mouse button twice in rapid succession.

**Keyboard**

**Click & Type:**
Click once where indicated and begin typing to enter your text or data.

**Selection:**
Highlights the area onscreen discussed in the step or task.

**Pointer Arrow:**
Highlights an item on the screen you need to point to or focus on in the step or task.

# INTRODUCTION

It's hard to believe the first Macintosh was introduced in 1984. Today, they're as popular as ever. The iMac, MacBook, Mac Pro, MacBook Air, and Mac mini all run Mac OS X Leopard. You can also run a Microsoft Windows operating system on any Mac with an Intel processor. Wait, there's more! Sync an iPod, iPhone, or digital camera to your Mac to organize and share music, movies, and photos.

*Easy Mac Computer Basics* shows you how to set up an iMac and a MacBook, connect them to an iPod and iPhone, and work with a wide range of Apple software. Learn to do things such as synchronize your calendar (iCal) and Address Book with iTunes, play music or movies, organize photos, surf with Safari, and get a handle on text with Pages. Using Macs with iPods and iPhones with OS X Leopard and OS X applications is the focus of this book. Although nearly all the iPod and iPhone tasks in this book show Mac OS X, doing the same task with iTunes on Windows is similar. This book also covers Boot Camp and various Windows computer tasks.

This book is divided into three parts: connecting and customizing Macs, working with applications, and maintaining Macs. The first part shows some elementary but necessary tasks. Part 1 shows you how to set up your Mac and connect it to an iPod or iPhone. Parts 2 and 3 focus on Mac OS X basics such as customizing Mac OS X and selecting, moving, and finding files and folders. Part 4 covers some common tasks with TextEdit, copy/paste, and creating PDFs with your text documents.

The second part of the book covers connecting to the Internet, setting up a wireless home network, and some popular Apple applications: iTunes, iPhoto, Pages, iChat, iCal (calendar), Address Book, and Photo Booth. Learn how to set up a wireless back up with Time Machine and Time Capsule, surf with Safari, organize your music, movies and photos; set up and sync calendar and contact information from your Mac to your iPod or iPhone; and chat with your buddies or create a great-looking document with Pages!

Parts 14, 15, 16, and 17 focus more on your Mac hardware. Part 15 walks you through setting up Boot Camp, running Boot Camp and configuring your Mac to install Windows Vista. Parts 14, 16, and 17 show you how to connect and remove devices, add security to your Mac, and maintain it.

You can read this book from beginning to end, starting gradually and learning as you complete each chapter. If that doesn't float your boat, you can pick any task and dig in to *Easy Mac Computer Basics* and use this book as a reference. Either way, *Easy Mac Computer Basics* lets you see it done, and then do it yourself.

## SETTING UP AND CONNECTING YOUR MAC WITH IPOD AND IPHONE

Macs are more popular than ever. Today's Macs differ significantly from the first 128K Mac Plus introduced in 1984. Many aspects of the Mac that made it cutting-edge technology in 1984 are still what makes today's Macs so desirable; the computer exterior, keyboard, mouse, along with Mac OS X and every application—all are beautifully designed and extremely functional. Apple's iPod is the most popular music and movie player on the market, and the iPhone is a favorite all-in-one device for millions, too.

Part of the beauty of the Mac, and probably a big reason why you purchased one, is the ease of use right out of the box. There's not a lot to getting your Mac up and running. If this is your first computer, however, or if you've never been the one to hook up the hardware, the first few tasks in this part are for you.

The first tasks show you how to set up an iMac and MacBook. The next tasks show you how to connect an iPod or iPhone to a Mac. Finally, the last tasks show you how to sync content from your Mac to an iPod or iPhone.

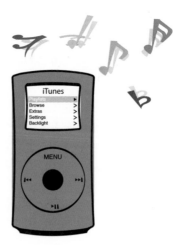

# GET TO KNOW YOUR MAC

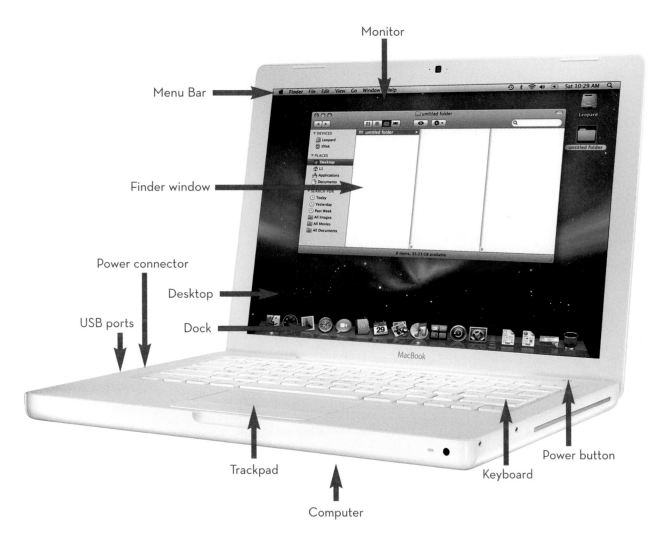

Monitor

Menu Bar

Finder window

Power connector

Desktop

USB ports

Dock

Trackpad

Computer

Keyboard

Power button

Courtesy of Apple

# SETTING UP AN IMAC

Apple's iMac is an all-in-one desktop computer—the monitor and computer are contained in one case; the keyboard and mouse are separate. This task shows you the four simple steps to set up your iMac.

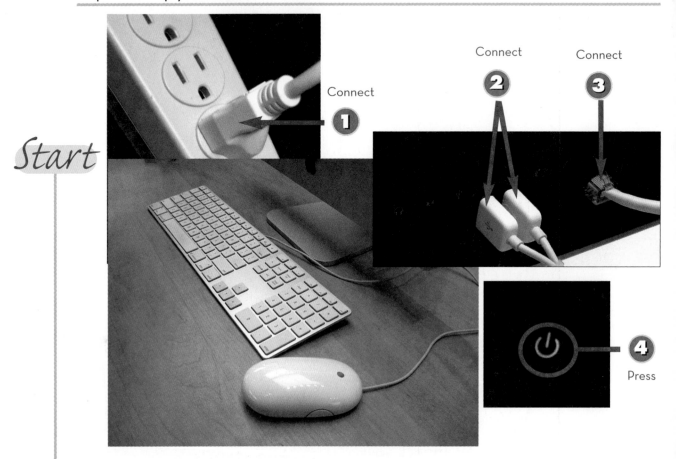

*Start*

Connect ①

Connect ②

Connect ③

Press ④

*End*

① Connect the power cord from the iMac to a power outlet. Place the iMac, keyboard, and mouse on a table or flat surface

② Connect the keyboard cable to a USB port. Connect the mouse cable to a USB port.

③ Connect one end of the Ethernet cable to your iMac and the other to an Ethernet hub or Internet modem.

④ Press the **Power** button. If this is the first time your Mac is powered on, follow the onscreen instructions to set up your Mac. After you've created an account and logged in the Mac Desktop appears.

---

**TIP**
**The Mouse and USB Ports**
The mouse can connect to any USB port on the iMac, including the one on the keyboard. On the iMac, the USB ports are located behind the monitor. On MacBooks, they're located on the left side next to the power connector port.

**NOTE**
**Turning Off Your Computer**
You can put your computer to sleep by choosing **Sleep** from the Apple menu. Alternatively, press the Power button and choose **Sleep**. Choose **Shut Down** from the Apple menu to turn your computer off.

# SETTING UP A MACBOOK

MacBooks are Apple's popular laptop computer. MacBooks have a built-in monitor, keyboard, trackpad, and DVD drive. This task shows you how to set up and power on a MacBook.

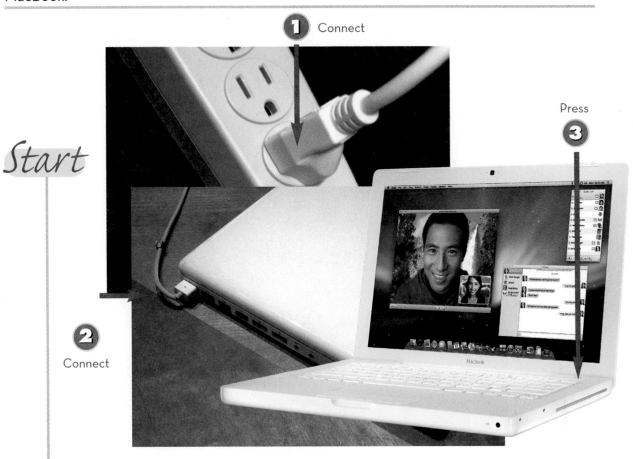

**1** Connect

*Start*

**2**
Connect

**Press**

**3**

 Connect one end of the power cord to a power outlet. The Mac's power adapter can connect directly to a power outlet with the "duck head" adapter or with the extension cable (shown).

 Connect the power cord to the MacBook.

**3** Press the **Power** button. The first time the MacBook starts, follow the onscreen instructions to create an account. The Mac automatically logs in with this account.

*End*

---

**TIP**
### External USB Devices
You can connect a full-size external keyboard or mouse to the USB ports on your MacBook if you get tired of using the built-in keyboard and mouse You can also connect monitors, printers, hard drives, and more. To find out how to connect devices, go to Part 14, "Adding New Devices."

**NOTE**
### Put Your MacBook to Sleep
Instead of powering off your computer, you can put it to sleep. Just close the MacBook lid and the computer will go to sleep. To wake your MacBook from sleep, open its lid.

# NAVIGATING THE DESKTOP

The desktop appears on your screen after Mac OS X starts. The desktop enables you to access any storage devices, applications, files, and DVD or CD media on or inserted into your computer. The Dock appears on the bottom of the desktop and provides easy access to applications and files. This task explains each desktop element.

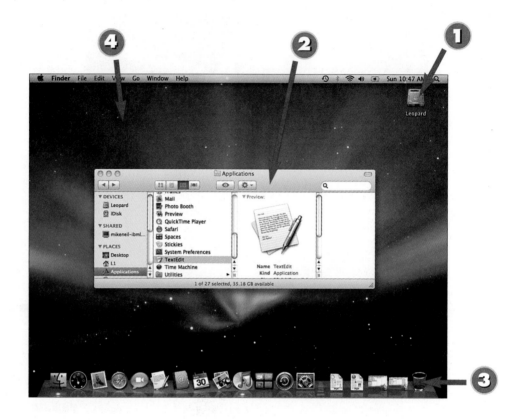

(1) The hard drive stores the operating system (Mac OS X) and all the files and folders on your computer.

(2) Folders open into windows. Folders can store files and more folders.

(3) Remove files or folders by placing them in the Trash. Then choose **Finder ▸ Empty Trash** to remove the files from your Mac.

(4) The desktop is a folder that is always open.

*End*

**NOTE**

**Find Out More About Files and Folders**

To find out more about how to work with files and folders, go to Part 2, "Working with Files and Folders."

**NOTE**

**Find Out More About Mac OS X Settings**

To find out more about Mac OS X settings, go to Part 3, "Customizing Mac OS X Leopard."

# NAVIGATING THE DOCK

The Dock is located at the bottom of the desktop. You can move it to the side and adjust whether it hides when not in use, or always remains visible. Applications, folders, and files can be added or removed from the Dock. This task navigates the icons in the Dock.

*Start*

**① Click**    **② Click**    **④ Click**    **③ Click**

**①** **Application icon in the Dock**. This program is not running. Click the icon to start the program.

**②** **Active application in the Dock.** The white dot indicates this program is running.

**③** **Downloads Folder.** Any files downloaded from a website are placed in the Downloads folder, which resides inside the Documents folder. Access it from the Dock icon or in your User folder in Finder.

**④** **Documents Folder**. This is the default location for storing files on your Mac. The Downloads, Music, Movies, and Pictures folders are located in the Documents folder.

*End*

---

 **NOTE**
**Find Out More About the Internet**
To find out more about how to connect to the Internet, go to Part 6, "Connecting to the Internet."

 **NOTE**
**Find Out More About Applications**
To find out more about applications, go to Part 4, "Installing and Using Applications."

# NAVIGATING FINDER

Finder is the door to Mac OS. It lets you see all the files and access all the features in the operating system. This task shows you some of the basic elements of Finder.

**Click**

**Click**

*Start*

**3 Click**

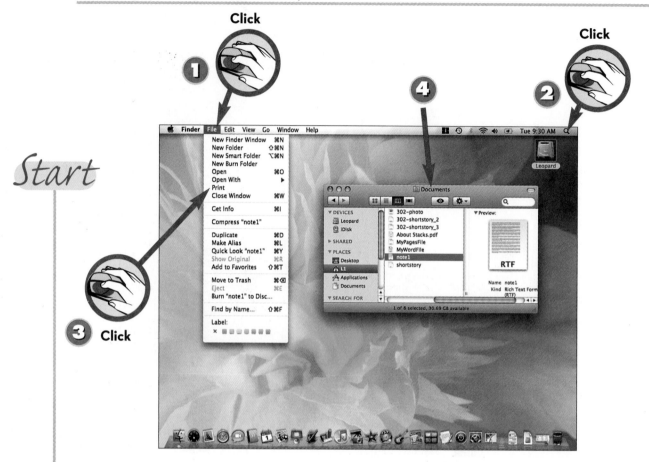

**1** **Finder Menu bar**. Clicking on the desktop brings you to the Finder application. The File, Edit, View, Go, Window and Help menus enable you to view or customize files and folders on your Mac.

**2** **Search**. Type a word or words to search for matching files and folders on your hard drive.

**3** **Print**. Open a Finder window, select a text or image file, and choose the **File > Print** menu. The file is sent to the printer connected to your Mac or connected via a wired or wireless network.

**4** **Finder window**. Navigate files and folders stored on your hard drive. Choose from 4 different views: Icon, List, Columns, and Cover Flow.

*Continued*

 — **NOTE**

**Find Out More About Mac OS X Settings**
To find out more about Mac OS X settings, go to Part 3, "Customizing Mac OS X Leopard."

**Click**

**Click**

8

5

7 **Click**

6 **Click**

5 **Files**. Text, graphics, page layout, photos, and movies are examples of some of the different kinds of files your Mac can work with.

6 **Menu bar shortcuts**. Some of the applications installed on your Mac can be easily access from their shortcut menus located on the menu bar.

7 **Application Menu**. The application menu shows the name of the application and provides menu commands for that application.

8 **Apple Menu.** The Apple menu is always visible regardless of the application running in the foreground. It contains important commands such as Software Update, System Preferences, and Shutdown.

*End*

---

**NOTE**

**Help Menu**

Each application installs help information. Select **Help** > **Mac Help** in Finder to access the Mac OS X help files.

**NOTE**

**Find Out More About Files and Folders**

To find out more about files and folders, go to Part 2, "Working with Files and Folders."

# CONNECTING AN IPOD TO A MAC

Apple's iPod is the most popular MP3 and movie player available today. After you connect your iPod to a Mac via its dock, you can transfer the music and movies you want on your iPod. This task shows you how to connect the iPod to your Mac with a manual sync configuration. You can also follow these steps to connect an iPod Touch to your Mac.

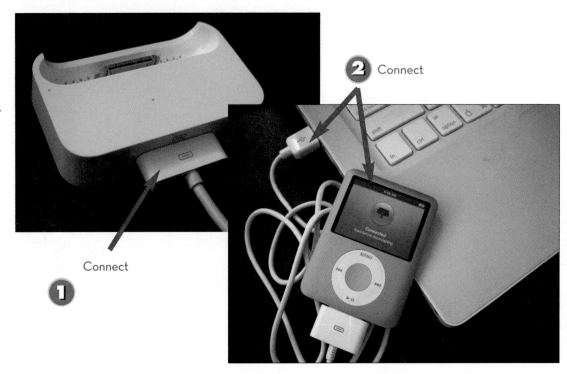

**Start**

**2** Connect

Connect

**1**

**1** Connect the iPod connector to the iPod dock.

**2** Connect the USB connector to your Mac. iTunes is set to automatically open whenever you dock an iPod to a Mac. To disable this behavior, un-check **Open iTunes when this iPod is connected** in the **Summary** tab.

Continued

**NOTE**

**Sleeping and Waking Your iPod**

Hold down the **Play/Pause** button to put your iPod it to sleep. Pressing the **Menu**, **Play/Pause**, or center button wakes it.

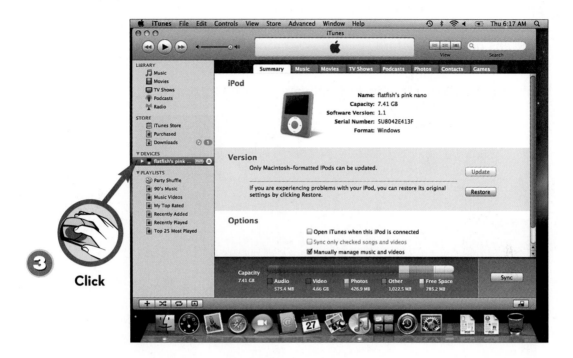

**Click**

③

③ Select your iPod under **Devices** in the iTunes sidebar. View the summary information for your iPod.

*End*

**TIP**

**Free Music and the iTunes Store**

If you don't have any music in iTunes, go to the iTunes store. Free music and TV show downloads are available. The free music title changes every Tuesday. You can use these files to test syncing and playing music and movies on your iPod.

# CONNECTING AN IPHONE TO A MAC

The iPhone is Apple's cell phone that has all the great music and movie-playing capabilities of an iPod. Like the iPod, Apple's iPhone works with iTunes. However, because it is a phone, the first time you connect it to iTunes you need to set up the phone service before you can sync any data to it. Before you can synchronize any data to your iPhone, you must either pick a cell phone provider or migrate an existing cell phone account to your iPhone.

This task shows you how to connect your iPhone to your Mac.

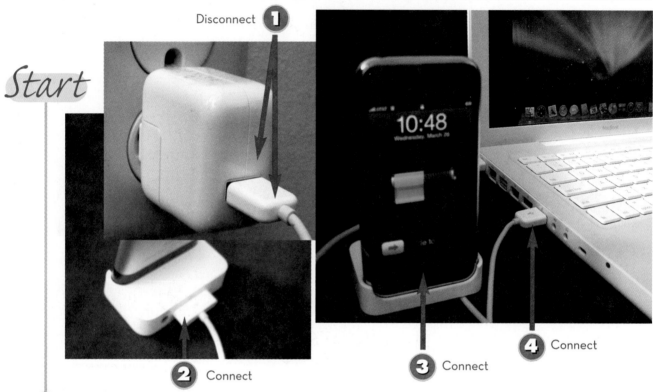

Disconnect **1**

*Start*

**2** Connect

**3** Connect

**4** Connect

**1** Disconnect the USB connector from the power module connected to a power outlet.

**2** Connect the iPhone connector to the iPhone's Dock.

**3** Set the iPhone in its Dock.

**4** Connect the USB connector to your Mac.

*Continued*

**TIP**

**Charging Your iPhone**

When your iPhone or iPod is connected to a Mac, its battery automatically starts recharging.

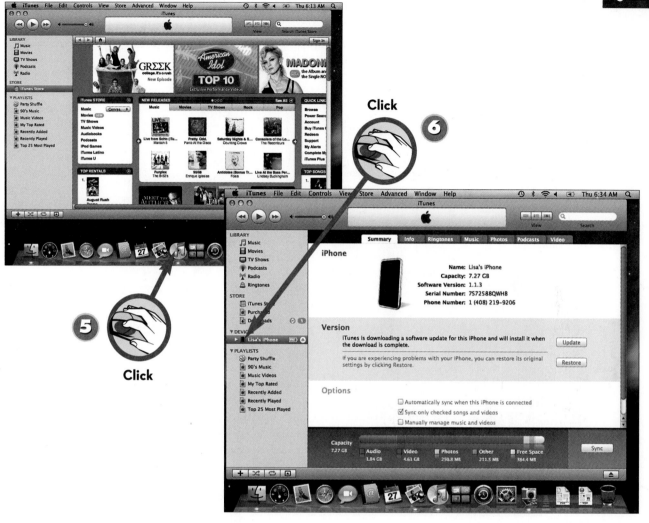

**Click**

**Click**

5 Open iTunes. iTunes opens automatically when your iPhone is docked to your Mac. To disable this, uncheck **Open iTunes when this iPod is connected** in the Summary tab.

6 Select the iPhone under **Devices** in the sidebar. You'll see details about your phone, including the capacity, software version, and serial number on the **Summary** tab.

*End*

---

📝 **NOTE**

**Powering Off Your iPhone**

Hold down the **Power** button for 3 to 5 seconds until the Slide to Power Off screen appears. Slide the red arrow to the right to power off your iPhone.

 **TIP**

**Airplane Mode on the iPhone**

Airplane mode disables wireless cell phone capabilities on your iPhone. To turn off the cell phone on your iPhone, choose **Settings** and turn on **Airplane Mode**. An airplane icon appears at the top of the home screen when your iPhone is in Airplane Mode.

# SYNCING CONTENT TO AN IPOD

When your iPod is connected to your Mac, you can copy music and movies to it using iTunes. This task shows you how to synchronize music and calendar data on your Mac with your iPod.

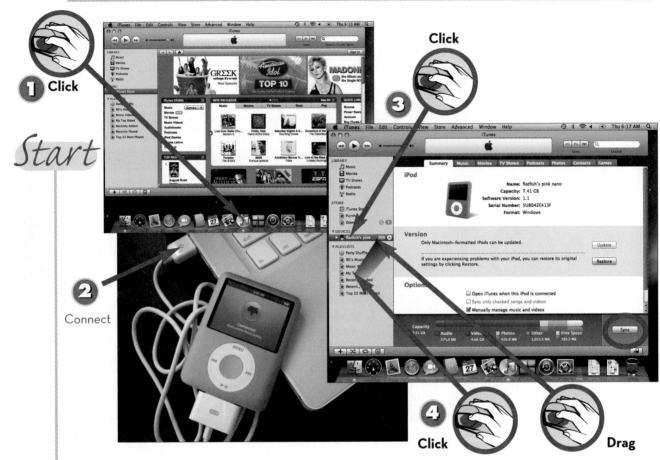

**Click**

**Click**

*Start*

**Connect**

**Click**

**Drag**

**1** Click the iTunes icon on the Dock to open iTunes.

**2** Place the iPod in its dock and be sure the dock is connected to your Mac.

**3** Select the iPod in iTunes. When you connect the iPod for the first time it is empty and iTunes is set to automatically sync whenever the iPod is docked.

**4** Drag and drop a playlist onto the iPod in the Devices list, and then click the **Sync** button. Do not disconnect the iPod while the playlist is syncing.

*Continued*

---

**TIP**
### Locking and Unlocking Your iPod
If you're listening to music or watching a movie and you want to disable the click wheel, lock your iPod. Slide the **Lock** button to the right to lock it. Slide it left to unlock it.

**NOTE**
### Disable Automatic Syncing
When you first set up your iPod, it is set to sync every time you connect it to your Mac. Choose **iTunes** > **Preferences** and then on the **Syncing** tab, check the **Disable automatic syncing for all iPhones and iPods** to turn off automatic syncing.

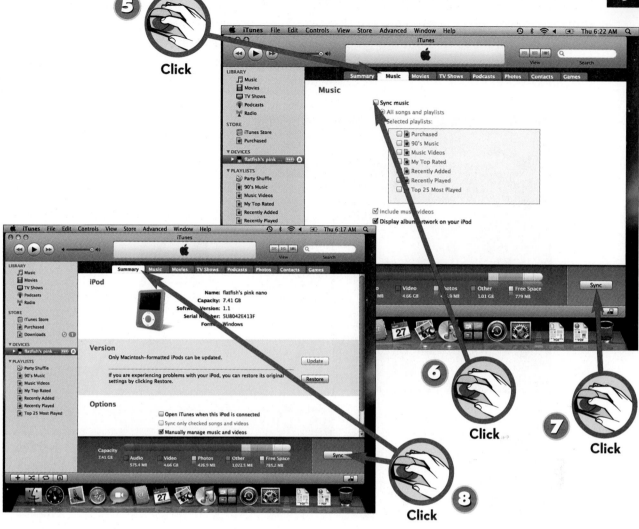

Click

Click

Click

Click

**5** Select the **Music** tab.

**6** Check the **Sync music** check box if you want to select playlists in iTunes to copy to your iPod.

**7** Click the **Sync** button to update your iPod.

**8** Select the **Summary** tab and click **Sync**.

*End*

# SETTING UP AND SYNCING CONTENT TO AN IPHONE

This task shows you how to configure iTunes to synchronize data on your Mac with your iPhone. If you want to find out more about working with music, movies, photos, calendar data, or the Address Book, see the parts later in this book that focus on iTunes, iPhotos, iCal, and Address Book.

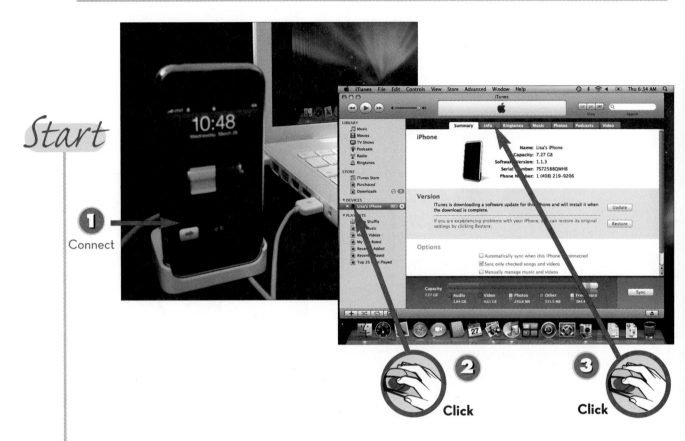

*Start*

**1** Connect

**Click**

**Click**

**1** Connect the iPhone to your Mac. iTunes opens automatically.

**2** Select the iPhone under **Devices** in the Source pane. View the information about your iPhone on the **Summary** tab.

**3** Click the **Info** tab.

*Continued*

**TIP**

**Learn More About iCal**

To find out more about how to use iCal with your Mac and iPhone, go to Part 9, "Managing and Syncing Your Calendar with iCal."

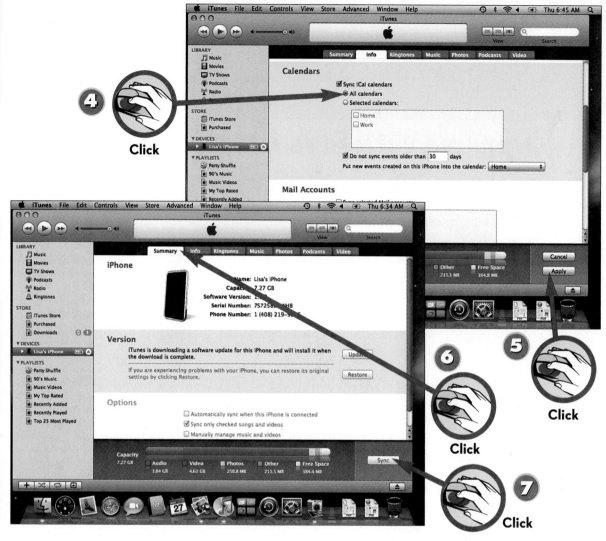

**4** Select the **Sync iCal Calendars** check box and choose settings for how you want iCal to sync with your iPhone.

**5** Click **Apply**.

**6** Select each tab in the iTunes window. If you make any changes, click the **Apply** button. iTunes syncs the data to your iPhone.

**7** Click the **Summary** tab in iTunes. Click the **Sync** button.

*End*

**TIP**

**Disconnecting Your iPhone**

Click the **Eject** button for the iPhone in iTunes to disconnect it from your Mac.

## WORKING WITH FILES AND FOLDERS

The fundamental starting point of learning how to use your Mac is understanding how to work with files and folders. Files store data—anything from images to graphics, music, movies, words, numbers, and so on. You can do a lot of different things with the files on your Mac, such as print, share, and edit them. Your Mac came with a lot of different types of files already on it, and with the use of certain applications such as those included with Mac OS X, iLife, and iWork, you can create your own files that contain data. You can copy pictures from your camera to your Mac, and those also become files that you can store, organize, edit, and share. You can also copy music, movies and photos from your Mac to an iPod or iPhone.

Folders enable you to organize your files, similarly to a filing cabinet. The hard drive is a drawer in the cabinet and each folder can store zero, one, two or hundreds of pieces of paper, or files. Folders can also store other folders; which in turn can store files. If you had to make a map of the folders and files on a hard drive it would resemble a tree.

This part shows you how to navigate, select, move, copy, delete, and share files and folders on your Mac. The first three tasks explore Finder windows, showing you how to navigate files, move and resize windows, and change the window view. Next, learn how to select, move, copy, and delete files and folders. The last set of tasks show you how to share, search for, rename, and compress files.

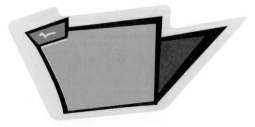

# EXPLORING A FINDER WINDOW

View options

Maximize window

Minimize window

Folder name

Close window

Show/hide toolbar

Next/previous window view

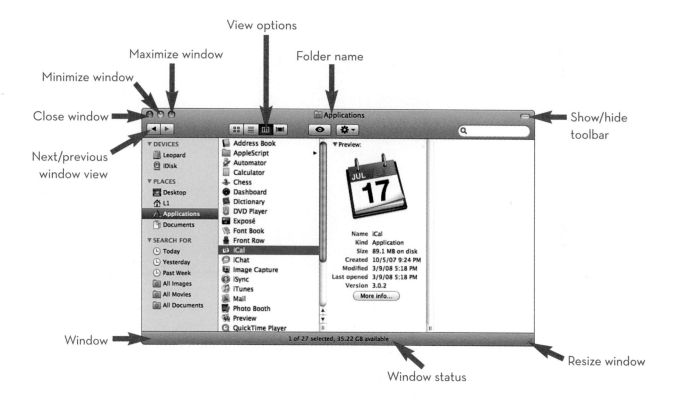

Window

Resize window

Window status

# SHOWING AND HIDING WINDOWS

Before you can work with files and folders, you need to understand how to see them. Folders open into windows. Opening more than one window can make it difficult to access files on your desktop. This task shows you how to hide all windows with the press of a button.

*Start*

**Click**

**Double click**

Press F11 a second time

Press F11

**1** Choose **File** > **New Folder** from the Finder menu.

**2** Open the folder. Double click a folder to open it. Similarly, double-click a file to open it.

**3** Press the **F11** key on the keyboard. All windows move to the nearest edge of the screen.

**4** Press **F11** again. All open windows reappear onscreen.

*End*

**NOTE**
**Learn More About Mac OS X Settings**
To find out more about how to customize Mac OS X, go to Part 3, "Customizing Mac OS X Leopard."

**NOTE**
**More Desktop Function Keys**
Finder is an application. Other programs, such as Text Edit, and iTunes have their own windows. Press **F9** to show all open windows onscreen. Press **F10** to simultaneously show all open Finder windows.

# MOVING AND RESIZING WINDOWS

Moving and growing or shrinking a window are a few of the most common changes folks make so that they can see folder contents, or access frequently used files or folders. This task shows you how to move and resize windows.

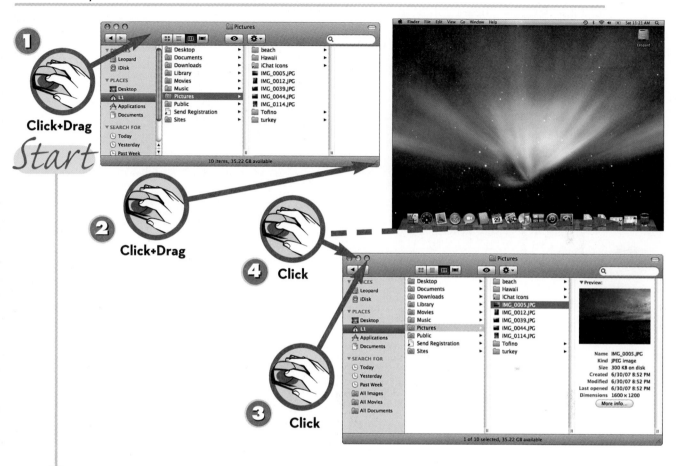

**1** Click the toolbar of the window and drag to move it around the desktop.

**2** Click and drag the lower-right corner of the window to change the window's size.

**3** Click the green **Maximize** button to enlarge the window.

**4** Click the yellow **Minimize** button to minimize the window to the dock. Click the minimized window on the dock to return it to the desktop.

*End*

---

**TIP**

**Hide Toolbar Buttons**

Click the button in the upper-right corner of the window to hide the sidebar and all the toolbar buttons in a window.

**NOTE**

**Toolbar Buttons**

The Toolbar buttons in every Finder window enable you to customize the folder and file view, view a Quicklook image of a file or view a slideshow, search for files, and more.

# CHOOSING A VIEW

Each Finder window can show one of four views. Each view provides a different way of viewing the folders and files in a window. Some, such as Cover Flow view and Icon view, work better with photos or graphics. Others, such as Columns view, are great for navigating folders. This task shows you activate each window view.

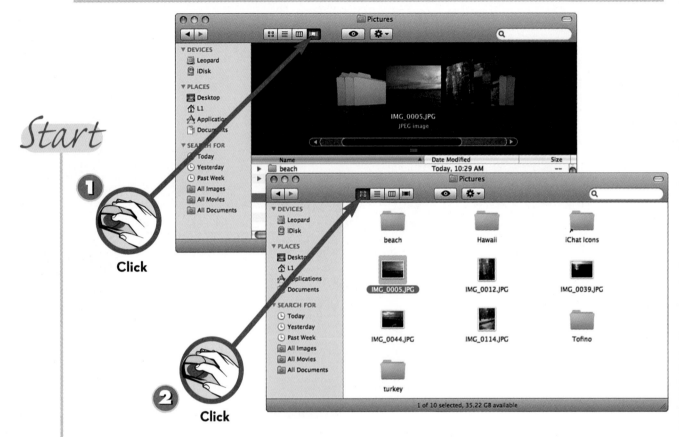

*Start*

**Click**

 **Click**

**Click**

1. In an open window, click the **Cover Flow view** button to see the files appear as pictures in the window. Drag the scrollbar to flip through the files.

2. Click the **Icon view** button to see each file and folder as thumbnails in the main part of the window.

*Continued*

---

**TIP**

**Show the Path Bar**

Choose **View > Show Path Bar** to display the path (the folders and sub-folders in which a selected file is stored) at the bottom of each window. Alternatively, ⌘-clicking the name of the folder also displays its path. This proves helpful when you are viewing files in Icon or List view.

**NOTE**

**Keyboard Shortcuts**

Each window view has a keyboard shortcut. Press ⌘-1 to show Icon view, ⌘-2 to show List view, ⌘-3 for Columns, and ⌘-4 for Cover Flow view.

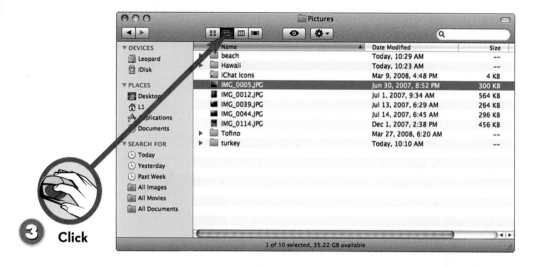

**3** Click

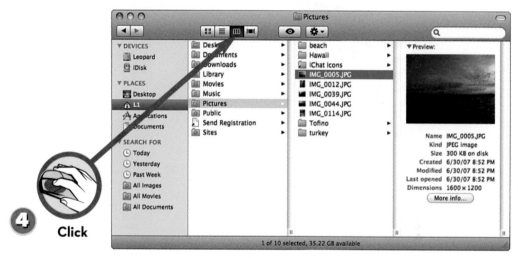

**4** Click

**3** Click the **List view** button to view the file and folder names as a list in the main window.

**4** Click the **Columns view** button to view the folders and files in separate columns. This proves especially useful when viewing multiple files within folders.

*End*

# SELECTING AND MOVING FILES

You can select one or more files or folders by holding down a modifier key, such as the Shift or ⌘ key while clicking on a file or folder. After the files and folders are selected you can move them to a new location. This task shows you how to select and move more than one file or folder at a time.

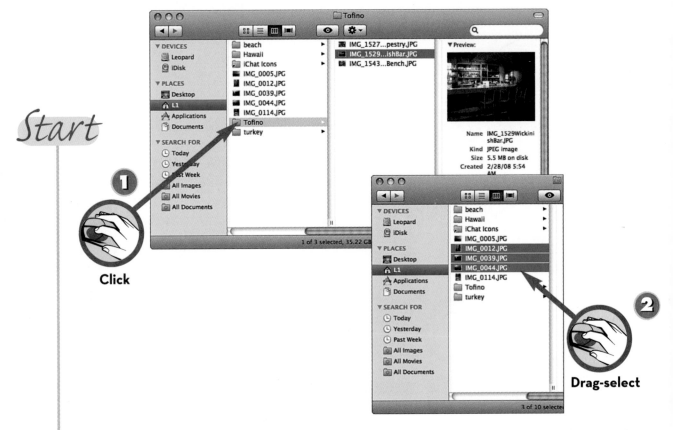

*Start*

**Click**

**Drag-select**

① Click a file and drag it onto a folder. Release the mouse button to move the file into that folder.

② Drag over a series of files or folders to select them. You can then move them as a group to another folder location if you want by dragging and dropping.

*Continued*

**TIP**

**Assigning Labels**

Assigning a color to a file can help you find the file you want a little faster. Select a file and choose a label from the **Edit** menu in Finder. Alternatively, Control-click the file and pick a color. The color appears around the file or folder icon and file name.

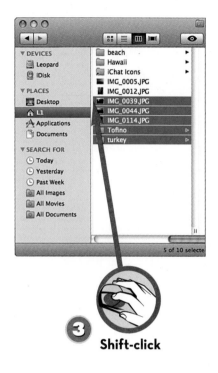

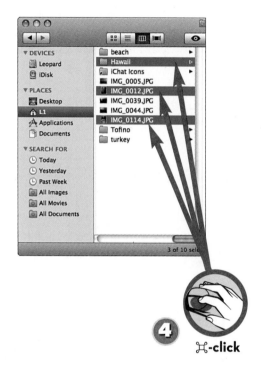

**Shift-click**

**⌘-click**

③ Click a file or folder, and then Shift-click another file or folder to select a continuous group of files or folders. This works the same as dragging over a group of files or folders to select them.

④ ⌘-click to select files that are not next to each other.

*End*

**NOTE**

**Highlight Color**

To find out how to back up your files with Time Machine, go to Part 17, "Taking Care of Your Mac."

**NOTE**

**Viewing Files on an iPod**

You can select files or folders using the methods in this task. Next, drag and drop them onto an iPod to copy them to that iPod. The same view settings apply when viewing files on an iPod. To find out more about how to use an iPod as a hard drive, go to the task "Using an iPod as a Hard Drive" in Part 14.

# COPYING A FILE OR FOLDER

You can copy a file or folder in a couple of different ways. The easiest way is to drag and drop files. But you can also use menu commands, as you'll see in steps 3 and 4 below.

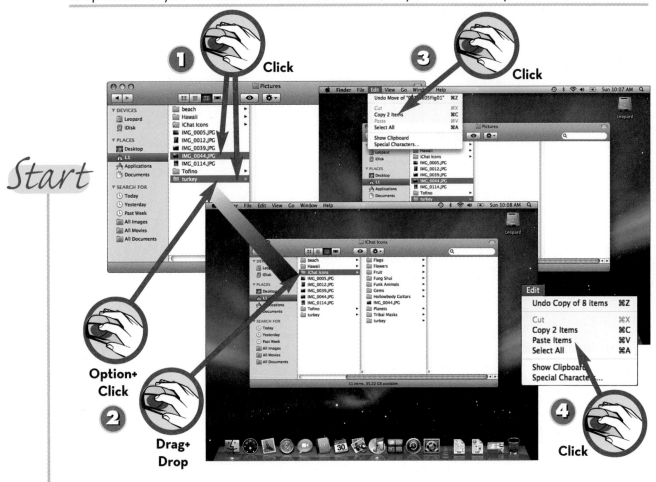

**Start**

Click

Click

Option+
Click

Drag+
Drop

Click

1. Select the file or folder using one of the methods given in the preceding task.

2. Hold down the **Option** key while you drag and drop the file or folder in a new location.

3. Alternatively, choose **Edit** > **Copy** in the menu bar.

4. Open the folder where you want to move the file or folder and choose **Edit** > **Paste Items**.

*End*

---

 **NOTE**

### Cutting Versus Copying

The Edit > Cut command removes the original file from its original location. The Edit > Copy command leaves the original file as-is. Choosing Edit > Paste places the cut or copied file in the new location.

 **TIP**

### Copying Files with the Same Name

Select one or more files and choose **File** > **Duplicate** to copy them. The word *copy* appears at the end of each duplicated file's file name, just before the extension. For example, duplicating **untitled.rtf** produces **untitled copy.rtf**.

# DELETING A FILE OR FOLDER

As you create and share files, you might reach a point where you want to remove files or folders. This task shows you how to delete files, but the process works the same for folders.

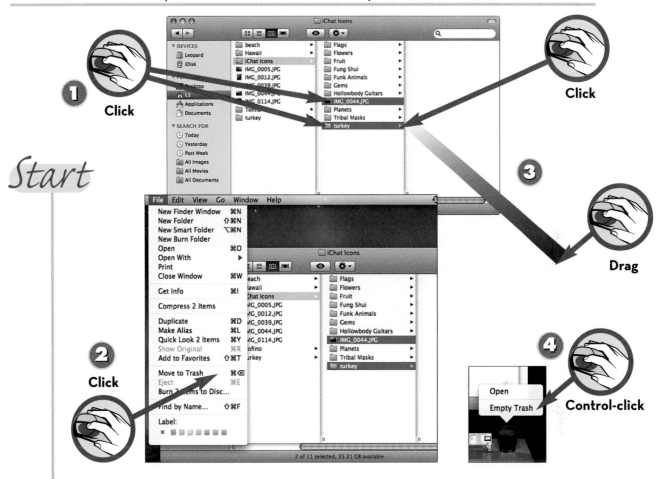

*Start*

**1** Click

**2** Click

**3** Drag

Click

**4** Control-click

2 of 11 selected, 35.21 GB available

Open
Empty Trash

**1** Select a file or folder.

**2** Choose **File** > **Move to Trash** from the menu bar. The selected file moves to the Trash.

**3** Alternatively, you can click and drag the file or folder to the Trash icon on the dock. When the icon is highlighted, release the mouse button.

**4** Control-click the trash and select **Empty Trash** to delete the files from your hard drive.

*End*

---

**TIP**

**Deleting Without a Warning**

Hold down the **Option** key while selecting **Empty Trash** if you want to the delete the files without seeing a warning that your files are being permanently deleted.

**NOTE**

**Secure Emptying Trash**

Choose **Finder** > **Secure Empty Trash** to completely remove the files in the trash from your hard drive. This can take awhile compared to just emptying the trash, which only removes the files when the space on the disk is overwritten by other files.

# SHARING FILES AND FOLDERS

File Sharing enables you to access files if you have a second computer. Of course, you can also share files with others. This task shows you how to turn on File Sharing.

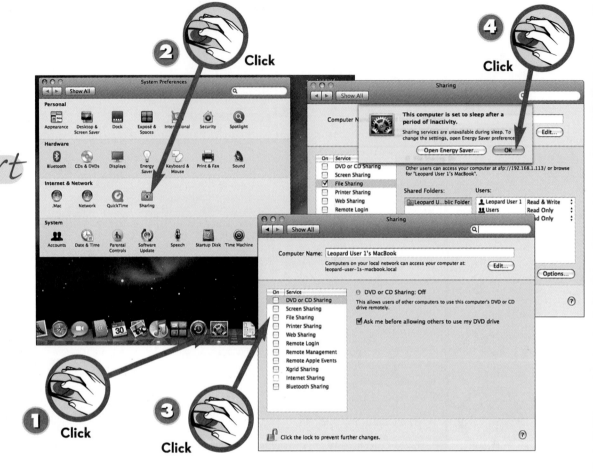

**Click**

**Click**

*Start*

**Click**

**Click**

**Click**

**1**   Choose the **Apple > System Preferences** menu or click its icon on the dock.

**2**   Click the **Sharing** icon.

**3**   Click the **File Sharing** check box to turn on File Sharing. If a check mark already appears in the box, File Sharing has already been turned on.

**4**   If you're sharing files on a MacBook, an alert appears the first time you turn file sharing on. Click **OK**, and then close the Sharing window.

*End*

**TIP**

**Your Public Folder**

When File Sharing is turned on, most users who access your Mac will be able to access files on your machine only if you place them in the Public folder. You can add user accounts to limit access to files on your machine.

# FINDING FILES OR FOLDERS USING SPOTLIGHT

Spotlight is the Mac OS X desktop search engine. As you create, move, or delete files, Spotlight runs quietly in the background and can help you find any file or folder it has indexed.

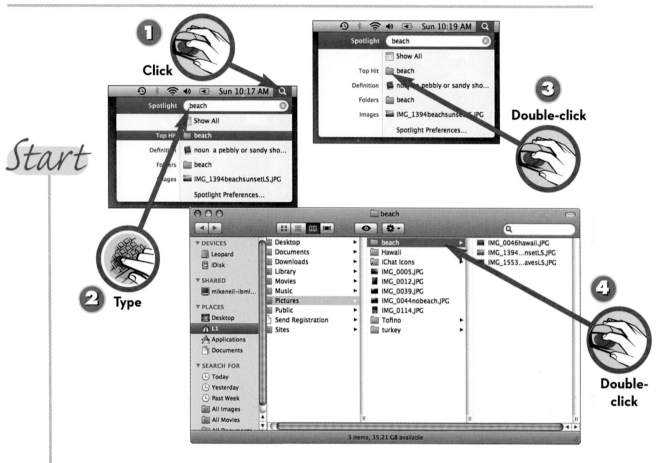

*Start*

**Click**

**Type**

**Double-click**

**Double-click**

*End*

**1** Open Spotlight by clicking the **Magnifying Glass** icon in the status bar.

**2** Type a word or words you want to search for.

**3** Double-click a file or folder in the results list to open it.

**4** View or open the file as you like. If the original application is not installed, The Preview application opens image files; text files open in Text Edit.

**TIP**
**Hints for Naming Files**
Sometimes adding the date or time to the name of the file can help you find a photo or other file that you may have more than one copy of on your hard drive.

**NOTE**
**Keyboard Shortcut**
Press ⌘-**F** in Finder to open the Find panel. The Find panel provides a wider range of criteria you can use to search for files on your Mac.

# RENAMING A FILE OR FOLDER

New folders get a default name of Untitled. Changing the folder name can help you organize files, for example, by date. You can also be creative and rename files to reflect an event, person, place, or thing.

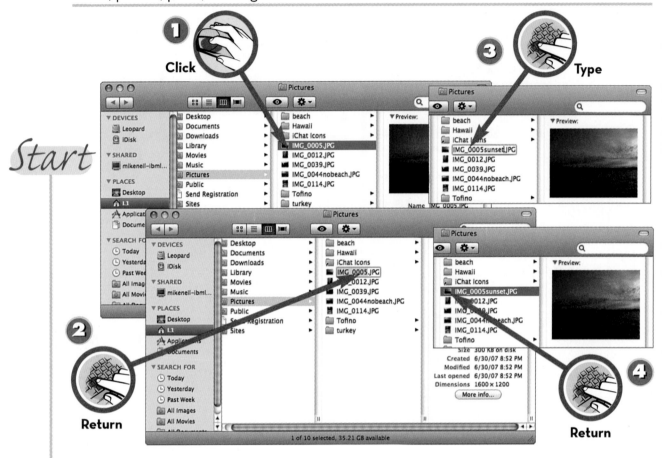

*Start*

**Click**

**Type**

**Return**

**Return**

*End*

① Select a file or folder. (See the task "Selecting and Moving Files" earlier in this part if you need help.)

② Press **Return**.

③ Click in the filename and type a new name. Press the **left-** and **right-arrow** keys to navigate each letter. Be careful not to change the extension (the letters after the period) because that could cause the file to be unusable.

④ Click a blank area on the desktop, or press the **Return** key, to apply your changes.

**NOTE**

**Show or Hide File Name Extensions**

Mac OS X enables you to hide the file name extension for any file. To do this, select a file and choose the **File > Get Info** menu or press ⌘-I. Uncollapse the **Name and Extension** section and check the **Hide extension** checkbox.

**TIP**

**Window Views and File Names**

All the characters in a long file name may not be visible in List or Columns view. Widen the column in List view to view more of the file name, or in Column view, double click the 2 vertical lines at the bottom of the divider to resize the window.

# COMPRESSING FILES AND FOLDERS

If you're sending a file or folder over Mail, or sharing it on the Internet, compressing the files can help send that email faster. This task shows you how to compress a folder of files.

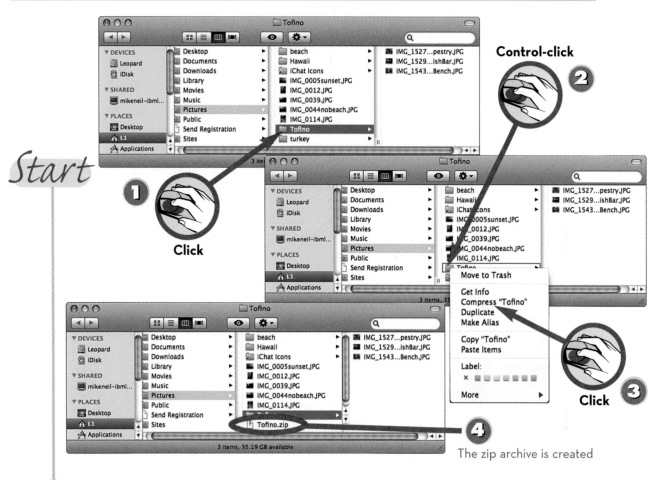

 *Start*

**Click** ①

**Control-click** ②

Move to Trash

Get Info
Compress "Tofino"
Duplicate
Make Alias

Copy "Tofino"
Paste Items

Label:
× ■ ■ ■ ■ ■ ■

More ▶

**Click** ③

Tofino.zip ④

The zip archive is created

 *End*

① Select a file or folder.

② Hold down the **Control** key and click the folder. A contextual menu opens.

③ Choose **Compress (name of the folder or file)** from the context menu. Mac OS X displays a menu bar while the files are being compressed..

④ The zip archive is created.

## TIP
**Uncompressing Files**
Double-click the zipped folder to decompress the files. A folder with each file will appear in the same window as the zip archive.

## NOTE
**Attaching an Archive to Email**
If you have one or more files you want to send in an email, place the files in a folder. Select the files and create an archive, as shown in this task. Drop the resulting zip file into an email and send it. Check the **Send Windows-Friendly Attachments** check box in the Attachment window in the Mail application to enable recipients to open any attachments.

# CUSTOMIZING MAC OS X LEOPARD

Mac OS X is the operating system software for Macs. The operating system is sort of like the "manager" of your Mac. It tells the Mac to start up, shut down, open a file, start an application, and so on, based on your interactions and settings that you can customize. The current version of the Mac operating system as of the printing of this book is called Leopard and is version number 10.5.

You can customize settings such as the keyboard and mouse interaction rates, the desktop picture or screen saver in the System Preferences application. For viewing files, you can customize the way files appear in the windows on your desktop.

This part shows you how to adjust keyboard, mouse, date and time, desktop, and screen saver settings. Adding icons to the dock, renaming your Mac, and selecting a startup disk are also explained in the following tasks.

# SYSTEM PREFERENCES

Change the desktop
picture or screen saver

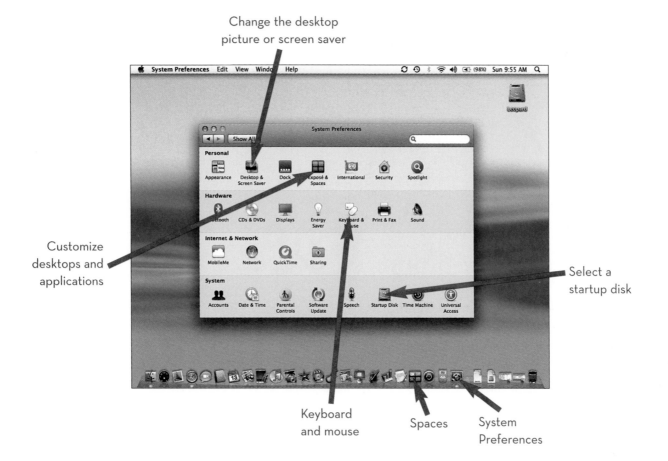

Customize
desktops and
applications

Select a
startup disk

Keyboard
and mouse

Spaces

System
Preferences

# CUSTOMIZING FILE AND FOLDER VIEWS

Each window can have custom settings. You can customize window settings in the Show View Options panel. Each Finder window view, such as Icon, List, Column, and Cover Flow can have custom View Options. This task shows you the view options you can adjust for the Column view.

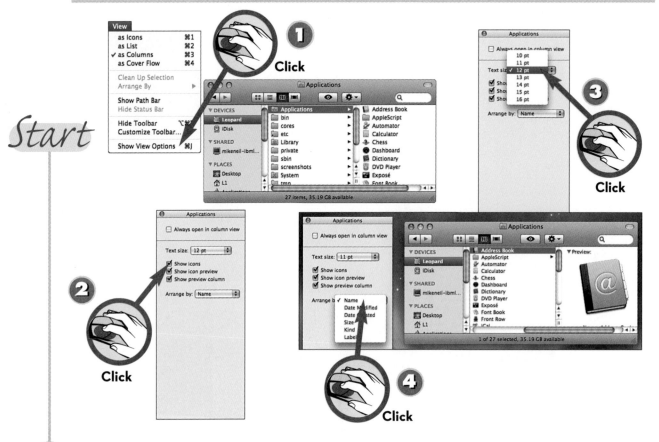

1. Open a window. Select the **Column View** button. Select **View** > **Show View Options**.

2. Choose your icon options. The options vary depending on the view selected in the Finder window.

3. Change the size of the text.

4. Select your arrange options.

 **End**

**Start**

---

### TIP
**Finder Preferences**

Set the default folder that appears when a new window is created from the Finder Preferences General panel. To view Finder preferences, choose **Preferences** from the **Finder** menu.

### TIP
**View Files on Devices**

The same view settings apply when viewing files on an iPod if your iPod is set to Enable Disk Use. To find out more about how to use your iPod as a hard drive, go to Part 14, "Adding New Devices", and check out the "Using an iPod as a Hard Drive" task.

# CUSTOMIZING THE TOOLBAR

Control-click the toolbar of any window to access custom icons. You can add or remove icons from the Customize Toolbar sheet. This changes the toolbar for every open Finder window.

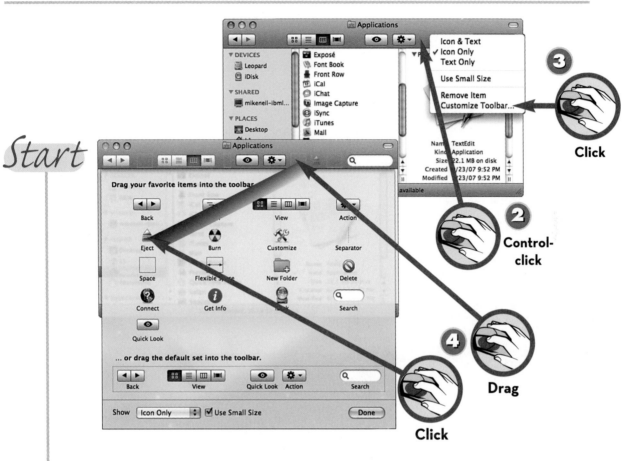

1. Open a window.

2. Hold down the **Control** key and click in an open area of the toolbar.

3. Choose **Customize Toolbar** from the context menu. Alternatively, select **View** > **Customize Toolbar** from the Menu bar.

4. Click and drag icons from the drop-down sheet and drop them on the toolbar to add them.

## TIP
### Toolbar Icon Options
You can use four settings to customize the toolbar appearance in Finder or application windows. You can show icons, icons with text, text only, or small or large size icons. ⌘-**click** the button in the upper right corner of the window to cycle though each Toolbar setting.

## NOTE
### Removing Icons from the Toolbar
Hold down the ⌘ key and drag the icon off the toolbar to remove it from the toolbar.

# SETTING THE DESKTOP PICTURE

The desktop background is what seems to define the personality of a computer. One way to make your Mac your own is to customize what appears on the desktop. Photos are an excellent way to make your desktop background unique. Whether you have one photo or folders of photos, you can show them on your desktop.

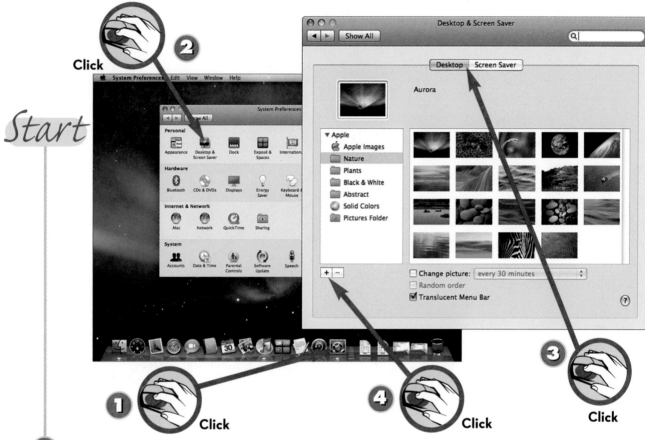

Start

1. Click the **System Preferences** icon on the dock to open the System Preferences window.

2. Click the **Desktop & Screen Saver** icon.

3. Select **Desktop**. The Desktop Picture options appear in the System Preferences window.

4. Click the + (plus sign) button to navigate to a folder that contains photos. Select the **Choose** button to select a file or folder. The folder appears in the left list in the Desktop window. Select it to choose a desktop picture.

*Continued*

---

**TIP**
**iPhoto Albums**
iPhoto albums can be used to select a desktop picture. You can also use any photos stored on your drive.

**NOTE**
**More Settings**
Check the **Translucent Menu Bar** option if you want your desktop picture to show through the menu bar. Check **Random Order** if you want Mac OS to shuffle the order of the images in the selected folder.

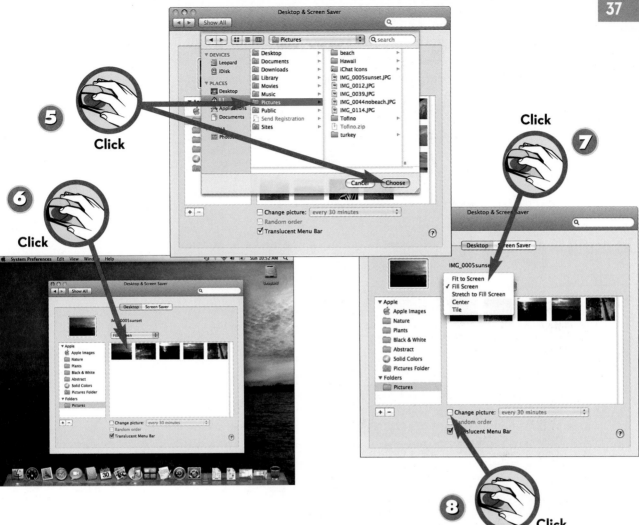

Click

Click

Click

Click

Click

**5** Select the folder that contains the images you want to use for your desktop picture and click **Choose**.

**6** Select a folder containing multiple files or select a single file to use as your background.

**7** Select options from the pop-up menu. The desktop picture will change to match the setting you choose.

**8** Check **Change picture every** and choose the interval for changing the desktop picture.

*End*

---

**NOTE**

**Optimal Image Dimensions**

Because the desktop is usually in a landscape orientation, photos that are in portrait orientation do not work as well as desktop pictures.

**NOTE**

**Desktop Background Shortcut**

**Control-click** the desktop to show the Desktop context menu. Choose the **Change Desktop Background** command to show the Desktop Preferences window.

# CUSTOMIZING THE SCREEN SAVER

Like desktop pictures, screen savers are both entertaining and functional. This task shows you how to select photos for you screen saver and customize hot keys. You will also set the timer for when the screen saver is activated.

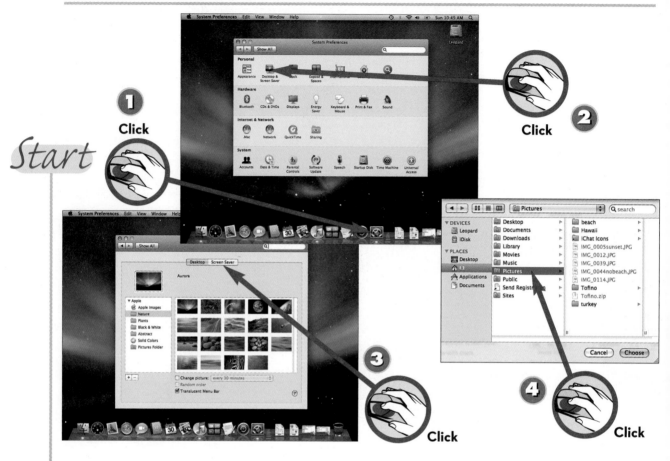

**1**   Click the **System Preferences** icon on the dock to open the System Preferences window.

**2**   Click the **Desktop & Screen Saver** icon.

**3**   Click the **Screen Saver** tab.

**4**   Select a folder that contains the image you want to use as your screen saver and click **Choose**.

*Continued*

---

**NOTE**

**Shortcuts**

Click **Hot Corners** to assign hot corners to enable or disable the screen saver manually. After you set a hot corner, you just move your cursor to the corner that you chose and your screen saver will start immediately rather than waiting the set amount of time for activating.

**TIP**

**Energy-Saver Options**

Make sure your machine is not set to go to sleep before your screen saver activates. Go to the **Energy Saver** panel in System Preferences to adjust these settings. A warning appears in System Preferences if the screen saver is set to activate after the machine is set to sleep or shut down.

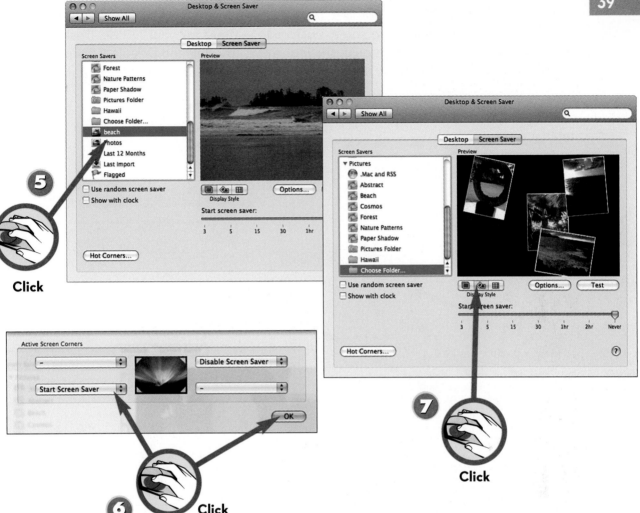

**Click**

5  Select an iPhoto album.

6  Select the **Hot Corners** button in the Screen Saver window. Pick **Enable** or **Disable Screen Saver** from the drop-down menu. Click **OK**.

7  Choose a display style for the screen saver images. You can choose from Slideshow or Collage. If iPhoto is installed, the Mosaic option is available.

*End*

**NOTE**
**Randomize Screen Savers**
Check the **Use Random Screen Saver** check box to have Mac OS X randomly pick any of the screen savers in the list when it goes to Screen Saver Mode.

**NOTE**
**Screen Saver Options**
Select the **Options** button to customize screen saver settings. Settings in the Options sheet vary depending on the Screen Saver and Display Style selected in the Screen Saver window.

# ADJUSTING MOUSE SETTINGS

The mouse preferences enable you to customize settings for your mouse. Desktop Macs with a traditional one-button mouse show only the Tracking and Double-Click speed settings. Trackpads on MacBooks support the additional settings shown in this task.

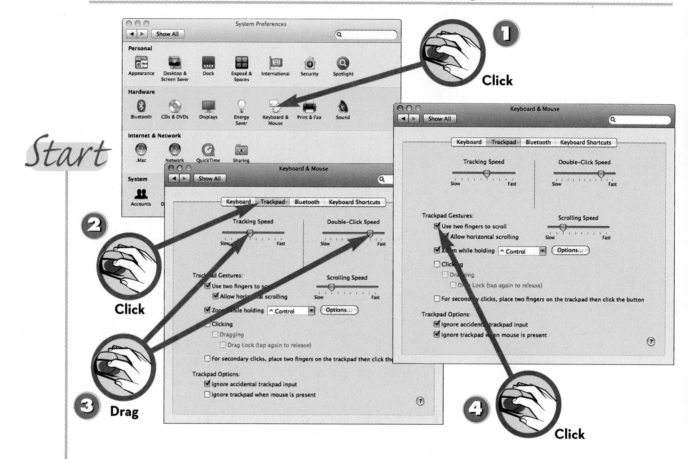

*Start*

*End*

**1** In the System Preferences window, click the **Keyboard & Mouse** icon.

**2** Select **Trackpad** if you have a MacBook like I do. If you have a Mac that uses a traditional mouse, select **Mouse**.

**3** Drag the slide control to set the tracking or double-click speed.

**4** Change any of the available options so that your trackpad works the way you want it to.

**NOTE**

**Mighty Mouse**

Some mice, like Apple's Mighty Mouse, have more features than a one-button mouse. The Mouse System Preferences panel will show different settings for the Mighty Mouse in comparison. For example, Mighty Mouse enables you to assign custom keys, such as F12, to any of its four buttons.

# CHANGING KEYBOARD SETTINGS

There are three main settings for keyboards: adjusting the key repeat and delay until repeat rates, and a check box for changing the function key behavior. You can also customize keyboard shortcuts and choose how tabbing behavior works in applications. This task shows you how to customize keyboard and keyboard shortcut settings.

**Start**

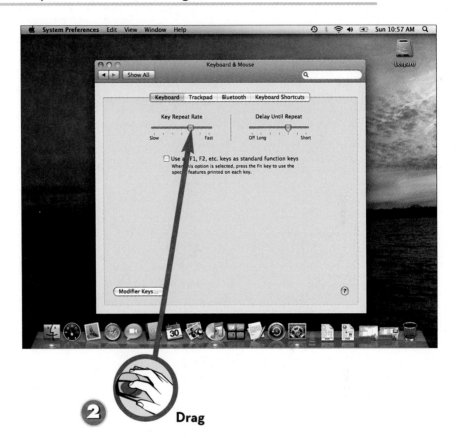

**1** Click

**2** Drag

**1** Click the **Keyboard & Mouse** icon in the System Preferences window.

**2** Adjust the **Key Repeat Rate** or **Delay Until Repeat** by dragging its slider.

Continued

## NOTE
**Keyboard Shortcuts**
Aside from the essential task of typing, the next most powerful keyboard feature is typing keyboard shortcuts to access menu commands or tools in applications.

## NOTE
**Keyboard Keys**
Most desktop keyboards have the standard alphabet keys, 15 function keys, navigation (arrow) keys, and page and home/end page, and a number keypad. MacBooks have smaller keyboards, supporting only 12 function keys with the alphabet keys.

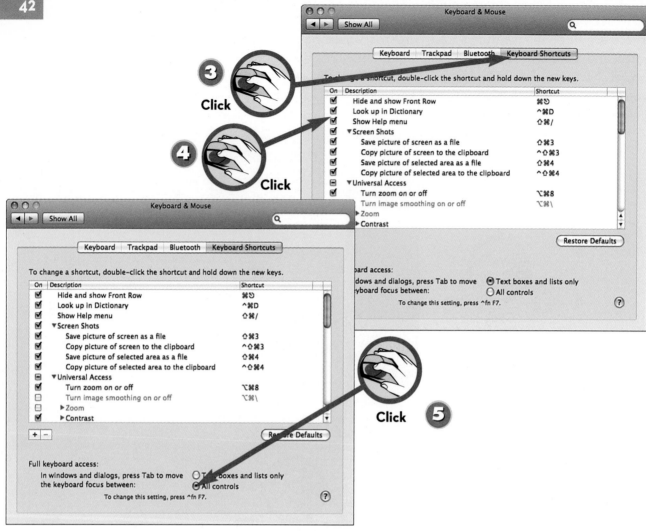

**3** Click

**4** Click

**5** Click

**3** Select **Keyboard Shortcuts**.

**4** Select or deselect settings.

**5** Choose **All Controls** to enable tabbing in application windows, such as Inspectors.

*End*

**TIP**

**Macs and External Keyboards**

If you prefer to type on a standard keyboard, if it has a USB connector, you can connect it to your Mac or MacBook and continue typing away.

# CHANGING THE DATE AND TIME

The date and time settings can help you and your applications stay on time. Mail, applications, and the Finder use the system date and time to identify when a file is created or modified, received or sent. This task shows you how to set the date, time, and location on your computer.

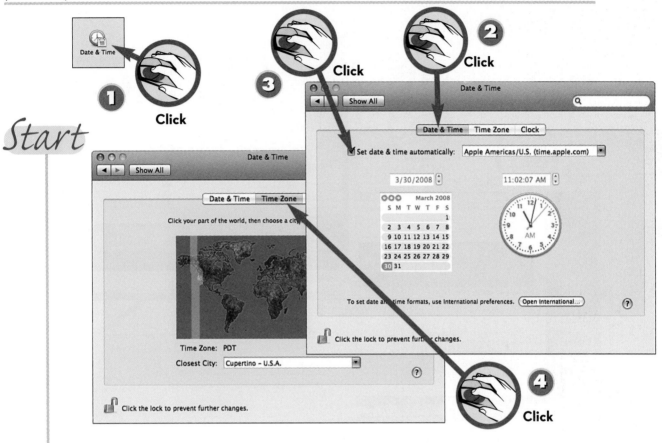

*Start*

*End*

1. Click the **Date & Time** icon in the System Preferences window.

2. Select **Date & Time**.

3. Check **Set Date & Time Automatically**. Choose the continent from the drop-down menu. This is only necessary if your Mac is being set up for the first time, or if the date was accidently reset due to PRAM (parameter ram) failure.

4. Choose **Time Zone**. Click the map to change your location. This can come in handy if you want to use your Mac as a clock while traveling.

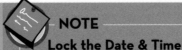

## NOTE
**Location, Location, Location**
Aside from the date and time, the location may also be used by some websites to decide which language to show on a web page.

## NOTE
**Lock the Date & Time**
Click the lock in the lower-left corner of the Preferences panel to lock the Date & Time settings.

# WORKING WITH SPACES

Spaces is new to Leopard. Essentially, a space is a desktop that you can customize and save. You can assign which applications open in one or every space. This can help reduce window clutter when you work with certain applications.

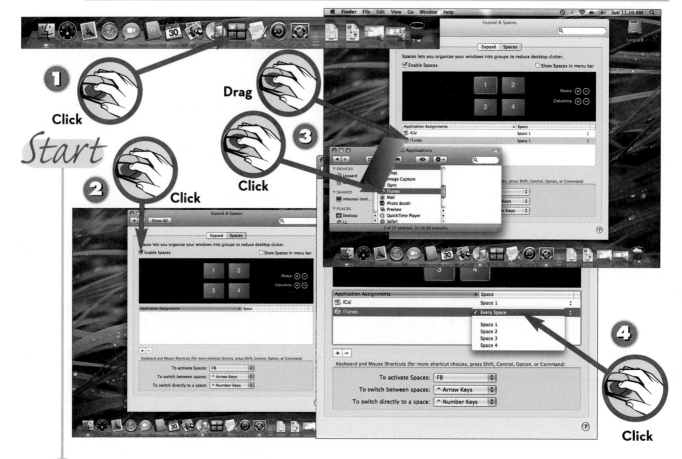

**1** Open the Spaces application by clicking its icon on the dock.

**2** Click **Spaces**, and then check the **Enable Spaces** check box.

**3** Drag an application to the Spaces window. Alternatively, choose the **+** button and navigate to the Applications folder to select applications you want to add to Spaces.

**4** You can now assign the application to one or more spaces. Choose **Every Space** to assign it to all available spaces.

*End*

## TIP
### Open Files in Any Space
Double-clicking a file in any space automatically launches the application in that space; the document window remains open only in this space. Go to the space for that application to view the file. Double click the file in a different space to open the application and document in that space.

## NOTE
### Keyboard Shortcuts
Press **F8** to activate Spaces. Ctrl-⌘ switches between spaces. Ctrl-Number key goes directly to a space.

# CUSTOMIZING ICONS ON THE DOCK

The dock is a 24/7 one-stop shopping destination for the applications and files you want to access quickly and easily. Dock settings are accessible from the System Preferences or the Apple menu.

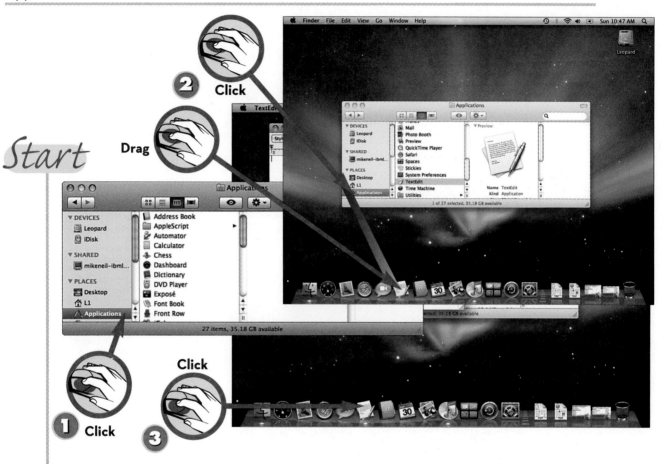

**1** Click the **Applications** icon in a Finder window to open the Applications folder.

**2** Drag the TextEdit application's icon to the dock. When space appears between two icons in the dock, release the mouse add the new icon to the dock.

**3** Click the **TextEdit** icon in the dock. A dot appears below the icon when the application is open.

*Continued*

---

**TIP**
**Customize Dock Settings**
Click the **Apple** menu and select **Dock** to view or change dock settings.

**NOTE**
**Keyboard Shortcuts**
If the dock is set to show, you can press ⌘-**Option-D** to hide it.

**Click** 4

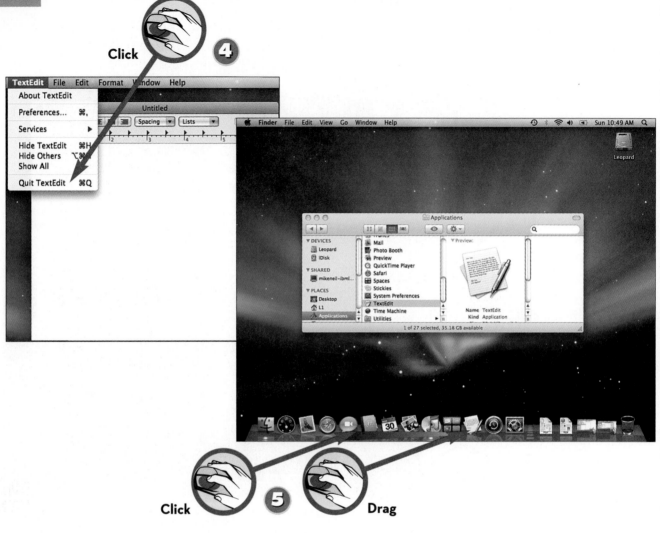

**Click** 5 **Drag**

4 Choose **TextEdit** > **Quit TextEdit**. The icon remains in the dock.

5 Drag the TextEdit icon to a new location in the dock.

*End*

**NOTE**

**Dock Preferences**

Adjust the dock's size, magnification level, position onscreen, and other options from the Dock Preferences window. Choose **Dock Preferences** from the **Apple** > **Dock** menu.

# CHANGING YOUR COMPUTER'S NAME

Your Mac's computer name is visible to other machines on the network. When you create an administrator account, Mac OS creates a computer name based on the username. This task shows you how to change your computer name.

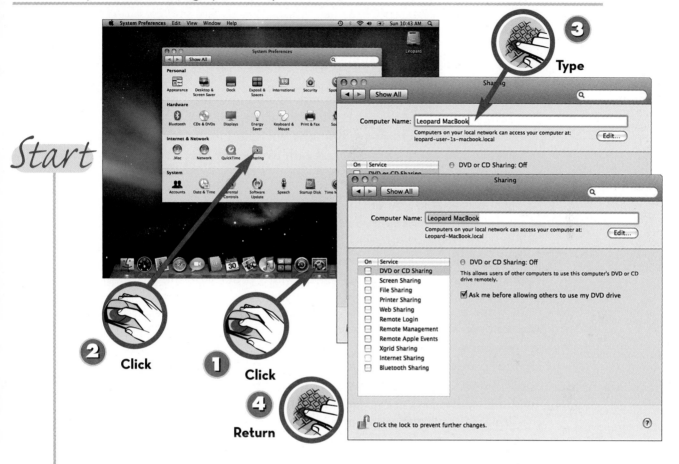

*Start*

**③ Type**

**② Click**

**① Click**

**④ Return**

**①** Click the **System Preferences** button in the Dock.

**②** Select the **Sharing** icon in the System Preferences window.

**③** Type a name for your computer in the Computer Name field.

**④** Press **Return**.

*End*

**TIP**

**What's in a Name**

You may want to include something unique about your computer to make it easier for others to find, such as Lisa's MacBook or Living Room iMac.

**NOTE**

**Computer Name Versus IP Address**

Some services don't recognize the computer name. If you're trying to access another Mac on the network, try typing the IP address, located in the **System Preferences > Network** panel of the machine you want to access, into the Connect to Server panel (⌘-K) in the Finder.

# INSTALLING AND USING APPLICATIONS

Apple includes many applications with every new Mac. Some—for example, TextEdit, Front Row, Address Book, iCal, iChat, and Safari—are located in the Applications folder. Other applications, such as iLife and iWork, are available separately. iLife comes preinstalled with every new Mac. iWork is available as a free 30-day trial from Apple's website.

Applications enable you to do a specific set of tasks on your computer. For example, TextEdit enables you to work with text. The Preview application enables you to view and edit PDF and image files. iLife enables you to view photos with iPhoto, listen to music and movies with iTunes, and more. iWork consists of three applications: Pages, a word processor and layout program; Keynote, a presentation program; and Numbers, a spreadsheet program.

Applications also have some common features, such as selecting text or images, copy and pasting text or images, and opening and savings files. This chapter provides some examples of common tasks that work similarly in most applications. Learn how to install and open applications; add and edit text in TextEdit; format text using the Font panel; copy and paste text; view images in the Preview application; and access music, photos, or movies from a remote control using Front Row.

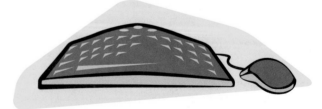

# MAC OS X APPLICATIONS

Applications folder

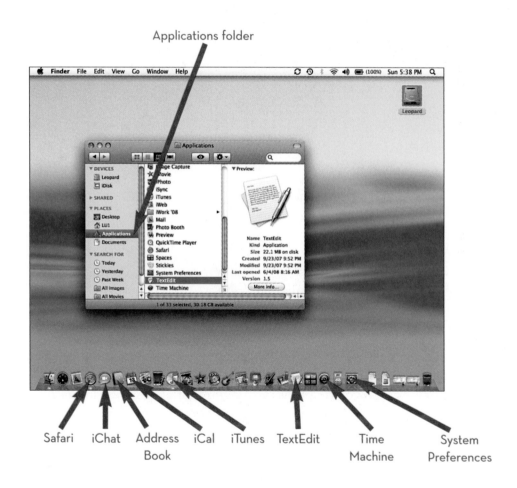

Safari    iChat    Address    iCal    iTunes    TextEdit    Time        System
                   Book                                     Machine     Preferences

# INSTALLING AND OPENING APPLICATIONS

Most applications have an installer that walks you through a series of screens that result in putting the application and its files on your computer. This task shows you how to install the iLife application suite, but the steps apply to any application you have to install.

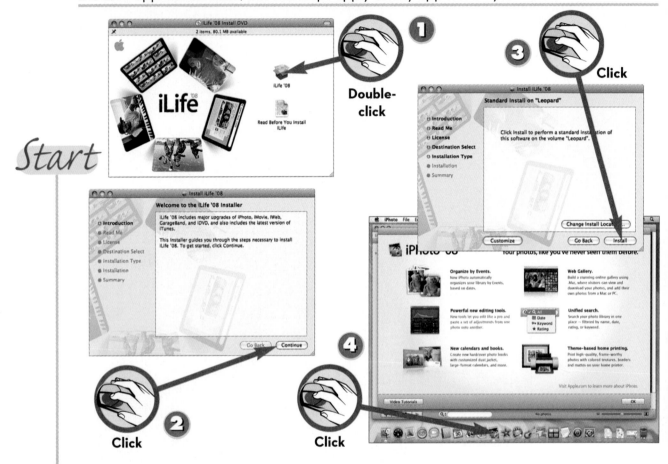

Start

Double-click

Click

Click

Click

**1** Insert the install DVD, and then double-click the **Installer** icon.

**2** The installer walks you through the process in a series of screens. Click **Continue** after reading and following each set of instructions.

**3** If for some reason you do not want the application installed in the Applications folder, click **Change Install Location** before you click the **Install** button.

**4** Open an application. Choose **Apple** > **Software Update** to check for the most recent updates for the Apple software on your Mac.

End

---

**TIP**
### Software Updates
After installing an application, be sure to follow step 4 and run the Software Updater to get the most recent updates for your Apple software. You might need to run the updater more than once. To find out more, go to "Checking for Software Updates," in Part 17, "Taking Care of Your Mac."

**TIP**
### Application Requirements
Before you install an application, be sure to review the requirements. Some applications require more memory or disk space than others.

# OPENING A FILE WITH TEXTEDIT

TextEdit is a basic word processing application that is included with Mac OS X. It is installed in the Applications folder. This task shows you how to open a file with TextEdit.

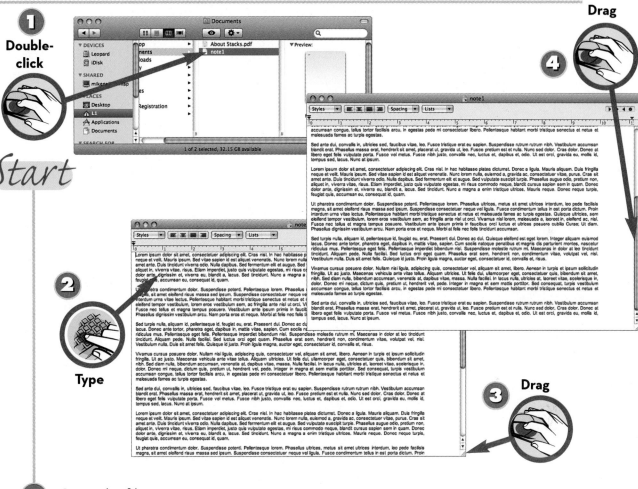

**Double-click**

**Drag**

**Type**

**Drag**

*Start*

*End*

1. Open the file.

2. Click on the canvas and type.

3. Drag to increase or reduce the window size.

4. Drag the scroll control to navigate the document.

---

**TIP**

**TextEdit File Formats**
You can open Rich Text (.rtf), Word (.doc), and Text (.txt) files with TextEdit.

**NOTE**

**More Windows: Widgets**
Widgets are applications that run in the Dashboard application. Press **F12** to view the clock, calculator, and default widgets; check out Apple's website to find more. Click the desktop to exit the Dashboard. To find out more about widgets, and download them, visit Apple's website at http://apple.com/downloads.

# WORKING WITH TEXTEDIT

As simple as it looks, TextEdit has quite a few features. You can access any font installed in Mac OS; apply shadow, bold, italic, and other font styles; change the text color, size, and more! This task shows you how to do some basic text editing in TextEdit.

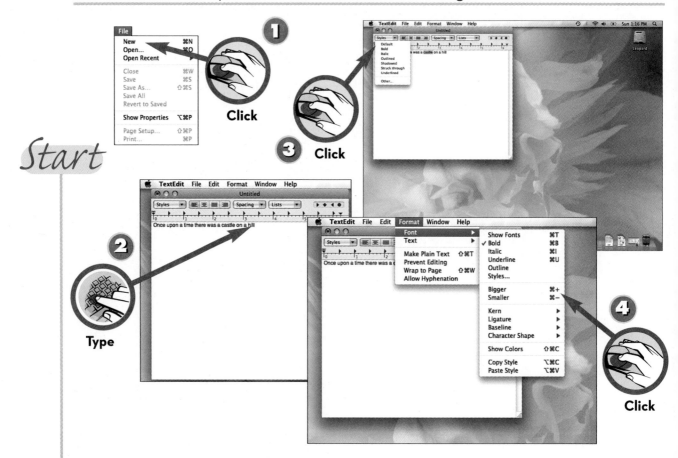

 Open TextEdit and choose **File** > **New** to create a new document.

**2** Type text in the document area.

**3** Select a word, and then click the **Style** drop-down to change the font style.

 Increase the font size by choosing **Format** > **Font** > **Bigger**.

*Continued*

---

**TIP**

**Drag and Drop**

If you are working in TextEdit and want to move some text to another application, try selecting the text and then dragging and dropping it onto the second application's window, or copy and paste the text.

**NOTE**

**Pages Versus TextEdit**

Pages is Apple's word processing and layout application that is bundled in the iWork application suite. To find out more about it, go to Part 5, " Using Pages."

**Double-click**

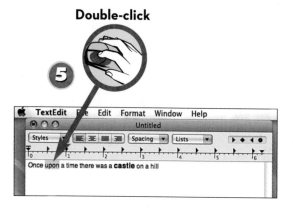

**5**

**Click**

**7**

**Drag**

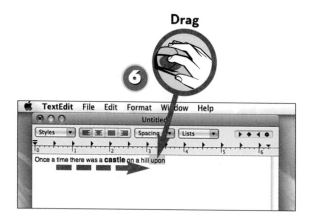

**6**

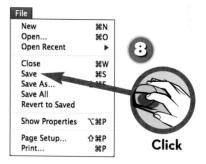

**8**

**Click**

**5** Select another word of text by double-clicking it.

**6** Drag and drop the selected text to a new location.

**7** Delete the selected text by choosing **Edit** > **Delete** (or pressing **Delete** on the keyboard).

**8** Choose **File** > **Save** to save the file. The first time the file is saved the Save As sheet opens and you can select where you want to save the file. Click the **Save** button to save the file.

*End*

**TIP**

**TextEdit Preferences**

Set the file format, window size, font, and other properties in the TextEdit Preferences window. Press ⌘-, (yes, ⌘ and the comma) to open the Preferences window.

**NOTE**

**Spotlight and TextEdit Properties**

If you want to use Spotlight to search for author, company, title, copyright, subject, keywords, or comments in a TXT or RTF file, choose **File** > **Show Properties** and type in any field. Save the file.

# COPY AND PASTING TEXT

Copying and pasting text enables you to duplicate or move text within the same document or to different documents or applications. This task shows you how to copy and paste text within the same document.

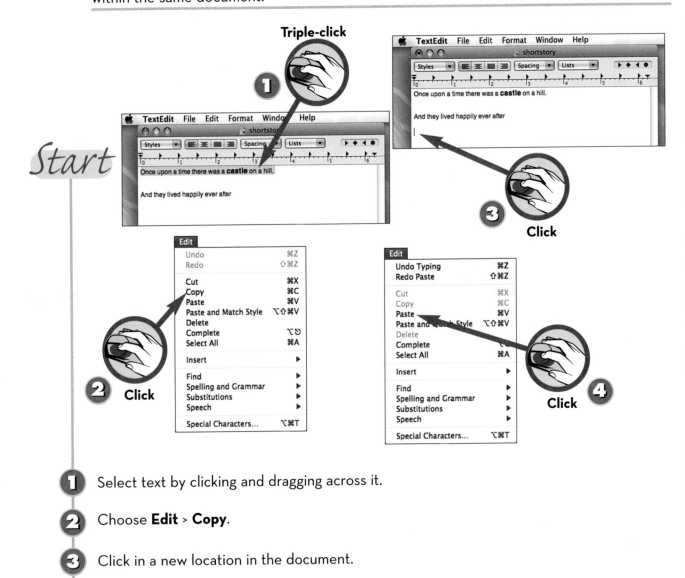

1. Select text by clicking and dragging across it.

2. Choose **Edit** > **Copy**.

3. Click in a new location in the document.

4. Choose **Edit** > **Paste**.

## TIP
### Clean and Dirty Documents
If the red circle in the document window is clear, the document is clean. If a gray dot appears in it, the document is dirty. Choose **File > Revert to Saved** to remove any unwanted edits.

## TIP
### Previewing Your Document
You can preview you document before printing it. Choose **File > Print**. Click the **Preview** button. The document opens in the Preview application. Check it out and make sure it looks the way you want it to before sharing or printing it.

# USING THE FONT PANEL

Each character you type is part of a font. Fonts are sets of alphabetic and numeric characters that follow a specific style. You can choose one or several fonts when working with text. Fonts are not created equal. Some have many different attributes, and others are relatively plain. This task shows you how to change the font family and size and how to work with some advanced font options.

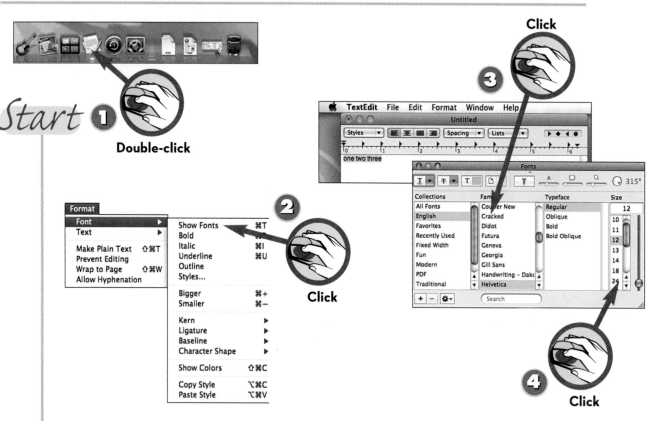

Start

**Double-click**

**Click**

**Click**

**Click**

1. Open TextEdit by double-clicking its icon on the Dock.

2. Choose **Format** > **Font** > **Show Fonts** to open the Font panel (or press ⌘-**T**).

3. Click and drag over the text to select it, and then choose a different font family from the Family column in the Fonts panel.

4. Scroll up or down the Size column, and then click a size to change the font size.

*Continued*

**TIP**

**Navigating Font Collections**

The Font panel shows a list of fonts installed in Mac OS X Leopard. Select a Collection from the right section of the window to view smaller groups of fonts. Choose **All Fonts** to view all fonts in the Font panel window.

**TIP**

**Manage Fonts with Font Book**

Font Book enables you to preview, disable, and enable fonts. Choose **Manage Fonts** from the Font panel's Action menu to open the Font Book window. Select a font and click the **Action** menu to add, disable, or enable a font.

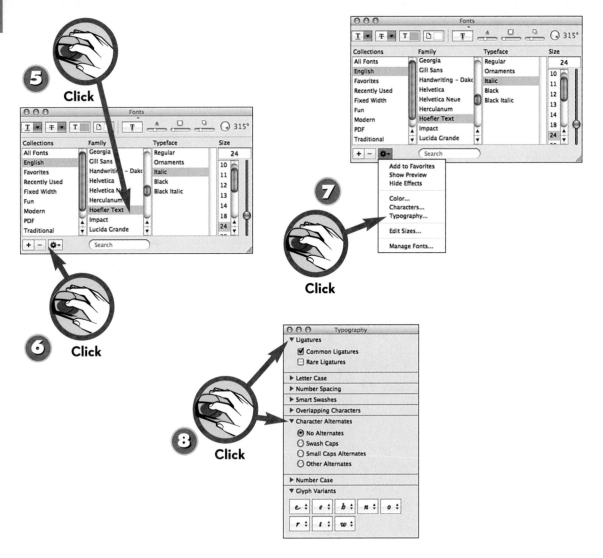

**5** With your text still selected, click the **Hoeffler Text** font in the Family column of the Font panel.

**6** Select the **Action** menu and view its menu list.

**7** Choose **Typography** from the drop-down list.

**8** Uncollapse arrows to view the font settings for this font family. Click a setting to apply it to your selected text.

*End*

**NOTE**

**Change Text Colors**

Select text in a TextEdit document. Open the **Font** panel and choose the color swatch at the top of the panel to open the Color Picker. Select a color to apply to the selected text from one of the color spaces. You can also choose **Color** from the Font panel's Action menu to open the Color Picker.

# USING FRONT ROW TO SURF YOUR MUSIC, MOVIES, AND PHOTOS

The Apple Remote is bundled with most Macs. It works like a remote control for a television, except it is for your Mac. You can use it to navigate photos, music, movies, TV shows, and more. This task shows you how.

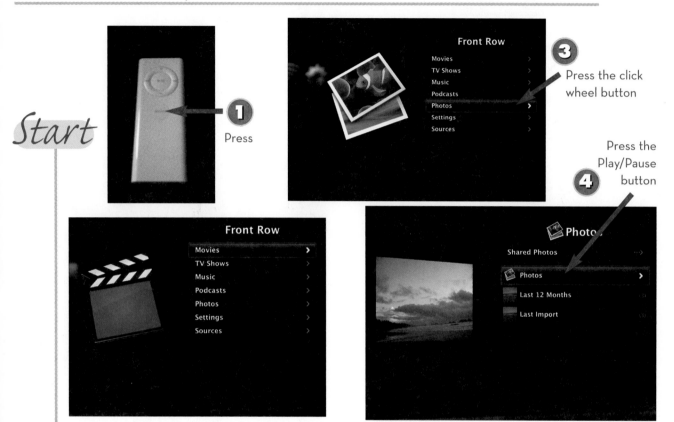

*Start*

Press ①

Press the click wheel button ③

Press the Play/Pause button ④

*End*

① Press the **Menu** button on the Apple Remote.

② Front Row opens on your Mac's desktop.

③ Press the top, left, right, or bottom of the click wheel to navigate the menu.

④ Press the center **Play/Pause** button to select any topic.

 **TIP**
**Returning to the Desktop**
From the Main menu, press **Esc** on the keyboard to exit the Front Row application and return to the desktop. Pressing Esc in any of the subcategories moves Front Row back a page.

 **NOTE**
**Turn Off the Infrared Receiver**
Open System Preferences and select **Security**. Check the **Disable remote control infrared receiver** check box to disable the remote control access to your computer.

# SHOWING AND HIDING APPLICATIONS

One way to reduce window clutter is to hide an application. When you hide an application, all of its windows are hidden. This task shows you how to hide a TextEdit window.

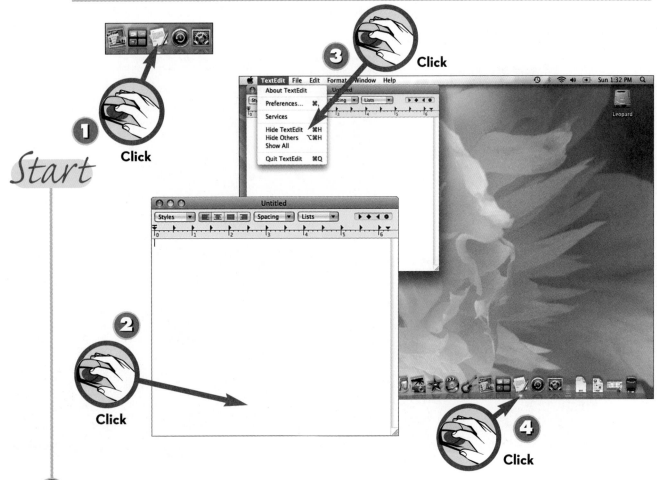

*Start*

**Click**

**Click**

**Click**

**Click**

*End*

1. Click the **TextEdit** icon on the dock. A new window opens.

2. Choose **File** > **New** to create a new window. Select the window.

3. Choose **TextEdit** > **Hide Text Edit**.

4. Select the **TextEdit** icon on the Dock to bring the window back into view.

 **TIP**
**Different Shortcuts for Different Apps**
Some applications, especially those that might have mapped ⌘-H to do something else, use **Control-⌘-H** to hide its app windows.

 **TIP**
**Function Keys**
Press **F11** to hide all open windows if you need a speedy way to view files on your desktop.

# SAVING A PDF FILE

If you have a Rich Text, Word, email, or text document that you want to share without allowing anyone to edit it, save the file as a PDF. You can send the PDF in email, publish it to a blog or website, share it online, or print it. Readers can view it, but cannot edit it. This task shows you how to open a file in TextEdit and save it as a PDF (Portable Document Format) file.

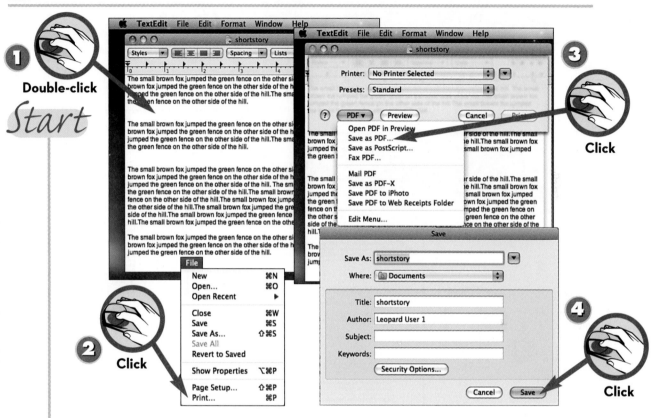

1. Open Text Edit. Open a file you want to share but don't want the reader to change.

2. Choose **File** > **Print**. The Print sheet opens.

3. Choose **PDF** > **Save as PDF**. The **Save** window opens.

4. Navigate to the folder where you want to save the file from the Where drop-down menu. Change the name for the file if you like, and then click the **Save** button. The PDF file is saved to your hard drive. Open it with the Preview application.

*End*

---

# USING PREVIEW TO NAVIGATE A PDF FILE

Now that you have created a PDF file, you can view it. Preview is the name of the program that enables you to view and print PDF files. This task shows you how to view and navigate a PDF file.

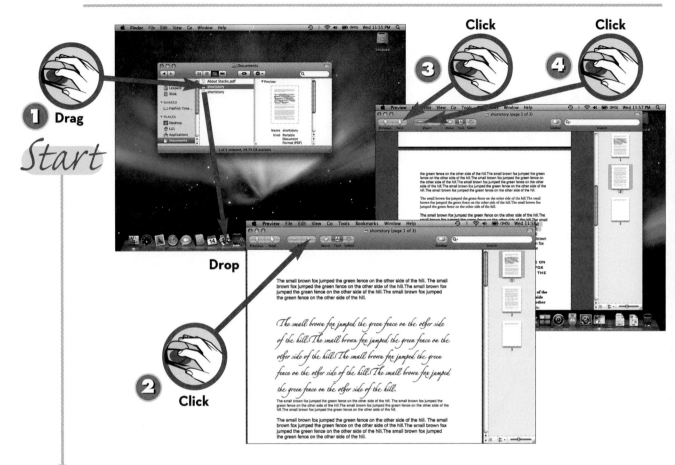

**Start**

**① Drag**

**Drop**

**② Click**

**③ Click**

**④ Click**

① Locate a PDF file on your hard drive and drop the file on the Preview app on the Dock.

② Click the **+** (plus) button on the toolbar to increase the zoom level.

③ Click the **Next** button on the toolbar. The next page in the document appears in the window. Conversely, click the **Previous** button to scroll back a page. You can also select a page from the sidebar.

④ Click the **–** (minus) button on the toolbar to decrease the zoom level. Alternatively, you can show the sidebar and select any page.

**End**

---

**TIP**
**Resizing the PDF Window**
Drag the lower-right corner of the PDF window to resize it. The scale of the document's text, images, and graphics grow or shrink as the window grows or shrinks.

**TIP**
**Printing the PDF**
You can print PDF files in the Preview app. Choose **File** > **Print** to show the Print sheet. Click the **Preview** button, and then click the **Print** button, or just click the **Print** button from the Print sheet.

# VIEWING PHOTOS WITH PREVIEW

In the previous task, you learned how to zoom and navigate the pages PDF. You can also view images in Preview (one or many images). This task shows you how to navigate images in Preview.

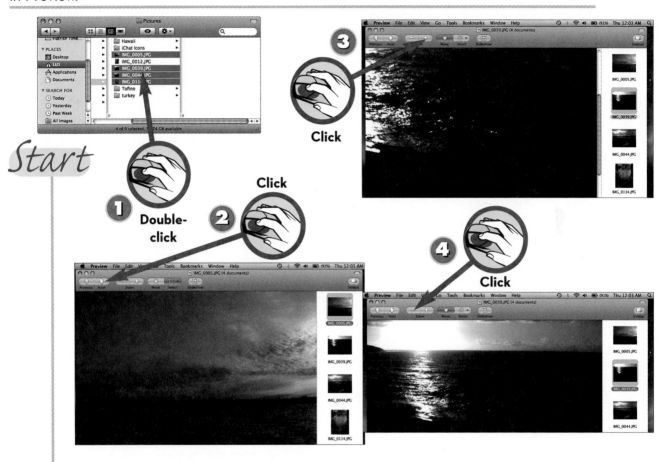

1. Select one or more JPG files in Finder and double-click to open them. Preview opens.

2. Click the **Next** button to view the next photo. Alternatively, select a photo from the sidebar to go directly to it. To return to the photo in step 1, click the **Previous** button on the toolbar.

3. Click the + (plus) button on the toolbar to increase the zoom level. Click the **Move** button on the toolbar and drag the cursor over the image to view different areas of the magnified image.

4. Click the – (minus) button on the toolbar to decrease the zoom level. The image becomes smaller in the window.

---

**TIP**

**Supported Image File Formats**

The Preview application enables you to view the following image file formats: JPEG, GIF, JPEG-2000, Microsoft BMP, OpenEXR, PDF, Photoshop, PICT, PNG, SGI, TGA, and TIFF.

**TIP**

**Changing Graphics Formats**

To save the image file as a different image file format, choose **File > Save As** or press ⌘-**Shift-S**. The Save As sheet opens. Choose an image format from the Format pop-up menu. Then click the **Save** button to save the file to the hard drive.

# USING PAGES

Pages is a word processing and page layout program. Pages is one of three programs in Apple's iWork suite, which includes Keynote, for presentations, and Numbers, for spreadsheets. The focus of these applications is to provide compatibility with rich-text, plain-text, and Microsoft Office files with a user-friendly set of common features to enable you to create presentations, spreadsheets, and text layout documents.

More than 100 word processing and page layout templates are included with Pages. Creating any file starts with a template. This chapter shows you some word processing basics and introduces you to some of the objects and layout-related features in Pages.

# THE PAGES WORKSPACE

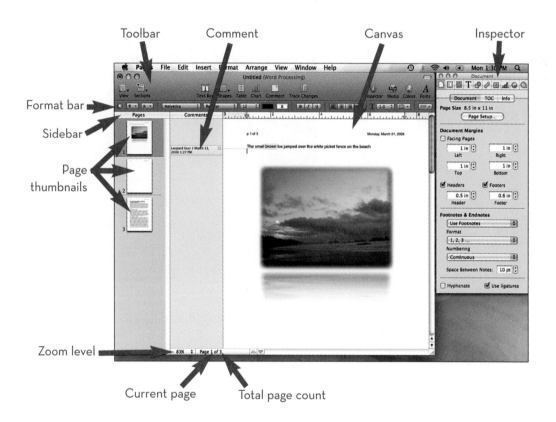

# INSTALLING IWORK '08

Apple provides a free iWork trial you can download from its website. The iWork '08 trial installs Keynote, Pages, and Numbers in an iWork '08 folder in the Applications folder on your Mac. This task shows you how to install iWork.

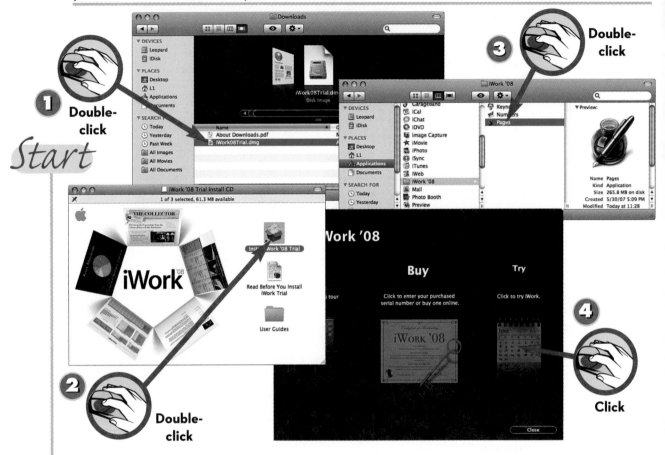

 *Start*

**1** Double-click the **iWork08Trial.dmg** file to access the installation files.

**2** Double-click the **Install iWork '08 Trial** icon. Follow the onscreen instructions.

**3** Double-click **Pages** in the **Applications** > **iWork '08** folder.

**4** Click the **calendar** icon in the Try section of the window.

*End*

 **TIP**

### iWork Requirements

iWork '08 requires a Mac with an Intel or PowerPC G4 or G5 processor, 512MB of memory, 1GB recommended, 32MB of video RAM, Mac OS X 10.4.10 or later, QuickTime 7.2 or later, iLife '08 recommended, and 1GB of available disk space

**TIP**

### Purchasing iWork

You can purchase iWork '08 anytime during or after the trial period. To purchase iWork, choose the Pages > Buy iWork menu. Follow the onscreen instructions and type the serial number to complete the purchase.

# CREATING A WORD PROCESSING DOCUMENT

Pages includes more than 100 templates for creating letters, envelopes, newsletters, cards, invoices, and so on. Each time you open Pages, the Template Chooser shows. Here you can navigate and select the template you want.

There are two types of templates: Word Processing and Page Layout. Page Layout documents only enable you to work with the floating layer in a document. Word Processing documents support a background, inline, and floating layer. This task shows you how to create a blank word processing document.

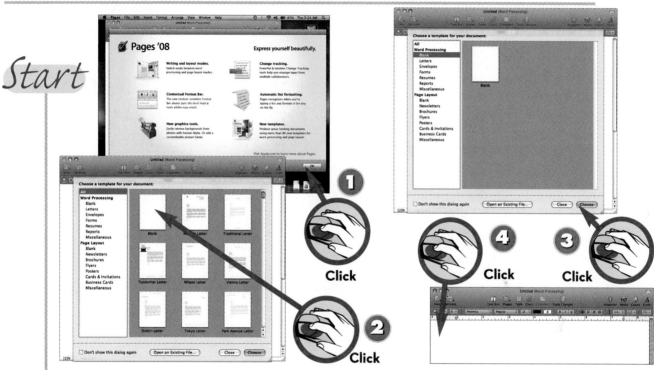

**1** A **Welcome screen** opens the first time Pages opens. Select a button in the window to learn more about Pages. Choose the **OK** button to close the window. Choose the **Help > Welcome to Pages** menu to open this window as you like.

**2** Click a template to select it. Here, I selected the Word Processing Blank template.

**3** Click the **Choose** button to open the template for editing.

**4** Click in the new document window to begin adding your own text to the template.

*Start*

*End*

---

**TIP**

**Don't Show Again**

Check the **Don't show this dialog again** check box if you do not want the Template Chooser to appear when Pages opens. Instead, a new window is created when Pages opens. A new Word Processing Blank template opens by default. Choose **File > New from Template Chooser** to access any templates.

**NOTE**

**Changing the Default Template**

Press ⌘-, to open the **Pages Preferences** window. Click the **Choose** button to select the template you want to use to create a new document.

# ADDING AND EDITING TEXT

Typing in Pages is similar to typing in TextEdit; what you see is what you get. Text appears on the canvas as you type, just like with TextEdit. Pages, however, also lets you type text in text boxes, shapes, tables, charts, and comments, which makes your documents much more flexible and visually appealing.

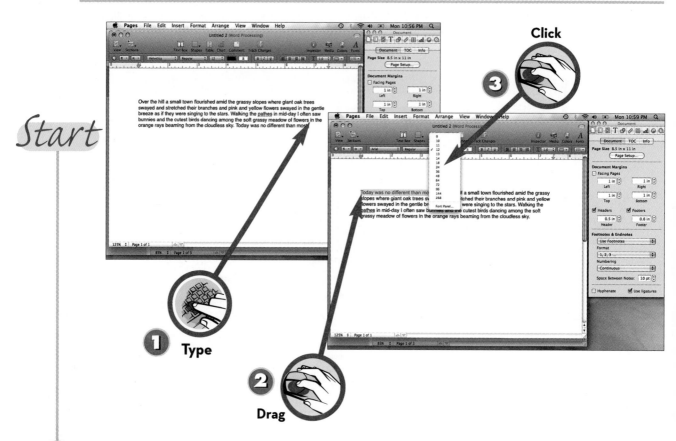

 *Start*

**1** Type

**2** Drag

**3** Click

**1** Type text on the canvas.

**2** Select text by dragging the cursor over it until one or more words are highlighted.

**3** Use the tools on the Format bar to change the selected text's formatting , such as selecting a new font size.

 *End*

---

**TIP**
**The Format Bar**
The Format bar, located at the bottom of the toolbar, enables you to format the font family, font face, color, styles, and much more. These font settings are also located in the Font panel (⌘-**T**).

**NOTE**
**Using Text from Another Document**
Select a rich-text or plain-text file and choose **Edit** > **Copy**. Then, click in the Pages document and select **Edit** > **Paste**. All the text in the file will appear in the Pages canvas. You can also drag and drop .rtf or .txt files onto the pages canvas.

# FINDING TEXT

Need to change the spelling of word or just not sure whether a term is in a document? You can find and replace text in Pages. Pages also has a Search panel that shows any matching search results in the sidebar. This task shows you how to find text with the Find panel.

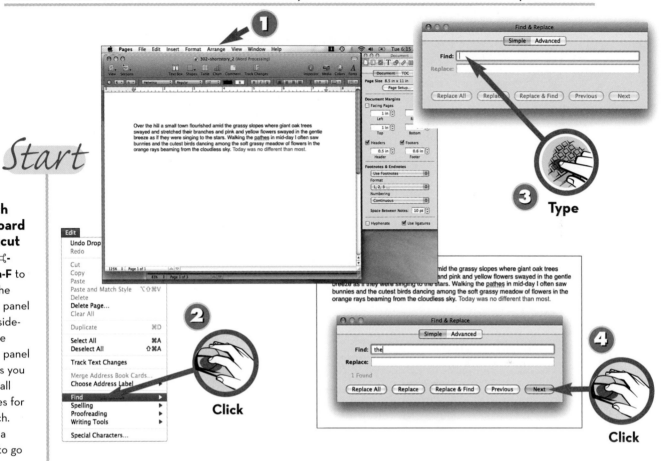

*Start*

**Type**

**Click**

**Click**

*End*

**1** Open a text file in Pages.

**2** Choose **Edit** > **Find** > **Find**.

**3** Type a word or words into the **Find** field and click the **Next** button (or press ⌘-**G**).

**4** If a match is found, the text is highlighted. If no matches are found, Not Found appears below the Replace field. Click **Next** to search for the next instance of the word.

**NOTE**

**Find Text in a Document**

Press **Find Next** or ⌘-**G** to search all text in the document continuously.

**TIP**

**Find and Replace**

You can directly type over the text you want to change, or type the replacement text in the **Replace** field of the Find panel. Choose Next to match the text you want to find. Then click the Replace button. Replace All changes all matching text in the document. Replace and Find replaces the highlighted text and finds the next match.

# ADDING AND EDITING SHAPES

Text boxes, shapes, tables, charts, and even images can be either *inline*, fixed on the page, or *floating*. You can drag floating objects to any page and move objects from floating to inline. This task shows you how to add a shape to the page, put text in it, and then edit it.

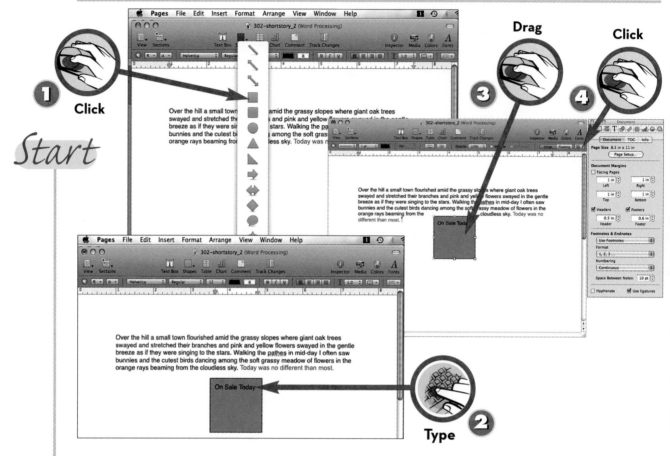

*Start*

**Drag** **Click**

**Click**

**Type**

1. Click the **Shape** button on the toolbar, and then select a shape in the drop-down list. The shape appears in the middle of the page.

2. Type some text in the shape.

3. Drag the shape around the canvas to reposition it.

4. Change the text-wrap setting for the shape by choosing a wrap setting from the Format bar. This changes the way the surrounding text wraps around the outside of the shape.

*End*

**NOTE**

**Create Custom Shapes**

Choose **Draw a Shape** from the **Insert > Shape** menu to create a custom shape. Click the canvas to create the points for the shape. Double-click at the ending location, or click the first point to close the shape.

**TIP**

**Editing Shapes**

To customize the shape's border, select the shape and then open the **Graphic Inspector**. To open the Graphic inspector, click the blue inspector icon in the toolbar and then select the Graphic button (square and circle icon) at the top of the inspector.

# WORKING WITH INLINE AND FLOATING OBJECTS

In a word processing document any shape, text box, image, table, or chart can be floating or inline. Floating objects can easily move from page to page. Text on the canvas wraps around it. Inline objects also wrap with the text, but are fixed and cannot move on the canvas. This task works with the Word Processing Blank template and shows you how to change an inline text box to floating.

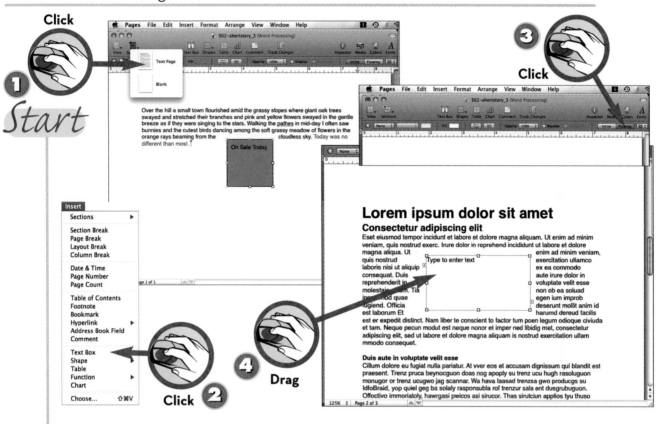

Choose **Sections** > **Text Page** from the toolbar. A page of text is inserted into the document. Click in the text on the canvas.

Choose **Insert** > **Text Box** from the menu bar. An inline text box is created. Drag the right and bottom sides of the text box to resize it.

Choose the **Floating button** from the Format bar. The text box is now in the floating layer.

Drag the text box to move it to a new location.

*End*

# WORKING WITH TABLES

If you want to organize text in a grid, consider using tables. Similar to tables in a spread-sheet, Pages tables enable you to customize the numbers of rows and columns. You can also use functions, navigate cells, and type text in them. This task shows you how.

**Click**

**Click**

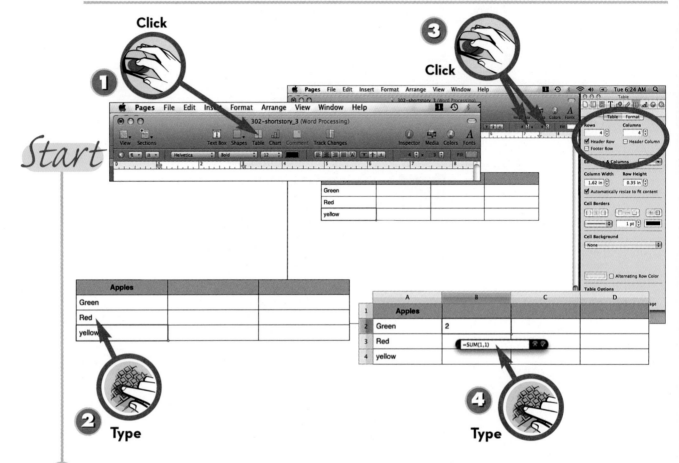

*Start*

**Type**

**Type**

*End*

1. Click the Table button on the toolbar to insert a table in your document.

2. Type text in a cell. Press the **Tab** key or arrow keys to select the next cell. Press ⌘-- to reduce the size of the text or ⌘-+ to increase the text size.

3. Add rows and columns using the buttons on the Format bar or the options in the Table Inspector.

4. Select a cell and type = to add a formula.

## TIP
### Custom Table Sizes
Hold down the **Option** key when selecting a table from the toolbar. Then drag to create a custom floating table on the canvas.

## TIP
### Cell Formatting
The Graphics and Table inspectors enable you to format a table or its cells. Like shapes, and text boxes, you can select a table or one of its cells and assign a custom color or image to the cell's background from the Graphic Inspector. Open the Table inspector to customize the size and shape of the table's columns, rows, or borders. .

# CREATING LINKED TEXT BOXES

Floating text boxes have a special attribute that enables you to create many text boxes that are linked together. Linking text boxes enables text to flow across pages in the floating layer or in a Page Layout document. This task shows you how to create a linked text box.

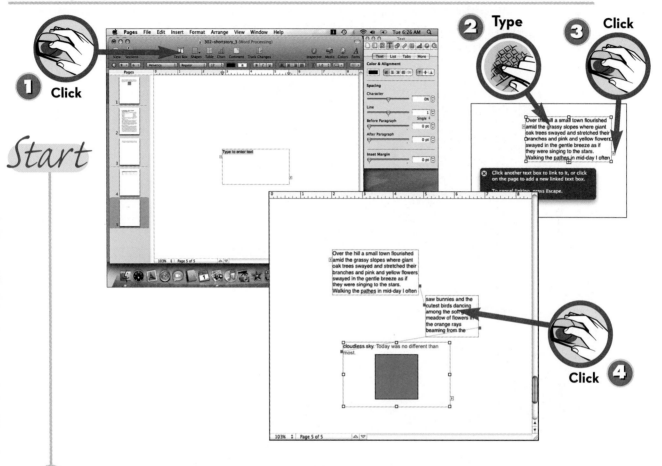

**Start**

**1 Click**

**2 Type**

**3 Click**

**4 Click**

---

**1** Click the **Text Box** button on the toolbar.

**2** Copy and paste, or type, several lines of text in the text box until you completely fill the text box and you can no longer see what is being typed.

**3** Click the blue box on the side of the text box.

**4** Click the canvas one or more times to create linked text boxes. The text that wasn't visible in the first text box appears in the linked text boxes. Choose the **File** > **Save** menu and save the file.

**End**

---

**TIP**

**Text Format in Linked Text Boxes**

Text in linked text boxes can be formatted just like text on the canvas. As the text box size changes, the text flowing across the text boxes automatically updates.

**NOTE**

**Removing a Link**

Click the blue box on the text box, and then press **Delete** to remove a link between linked text boxes.

# ADDING A PAGE BREAK

In a word processing document, you can format one or more pages with page, layout, or section breaks to group one or more pages in a document. A page break inserts a new page within a section. A layout break inserts a break in the layout, enabling you to customize column settings or margins. A section break inserts a new section in a document. This task shows you how to view page thumbnails and insert a page break into a word processing document.

*Start*

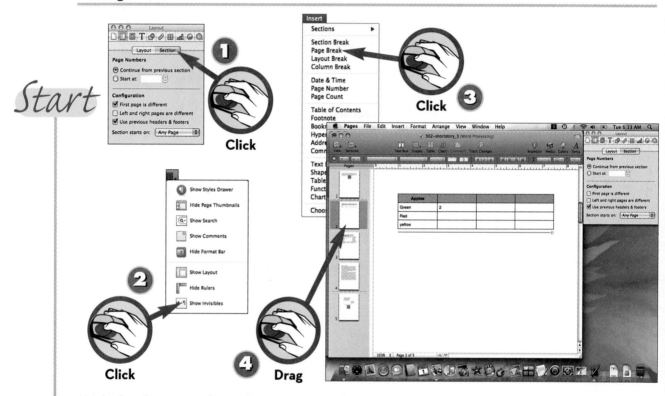

**Click**

**Click**

**Click**

**Drag**

With the document from the previous task open, Choose the Inspector button from the toolbar. Select the Layout Inspector (second icon from the left), and then click the **Sections** button. Here you can set page numbering and left or right layout ordering as you like.

Click the **View** button on the toolbar and select **Show Page Thumbnails.** The sidebar appears on the left side of the document

Click the canvas. Choose **Insert** > **Page Break**. A new page appears in the sidebar.

Select a page at the bottom of the sidebar and drop it below page 1.

*End*

 **TIP**
**Document Zoom Levels**
Set the document zoom level at the bottom of the window to 100% to view the document as it will be printed or viewed when exported to PDF or Word file formats.

 **NOTE**
**Shortcuts**
Press ⌘-Shift-I to show or hide invisibles. Press ⌘-Shift-L to show and hide the layout.

# WORKING WITH HEADERS AND FOOTERS

Repetitive information, such as page number or page count, can be added to the Header or Footer fields and will automatically increment for you (rather than you manually typing them on each page). This task shows you how to insert automated page count and page numbers into the Header field.

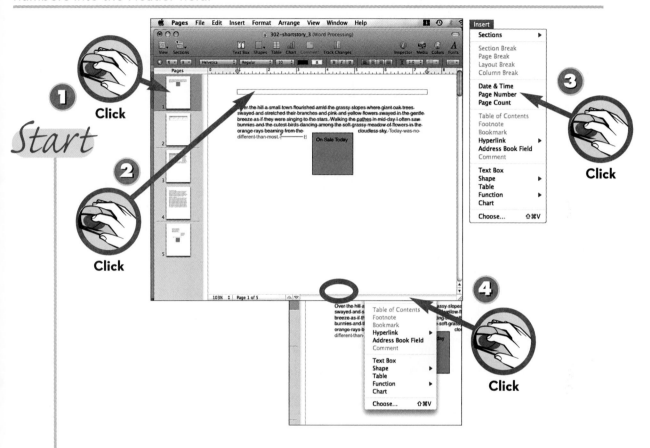

*Start*

**Click**

**Click**

**Click**

**Click**

**(1)** Continuing with the document you've been creating, select a page in the sidebar.

**(2)** Move the mouse toward to top of the page to show the header field, or select the **View > Show Layout** menu. Click in the **Header** field.

**(3)** Choose **Insert > Page Number**.

**(4)** Click in the Footer and select **Insert > Page Count**.

*End*

# INSERTING A FOOTNOTE

Footnotes are often used in research papers or other projects where you need to reference work belonging to someone else. You insert footnotes within the text on the page. Optionally, you can insert section endnotes or endnotes if you prefer. This task shows you how to insert a footnote.

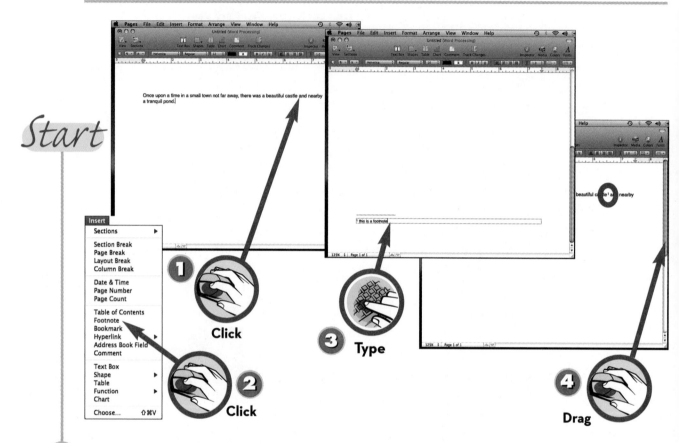

*Start*

**Click** **①**

**Click** **②**

**Type** **③**

**Drag** **④**

**①** Place the insertion point in the text where you want the footnote to appear.

**②** Choose **Insert** > **Footnote** from the menu bar.

**③** Type or drop text into the Footnote field.

**④** Press **Return**. Scroll up to the text to view the footnote superscript character.

*End*

**TIP**

## Footnotes and Selected Text

If you want to replace text with a footnote, select the word or words you want to remove, and then insert the footnote.

# SAVING A FILE

When you're ready to save your changes, save the file to your hard drive. This task shows you how to use the Save As menu command.

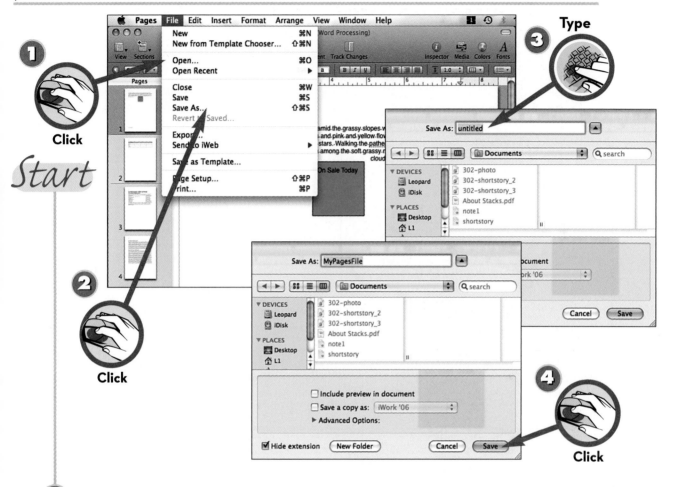

**Start**

**Type**

**Click**

**Click**

**Click**

 Open a text file or work with the one from the previous task.

 Choose **File** > **Save As** from the menu bar.

 Type a name and navigate to the folder where you want to save it.

 Click the **Save** button.

**End**

---

# PRINTING A DOCUMENT

If you have a printer configured on your Mac, you can print your document. The Preview application enables you to view your document before sending it to the printer. This task shows you how to preview and print a Pages document.

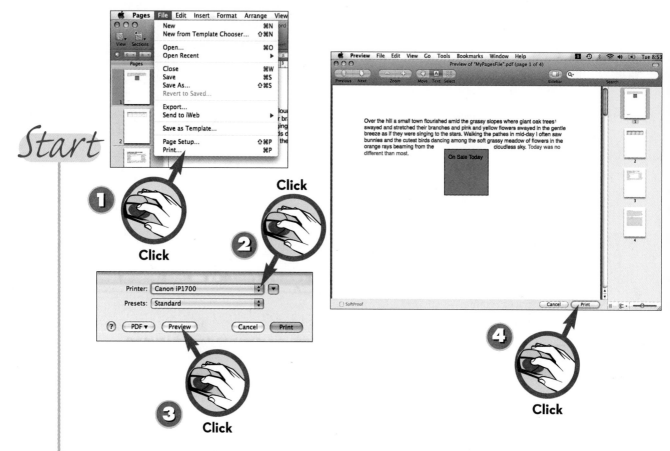

*Start*

*End*

1. With a file open that you want to print, choose **File** > **Print**.

2. Select a printer from the Printer list.

3. Click the **Preview** button. The Preview app opens. Scroll through the document to confirm it contains what you want to print.

4. When you're ready to print, click the **Print** button.

-TIP-
## Keyboard Shortcuts
Press ⌘-**P** to show the Print sheet. Press ⌘-**Shift-P** to open the Page Setup dialog. Here you can select the page size and scale. Page setup options are also available in the Document Inspector.

- NOTE -
## Adding a Printer
To find out how to add a printer to Leopard, go to Part 14, "Adding New Devices."

# CUSTOMIZING PREFERENCES

Customize the ruler, zoom level, new document, guide, table, and change tracking settings in the Preferences panel. You can also adjust auto-correction settings. This task shows you how to adjust ruler and auto-correct preferences.

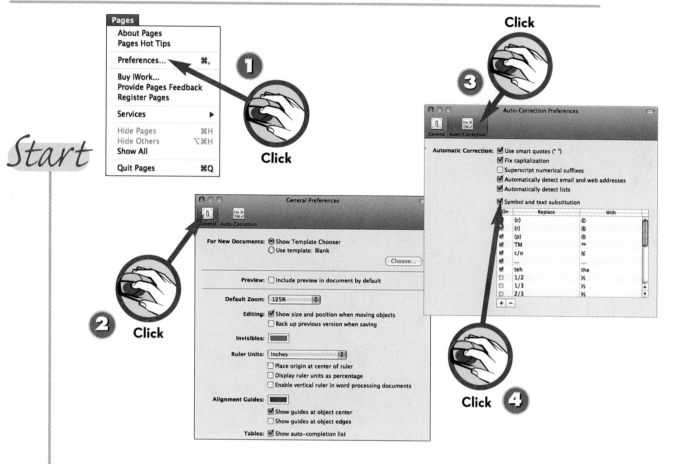

*Start*

*Click*

*Click*

*Click*

*Click*

**1** Choose the **Pages > Preferences** menu. The Preferences window opens.

**2** Select the **General Preferences** tab to view the General preferences panel. Click the **Ruler Units** drop-down to adjust the ruler's unit of measure.

**3** Click the **Auto-Correct** button to switch to the Auto-Correct Preferences panel.

**4** Adjust Auto-Correct Preference settings by checking or unchecking the check boxes.

*End*

-TIP-
**Spell Checking and Proofreading**
Pages flags misspelled words and some grammar errors. Choose **Edit > Spelling** or **Edit > Proofreading** to access settings for these features.

- NOTE -
**Keyboard Shortcuts**
Press ⌘-, to open the Preferences window. Press ⌘-W to close the Preferences window when it is the front window. Press ⌘-R to show and hide the ruler.

# CUSTOMIZING THE TOOLBAR

Customizing the toolbar in Pages works the same as the toolbars in Finder. This task shows you how to add and remove toolbar buttons.

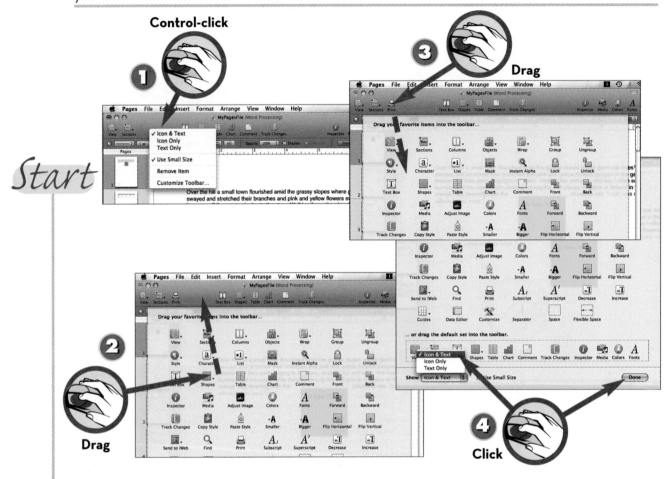

**Control-click**

**Drag**

**Start**

**Drag**

**Click**

**End**

1. Choose **View** > **Customize Toolbar** or Control-click the toolbar to use the context menu.

2. Drag an icon onto the toolbar to add it.

3. Drag an icon out of the toolbar to remove it

4. In the **Show** menu, choose **Small Size** to reduce the size of the icon on the toolbar. Click **Done** to save your changes and close the icon sheet.

**-TIP-**
**Default Toolbar**
Drag the default set onto the toolbar to return the toolbar to its factory-installed settings.

**-NOTE-**
**Keyboard Shortcut**
Press ⌘-**Option-T** to show or hide the toolbar in the selected document window.

# EXPORTING TO WORD

Microsoft Word and the Office application suite are the most popular applications on Macs and Windows computers. This task shows you how to export a Pages document to Word.

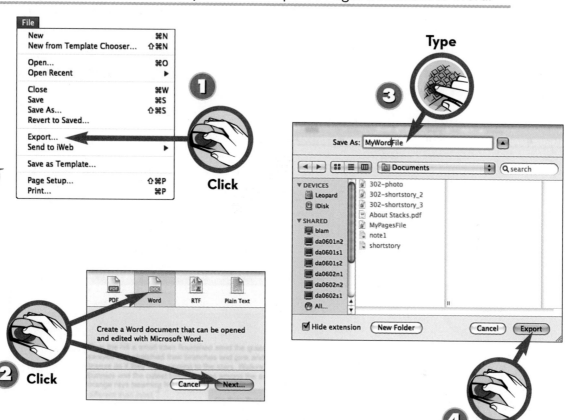

**Type**

**Click**

**Click**

**Start**

**End**

Using a document from previous tasks, choose **File** > **Export**.

Click the **Word** option on the Export sheet, and then click **Next**.

Type a name for the file.

Click **Export**.

# PRINTING A SPREADSHEET WITH NUMBERS

Numbers is the spreadsheet program in iWork '08. You can work with text boxes, shapes, and tables similarly to Pages and Keynote. However Numbers has a customized format bar for editing functions in tables, plus the capability to create functions across tables and sheets. The Print View option enables you to scale and layout the contents of a sheet as it would appear when you print it. This task shows you how to print a sheet with Numbers.

Start

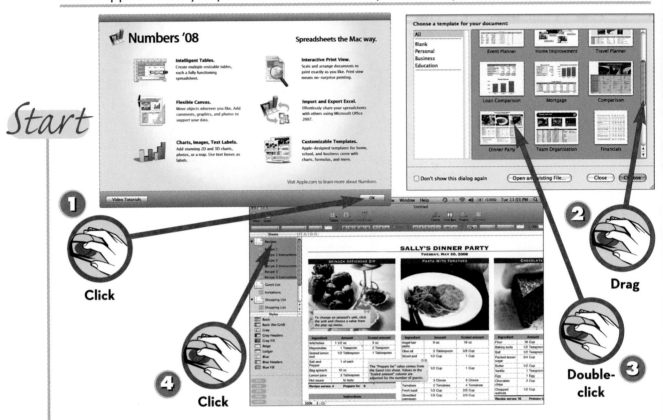

**Click**

**Click**

**Drag**

**Double-click**

① A Welcome screen appears the first time Numbers opens. Select a link to find out more about the features. Click the **OK** button to exit the Welcome window.

② The Template Chooser window opens each time you open Numbers or select it from the Dock. Drag the scroll bar to navigate the templates.

③ Double-click a template icon in the template chooser to create a new document. A new document window opens.

④ Select a sheet from the sidebar. The contents of the sheet appear on the canvas.

Continued

---

**TIP**

**Importing Excel Files**

To open a file created with Excel (Mac or Windows), drop one or more .xls file(s) onto the Numbers icon in Finder or on the Dock. Each worksheet in Excel appears as a sheet in Numbers.

**NOTE**

**Creating Charts from Tables**

Select a table or range of cells and choose a 2D or 3D chart from the **Chart** menu in the toolbar. The chart appears on the canvas populated with the selected data in the table.

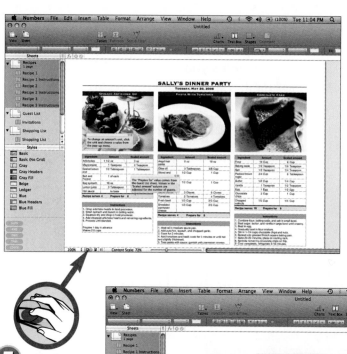

**Click**

**7**

**Click**

**5** **Click**

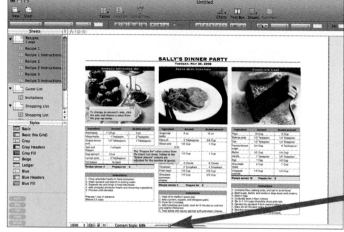

**6**

**Drag**

**5** Click the **Print View** button located at the bottom of the window. Or, choose the **File › Show Print View** menu. The canvas changes to a landscape page view.

**6** Drag the **Content Scale** slide control at the bottom of the window to shrink or grow the page contents.

**7** Choose the **File › Print Sheet** menu. The Print sheet appears. Select a printer and adjust any settings. Choose the **Print** button to print the document.

*End*

---

**TIP**

**Adjusting Margins and Paper Size**

To adjust margins and choose a page size, choose **View › Show Inspector**. Select the Document inspector to choose a Page Size. Choose the Sheet inspector to adjust margin settings.

**NOTE**

**Adding a Printer**

To find out how to add a printer to your Mac, go to Part 14, "Adding New Devices."

# PLAYING A SLIDESHOW WITH KEYNOTE

Create and playback presentations with Keynote. Keynote has similar table, text box, shape, and chart objects as Pages and Numbers. Keynote enables you to create slides with one or many themes (similar to templates in Pages and Numbers). This task shows you how to create and play a two-slide slideshow with Keynote.

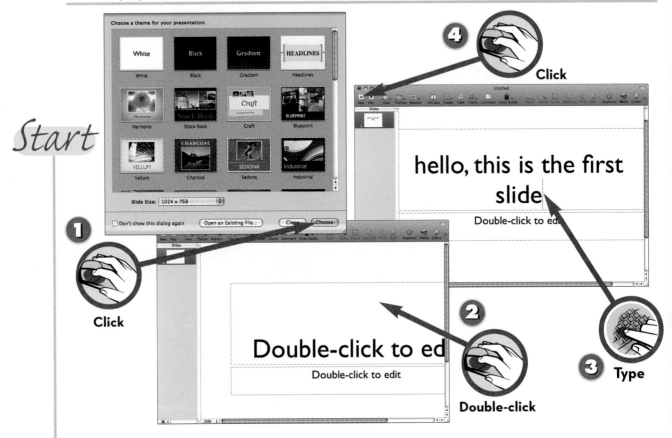

*Start*

Click

Double-click to ed

Double-click to edit

Double-click

hello, this is the first slide

Double-click to ed

Click

Type

**1** Select the **Keynote** icon in Finder or from the Dock to open the application. Click the **Choose** button, or press Return, to create a new document with the White theme.

**2** Double-click the text box on the canvas. The insertion point appears in the text box.

**3** Type some text into the text box. Press **Return** to end text editing, or click on the canvas.

**4** Click the **New** button in the toolbar to insert another slide. The new slide appears in the sidebar; its text appears on the canvas.

*Continued*

**TIP**
**Exporting to QuickTime**
Playback your slideshows on your iPod or iPhone. Choose the **File > Export** option in Keynote and choose **QuickTime** as the file format. Sync the QuickTime movie to your iPod Classic, Nano, Touch, or iPhone to view it.

**NOTE**
**Format bar shortcut**
Press ⌘-**Shift-R** to show the format bar in Keynote.

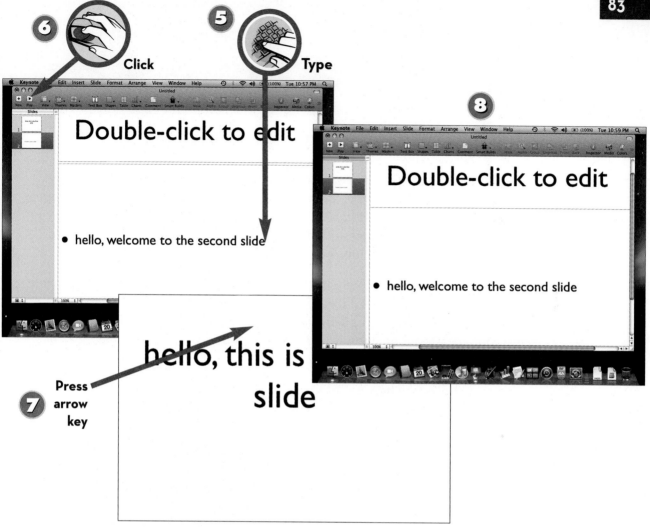

hello, this is slide

**5** Double-click the text box and type some text.

**6** Click the **Play** button in the toolbar to start a slideshow.

**7** View the first slide. Press the right arrow key to view the next slide. Conversely, press the left arrow key to view the previous slide.

**8** Wait for the last slide to end the slide show or press the Escape key to exit the slideshow and return to the Keynote window.

*End*

**TIP**

**What's a Master Slide?**

Master Slides enable you to change the look or format of a slide quickly and easily. You can select different master slides from the **Masters** button in the toolbar

**NOTE**

**Changing Themes**

Each slide in a document can use a unique theme. Choose a slide from the sidebar and click on the **Theme** menu in the toolbar to view or choose a different theme.

## CONNECTING TO THE INTERNET

The Internet consists of many, many computers that are connected together through a series of networks. Some computers are servers, hosting web pages; others store directory information and help computers see and find each other on the Internet. Browser software enables you to see web pages and other data stored on the Internet.

There are many different ways to connect to the Internet. In most cities, cable modems, which are offered through cable TV service providers, such as Comcast, are relatively popular. DSL (Digital Subscriber Line) provides Internet via telephone lines. You can also sign up for Internet access via cell phone providers.

This part shows you how to set up an Internet connection using a cable modem, surf the web with Safari, and use a MobileMe account to create web pages.

# THE SAFARI WORKSPACE

Refresh     Address field     Web page title     Search     Toolbar

Previous and
Next Page
buttons

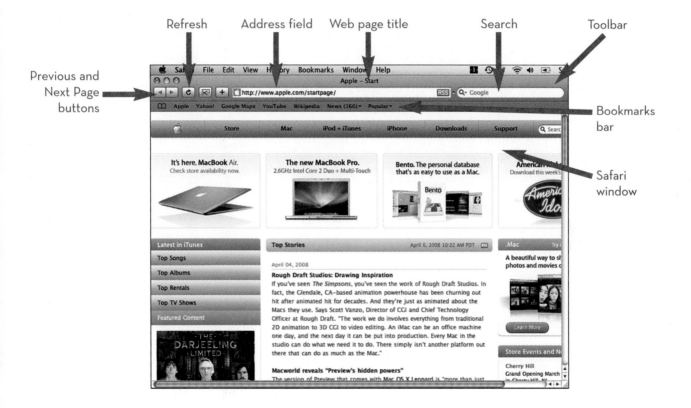

Bookmarks
bar

Safari
window

# SETTING UP THE INTERNET CONNECTION

Internet access through cable service is one of the most common ways that people access the Internet. The cable provider becomes your Internet service provider (ISP). They typically provide you with a cable modem that you connect to your cable connection and the Mac. This task shows you how to set up a cable modem.

 *Start*

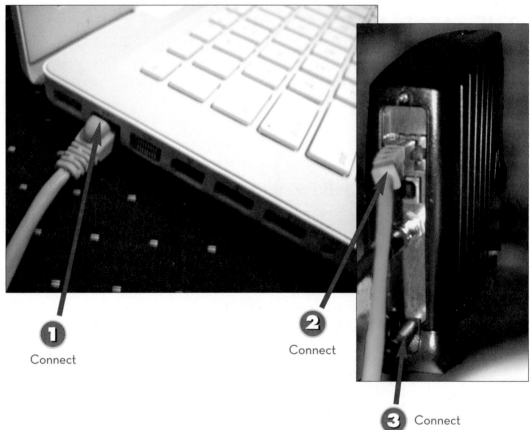

**1** Connect

**2** Connect

**3** Connect

**1** Connect an Ethernet cable to the Mac Ethernet port.

**2** Connect the other end to the cable modem. In this figure, the modem is connected to an AirPort base station. Connect the modem's power cord and plug it into an outlet.

**3** Connect the power cable to the Internet modem.

*Continued*

**TIP**
**Picking an Internet Service Provider**
Many Internet services are available to you: cable TV, telephone, satellite TV, or services provided through your cell phone plan. Review the plans available to you and choose the plan that best fits your needs.

**TIP**
**Connection Problems**
If your Internet modem for some reason cannot now connect to the Internet, check the service provider's web page for any known outages. Also, try powering the modem off and on.

**4** Press

**4** Press the power button on the modem. Wait for the connection lights to appear.

*End*

TIP

**Powering On the Modem**

Some modems power on when the power cord is connected to them. Others have an on/off switch. Read your modem's manual before connecting all the cables to familiarize yourself with the modem's basic features.

# SETTING UP A WIRED INTERNET CONNECTION

This task shows you how to set up an Ethernet Internet connection with automatically assigned addresses and DHCP. This is the default configuration for the Ethernet port. The steps show you where these settings are located in the System Preferences > Network window. After the Internet modem is connected to your network, try testing your Internet connection by surfing to a web page.

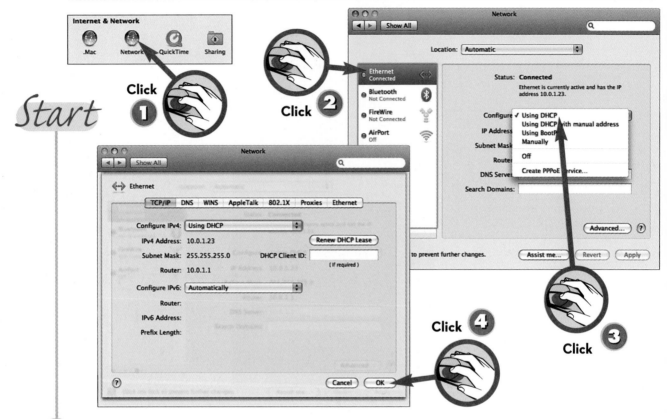

**1** In the System Preferences window, click the **Network** icon.

**2** Select the **Ethernet** connection.

**3** In the Configure list, choose **Using DHCP**. This is the default configuration. This DHCP setting allows the Mac to receive an IP address from the Ethernet router to enable network access.

**4** Alternatively, if you want to assign a static IP address to your Mac, click the **Advanced** button and select **Manually**. Type the IP address, subnet mask, and gateway IP addresses your ISP gave you to configure your Ethernet connection to the Internet into the panel, and then click **OK**.

*Continued*

## NOTE

### Dynamic IP Versus Static IP

A dynamic IP address is assigned by the router and the IP Address can change to enable your Mac to connect to the network. A static IP address is one that does not change and is usually assigned to you by a network administrator.

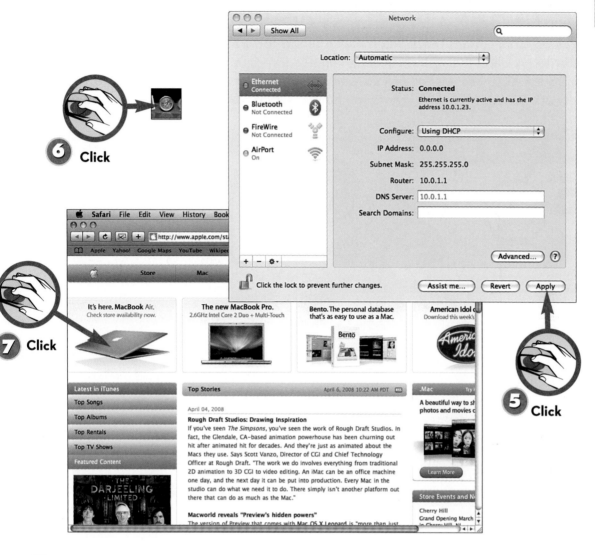

**5** Click the **Apply** button to save the changes.

**6** Click the **Safari** icon on the Dock to open Safari.

**7** View a web page such as www.apple.com to confirm the connection.

*End*

---

**NOTE**

**Cable Versus DSL**

If you're not sure which service to choose, look at the DSL services available in you area. Your location can determine the maximum throughput for your Internet connection. Conversely for cable, if there are lots of people accessing the Internet via cable modem, performance at peak hours is likely to be slower.

# SETTING UP A WIRELESS CONNECTION

Wireless connections to the Internet are similar to wired Ethernet connections to the Internet. A DHCP server, which assign an IP address to your Mac, is the most common configuration. Chances are you can connect to another wireless network without changing the network settings. This task shows you how to set up a DHCP wireless connection.

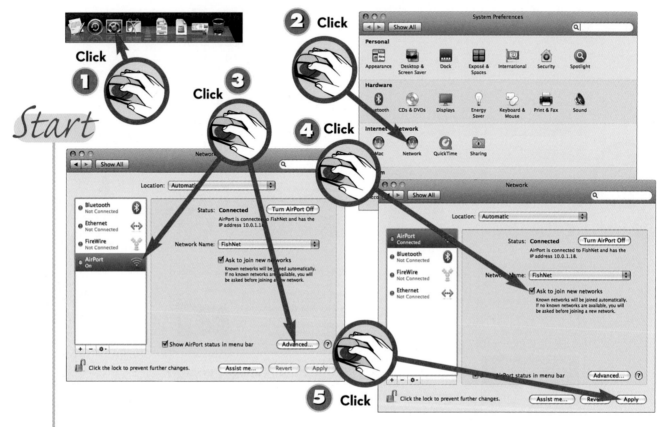

**Start**

1 Confirm that the AirPort Base Station is powered on. Click the **System Preferences** icon on the Dock. (See the tasks in Part 7 to find out more about how to set up an AirPort Base Station.)

2 Click the **Network** icon.

3 Choose **AirPort**. Click the **Advanced** button and choose **TCP/IP**. Then select **Using DHCP** from the drop-down menu. Click the **OK** button to return to the main Network window.

4 Check the **Ask to join new networks** check box.

*Continued*

---

**TIP**

**Network Status**

The Airport status in the menu bar shows the connection status as well as the strength of the wireless signal.

**NOTE**

**Secure Wireless Networks**

All available wireless networks are listed in the Airport menu. The networks that require a password show a lock icon on the right. Connecting to a secure network follows the same steps as connecting to a nonsecure network except you must type a password before connecting to it.

**Click**

**6**

**8** **Click**

**7** **Click**

**5** Click the **Apply** button to save your changes.

**6** View the wireless connection status in the menu bar.

**7** Click the **Safari** icon on the Dock.

**8** Refresh the page or surf to a new page.

*End*

**NOTE**

**Safari on iPod Touch, iPhone, and Mac OS X**

The Safari browser is available on Mac OS X as well as on the iPhone and iPod Touch. If you have favorite web pages on one device, consider choosing **File** > **Export Bookmarks** to import your favorite pages to another browser, such as FireFox or Internet Explorer, or to view with Safari on an iPhone or iPod Touch.

# SURFING THE WEB WITH SAFARI

Apple's Safari is the web browser for Mac OS X. it runs on Mac, iPhone, and iPod Touch computers, loading the full web page.

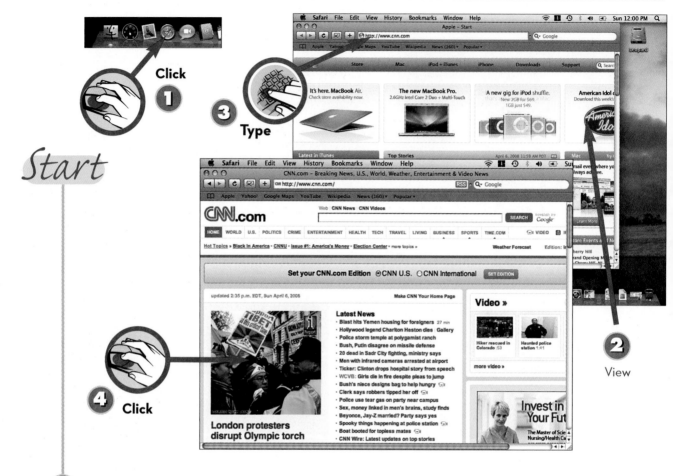

Click

Type

View

Start

Click

End

1. Click the **Safari** icon on the Dock.

2. View the web page.

3. Type the address (URL) of a page you want to view, and press **Return** to load the page.

4. Click a link.

**TIP**

### Setting a Default Web Page

In Safari, choose **Safari** > **Preferences** and click in the Home Page text edit field. Type a URL, such as www.google.com. Close the Preferences window. Open a new window in Safari to view the new home page.

# ADDING A BOOKMARK

Some URLs are relatively easy to remember (for example, cnn.com and google.com). Most are forgettable. One way to keep them at your fingertips is to create a bookmark. This task shows you how.

*Start*

**Type** ①

**Press Return** ②

③ **Click**

**Click** ④

① In Safari, type a URL in the **Address** field.

② Press **Return**.

③ Choose **Bookmarks** > **Add Bookmark**.

④ Click **Add**. View the new bookmark in the Bookmarks menu.

*End*

**TIP**

**Managing Bookmarks**

Choose **Bookmarks** > **Show All Bookmarks** to view all the bookmarks in Safari. Drag, rename, or delete the bookmarks to make them easier to find.

**NOTE**

**Add a Bookmark Shortcut**

Click the **+** (plus) button to the left of the URL field to add a bookmark, or press ⌘-**D**. Alternatively, drag a URL from the Safari toolbar and drop it in the bookmark bar to add it as a bookmark in Safari. Select the bookmark to load the web page.

# VIEWING MULTIPLE PAGES IN A WINDOW

In the old days, each web page opened in a separate window. Tabs in Safari enable you to store more than one web page in one Safari window to conveniently open a page that you view frequently without closing other pages you are viewing. This task shows you how to use web page tabs.

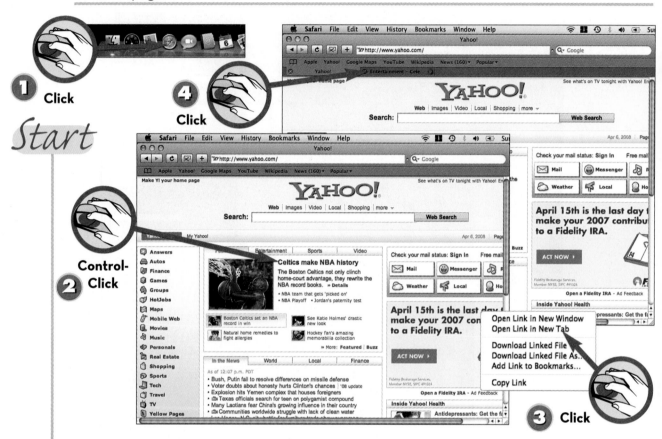

1. Open a web page in Safari.

2. **Control-click** a link. The context menu for the web page opens.

3. Select **Open Link in New Tab** from the context menu.

4. View the tab in the Safari window. Click it to view that page.

*End*

---

**TIP**

**Merging Pages**

If you have several windows open, you can merge them into one with tabs for the different pages. To try this out, open two or three windows in Safari, open a different web page in each, and then choose **Window > Merge All Windows**.

**TIP**

**Safari Alternatives**

Most web pages load successfully in Safari. If you find one that doesn't, try via the Firefox browser, which you can download from http://mozilla.com/firefox. Download the latest version for Mac OS X Leopard.

# CONFIGURING MOBILEME

You can configure your MobileMe (the service formerly known as .Mac) account from the Mac OS X System Preferences. This task shows you how to view iDisk information from the MobileMe panel.

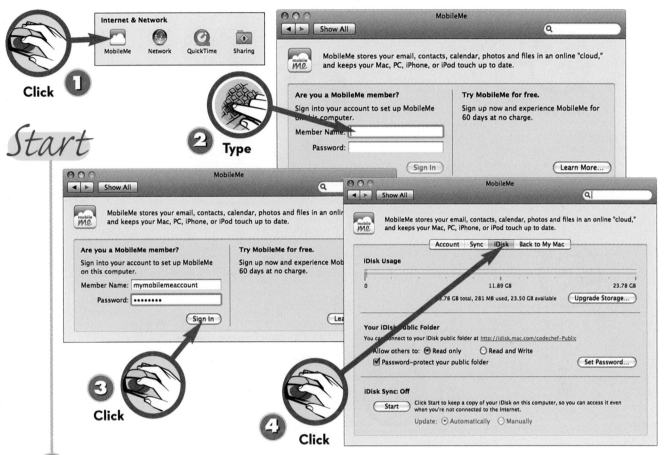

**Start**

**Click** **1**

**2** **Type**

**3** **Click**

**4** **Click**

**1** Open System Preferences and select MobileMe.

**2** Click in the **Member Name** field. Type your account information.

**3** Click **Sign In**.

**4** Select **iDisk** to view information about your account.

*End*

## TIP
### MobileMe and iTunes
If you plan to purchase music or movies in iTunes, you can use your MobileMe account to receive email about your iTunes purchases.

## TIP
### Movies on Your iPod
Movies purchased from the iTunes Store can be viewed on your Mac or on an iPod or iPhone. To sync the movie files, create a playlist of the movie or movies you want to put on your iPod or iPhone, and then click **Sync** in iTunes.

# ACCESSING FILES ON MOBILEME

Each MobileMe account includes iDisk access. This directory stores files created for MobileMe web pages, including iWeb domains. This task shows you how to mount the iDisk on your desktop.

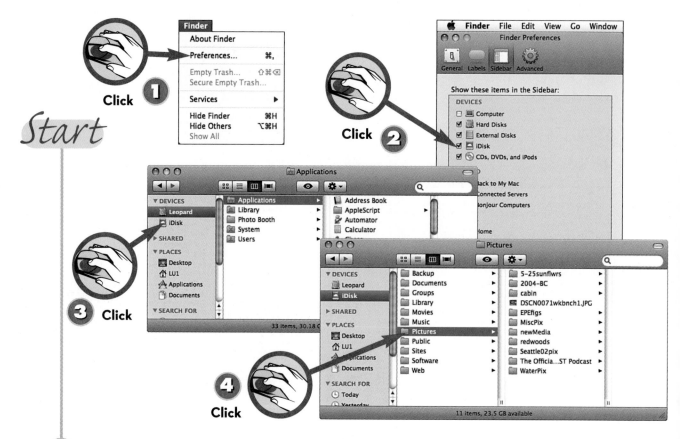

 **Start**

**Click** ①

**Click** ②

③ **Click**

④ **Click**

 **End**

① Choose **Finder** > **Preferences**.

② Check the **iDisk** check box.

③ Select **iDisk** in a Finder window.

④ Choose a folder on the iDisk.

---

**TIP**
**MobileMe Storage**
Each MobileMe account includes 10GB of storage. You can buy more if you like.

**TIP**
**MobileMe Services**
MobileMe accounts support Mail, galleries, Address Book, Home Page, and iCards. Navigate the MobileMe pages on http://mac.com to find out more about all you can do with your MobileMe account.

# CREATING A WEB PAGE ON MOBILEME

Although a MobileMe account is great for buying stuff on iTunes, it has lots of other great features. For example, you can publish web pages to your MobileMe site, iPod or iPhone. This task shows you how to publish a page from your MobileMe account.

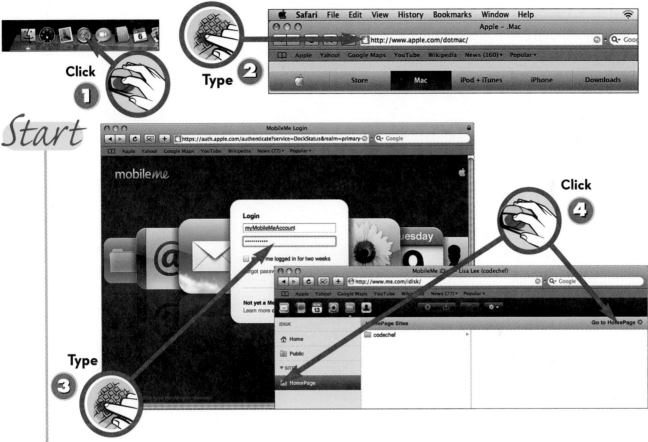

**Click** ①

**Type** ②

*Start*

**Type** ③

**Click** ④

① Click the **Safari** icon on the Dock to open Safari.

② Type **me.com** in the Address field and press **Return**.

③ Log in to your MobileMe account.

④ Select the **iDisk** (folder icon) button. Then choose the **Go to HomePage** link. Log in to your account again.

*Continued*

**TIP**

**Web Page Creation**

The MobileMe site provides a point-and-click interface to enable you to design a web page. Add text and photos and you're ready to publish your work and share it with the world.

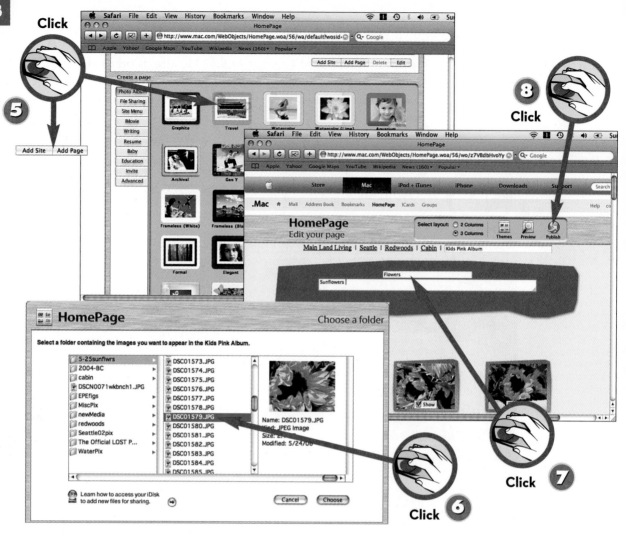

**Click** 5

**Click** 8

**Click** 7

**Click** 6

5 Select the **Add Site** button in the Home Page window to create a new site. If you already have a site, select the **Add Page** button. Choose an image for the page.

6 Navigate to a photo on your computer. Click the **Choose** button.

7 Select the files you want to use with the selected web page from the list of files. The selected images appear in the browser as you would see them if the page were published (viewable from someone else's browser.

8 Click the **Publish** button.

*End*

**TIP**

**MobileMe Mail**

MobileMe accounts include an email account which you can access by choosing the Mail hyperlink on the mac.com web page. You can use Safari to view, send and organize your MobileMe email.

# CREATING A PHOTO GRID PAGE WITH IWEB

iWeb is a website publishing application that is installed with iLife. You can publish one page or many to your MobileMe account using iWeb. This task assumes you have configured System Preferences > MobileMe to log into your MobileMe account. Follow these steps to learn how to create a web page with a set of image files using iWeb.

**1** Click

**2** Double-click

**3** Click

**4** Drag

*Start*

*End*

**1** Click the **iWeb** icon in the Dock. iWeb opens. (If you have not configured the MobileMe account in System Preferences > MobileMe, iWeb shows an alert asking you to log in. Type your login information and connect to MobileMe.)

**2** The template chooser window opens. Double click the **Photos** page from the template window to open it.

**3** Click the **Media Browser** button from the Toolbar. The Media Browser window opens.

**4** Drag over several images to select them and then drag and drop them onto a photo in the iWeb window. You can now view the images in the page.

---

**TIP**
### Create a Blog with iWeb
Select the **Blog** page from the template chooser window to create a blog page in iWeb.

**TIP**
### Change Themes
As your work on you iWeb pages, you may want to see page with a different template style. Choose the page and choose a different theme from the **Theme** menu in the toolbar.

# PUBLISHING A WEBSITE TO MOBILEME WITH IWEB

iWeb enables to you to create web pages by choosing many pages in a theme, or by mixing up theme pages. When you're ready to share your pages with the world, you can publish your website. iWeb sends your website to a folder that you can access from iDisk. Of course, you can also view your pages in Safari, or other browser. This task shows you how to create a web page with a set of image files using iWeb.

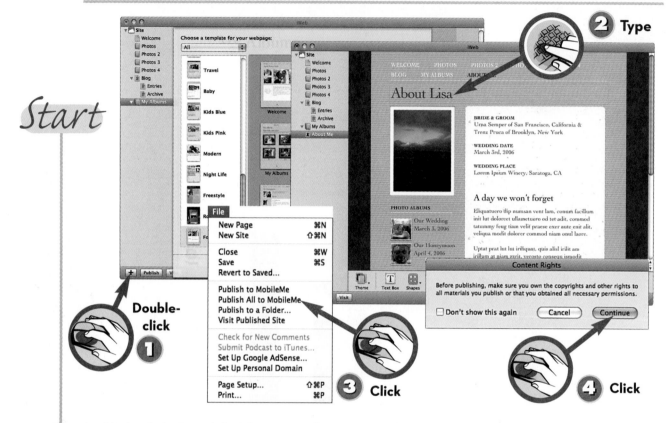

*Start*

**2 Type**

**Double-click 1**

**3 Click**

**4 Click**

1. In iWeb, click the + (plus) button in the main window to open the Template chooser. Insert as many pages as you like to create your website.

2. Edit text as you like.

3. Select the **File > Publish All to MobileMe** menu. An alert appears asking you if you want to publish your site.

4. Click **Continue** and wait for iWeb to publish your web pages. Open Safari and view the published pages.

*End*

**TIP**

**Saving Your Site**

Choose the **File > Save** menu or choose the **Save** button in the Alert when Quitting iWeb to save your changes. Publishing pages to MobileMe does not save your changes to your iWeb file on your hard drive.

**TIP**

**View Your Site**

After all of your pages are published to **MobileMe** you can view and navigate them with a browser. Choose **File > Visit Published** Site to view your web pages with Safari or the default browser on your Mac.

# SENDING FILES ATTACHED TO EMAIL

You can send a text document, image file, or zip archive as an email attachment using the Mail application. This is helpful if you want to share photos with family and friends, or other files. This task shows you how to send email attachments in email.

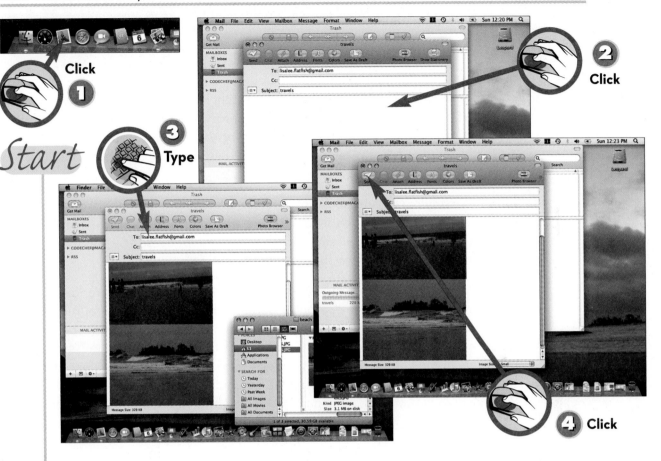

**Start**

**Click** ①

**Click** ②

**Type** ③

**Click** ④

① Click the **Mail** icon on the Dock to open Mail.

② Select the **New Message** button in the toolbar to create a new email window.

③ Open a folder that contains files you want to send, and drag and drop the files onto the email canvas. Type the email addresses into the To field.

④ Click the **Send** button to send the email.

**End**

**TIP**

**Sending Email from a Web Page**

Some web pages enable you to forward a URL (or an entire web page) in an email. Look for a hyperlink called "send to email" or something similar. Click on this hyperlink text and the Mail app opens. The Body of the email is populated with the address (URL) of the web page, and the contents of the page may also appear. Type the name of the recipient (you may want to include yourself). Click the **Send** button to send the email.

# SETTING UP A WIRELESS HOME NETWORK

A network enables you to navigate, listen, watch, print, or copy files between computers and other networked devices. Networks consist of computers and hubs (devices that propagate the network). Networks can be connected with wires or wirelessly. Most wireless connections use the Wi-Fi (Wireless Fidelity) standard.

There are many reasons to consider setting up a wireless home network. The obvious one is that you probably don't have a home prewired with Ethernet. The best reason to have a wireless home network is because you can use computers anywhere the wireless signal reaches.

The AirPort Base Station was the first popular network hub to use radio frequency (RF) signals to share computer data. There have been several AirPort models; the first model supported 802.11b—approximately 10 megabits per second data transfer rates. The current models are the AirPort Extreme Base Station and Time Capsule, which includes a hard drive with the wireless hub. These models support the Wi-Fi standard, including 802.11n (248Mbps), 802.11b (11Mbps), 802.11g (54Mbps). This part shows you how to set up a wireless network with Apple's AirPort Extreme Base Station.

# A WIRELESS INTERNET CONNECTION

AirPort Base Station

Connection status light

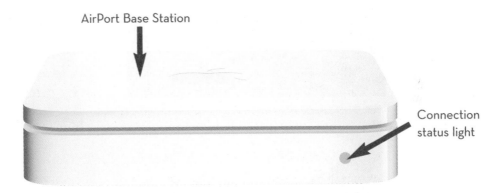

Courtesy of Apple

Courtesy of Apple

# SETTING UP AN AIRPORT EXTREME BASE STATION

AirPort Base Stations enable public or private wireless networks. You can configure one to connect to an Internet modem or to extend an existing wireless network to cover different floors or rooms in your home. This task shows you how to connect the AirPort hardware to a Mac.

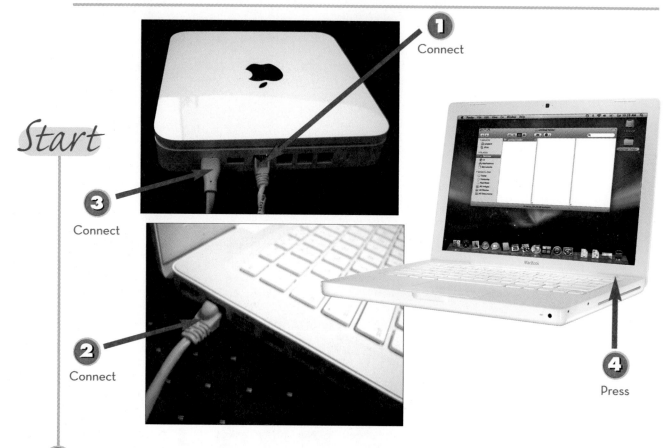

*Start*

**①** Connect

**③** Connect

**②** Connect

**④** Press

**①** Connect an Ethernet cable from the AirPort's Ethernet WAN port to the Internet modem.

**②** Connect a second cable from the AirPort's Ethernet port to a Mac. Power on the Internet modem.

**③** Connect the power cord to the AirPort Base Station.

**④** Power on the Mac.

*Continued*

**TIP**

**Powering On AirPort**

The AirPort Base Station powers on when the power cord is connected. There's no power on/off switch.

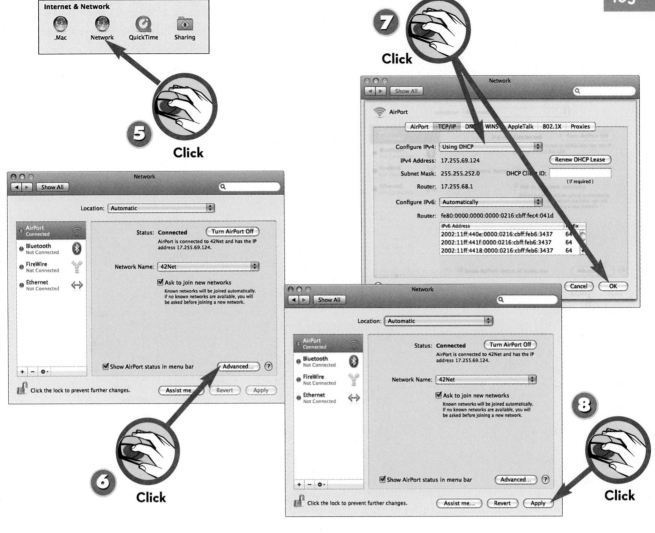

**Click**

**Click**

**Click**

**Click**

**Click**

**(5)** Open the **System Preferences** window and click the **Networks** icon.

**(6)** A list of network interface options appears on the left side of the Network window. Choose **AirPort**. Click the **Advanced** button.

**(7)** Select the TCP/IP tab. Choose **Using DHCP** from the Configure IPv4 drop-down list in the TCP/IP panel. Click **OK**.

**(8)** Click **Apply** to save all changes. After the AirPort base station is configured successfully, you can disconnect the Ethernet cables and connect to it with the AirPort card in your Mac.

*End*

---

 **TIP**

### Extending a Wireless Network

If you want to extend the range of the wireless network, add an AirPort Base Station and configure it to extend the existing wireless network. Place it within range of the other Base Station to extend the wireless network to more rooms or floors in your home.

 **NOTE**

### Network Connection for Setup

You can set up an Airport Base Station with a wired or wireless connection. For the first-time setup, I recommend using a wired Ethernet connection between the Mac and the Base Station.

# CONFIGURING AN AIRPORT EXTREME TIME CAPSULE

Time Capsule is the latest AirPort Extreme Base Station model; it has a hard drive that can work with Mac OS X Leopard's Time Machine. When a Mac is connected to the same network as the Time Capsule you can use the AirPort Utility program to configure and customize the AirPort Base Station or the hard drive as you like. Time Capsule enables you to back up files to the hard drive in the Base Station.

**Double-click**

**Type**

*Start*

**Click**

**Click**

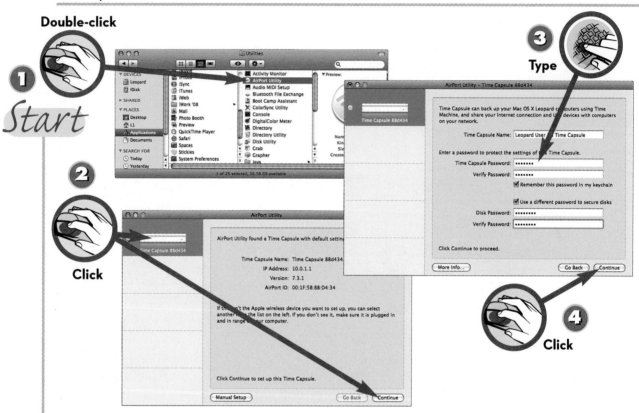

1. Open the **AirPort Utility** application. The program searches for AirPort Base Stations when it opens. Any AirPorts within range of your Mac appear on the left side of the AirPort Utility window.

2. Select **AirPort Extreme**. Click **Continue**.

3. Add a name and password. Click **Continue**.

4. Choose a wireless configuration for the Base Station. Click **Continue**.

*Continued*

## TIP

### Network Backups

The biggest benefit to having a networked hard drive is that Time Capsule works with Time Machine to automatically back up your files. You can access backups wirelessly as you like.

## NOTE

### Resetting Time Capsule

Each time you change the Time Capsule configuration, Time Capsule restarts. If your Mac fails to reconnect, press the **Reset** button on the back panel. Hold the **Reset** button down until the light in the front of the Time Capsule flashes, and then release it.

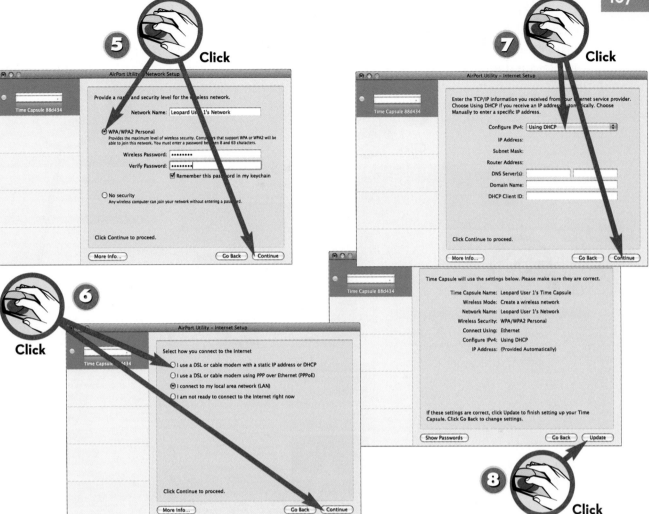

**5** Select **WP/WPA2 Personal** to add security to the network. Click **Continue**.

**6** Choose an Internet connection configuration. Click **Continue**.

**7** Choose **Using DHCP**. Follow the onscreen instructions. Click **Continue**.

**8** Review the summary. Click **Update** to send the settings to the Base Station.

*End*

---

**TIP**

**AirPort Preferences**

Choose **File** > **Preferences** to access AirPort preferences. The settings enable you to configure checking for updates.

**NOTE**

**Sleep and Wireless Networks**

When your Mac, iPhone, or iPod wakes from sleep, it will reconnect to a wireless network if Mac OS is set to remember login information for any available networks.

**TIP**

**What Is Time Capsule?**

To find out how to connect Time Machine to the Time Capsule hard drive, go to "Selecting a Time Capsule Drive," in Part 14.

# CONNECTING TO A WIRELESS NETWORK

Free wireless networking is available in some cities. Hotels, businesses, restaurants, and airports also offer free or paid wireless services. This task shows you how to connect to a wireless network.

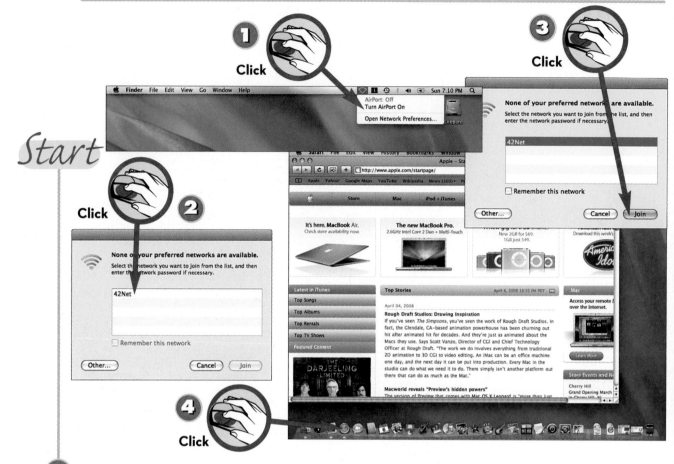

**Click** 1

**Click** 2

**Click** 3

**Click** 4

*Start*

*End*

1. Choose the **Turn AirPort On** option from the AirPort drop-down menu.

2. Select a wireless network from the list that appears.

3. Click the **Join** button. Wait for the AirPort connection to complete. Signal strength should appear in the menu bar.

4. Open **Safari** to begin browsing the web.

**TIP**
### Paying for Wireless Access
Most wireless networks, free or paid, require a name and password login prior to establishing the Internet connection. Read the online instructions or contact an admin if you are unable to log in to a wireless network

**TIP**
### Automatically Join Wireless Networks
Your Mac will automatically log in to wireless networks that you can access if you choose the **Remember any network this computer has joined** check box in the **AirPort** panel of the **System Preferences** > **Network** window.

# CHOOSING A DIFFERENT WIRELESS NETWORK

Your Mac can connect to a wireless network from the AirPort menu. This task assumes you have turned AirPort on and are already connected to a wireless network. It shows you how to change to a different wireless network.

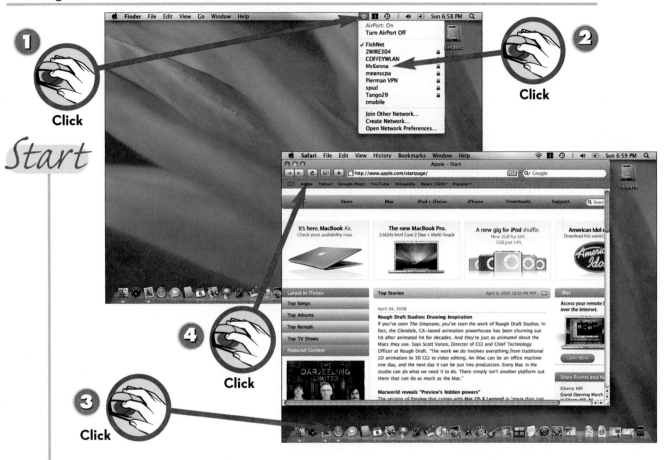

 *Start*

 *End*

**1** Click the **AirPort** drop-down menu. A list of wireless network appears.

**2** Choose a wireless network. Type a password if prompted. Wait for the wireless connection to complete.

**3** Open **Safari**.

**4** View a web page or type a URL to a new web page.

---

**TIP**

**Free Wireless Networks**

Choose the **Safari> Preferences** menu command and click the **General** tab. Choose the **Home Page** text field. Type a web address, such as **www.google.com**. Close the **Preferences** window. Open a new window in Safari to view the web page.

**NOTE**

**Understanding the AirPort Menu**

Wireless networks are not created equal. Networks showing a Lock icon indicate a password is required. Networks that don't appear to be locked may not necessarily be accessible.

# SHARING FILES WITH WINDOWS VISTA

There are many ways to share files with friends and family. You can send email, create a web page, or print them. Another alternative is to create a read-only folder and share it on the network. In Part 2, you learned how to turn on file sharing in "Sharing Files and Folders." This task shows you how to share files with Windows computers.

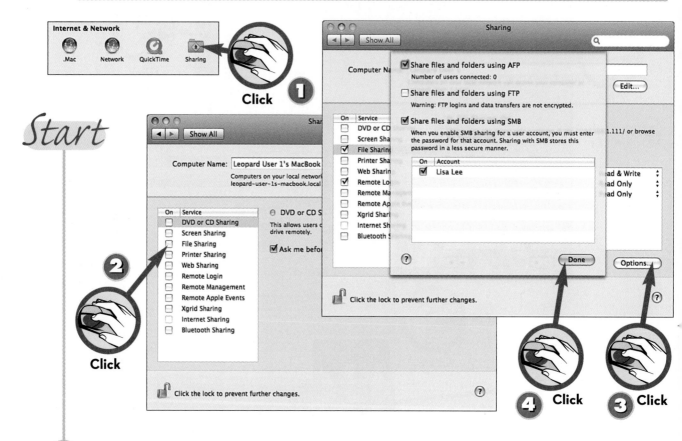

**1** Select the **Apple > System Preferences** menu command. Select **Sharing**.

**2** Check the **File Sharing** check box.

**3** Click the **Options** button.

**4** Select **Share files and folders using SMB**. The administrator user is selected by default. If you have multiple accounts on your Mac can select specific ones for smb. Click **Done**.

*Continued*

**TIP**

**Sharing and Security**

Creating a read-only folder allows folks who log on to your Mac to copy files to their computers, and prevents anyone from copying files to your Mac. Another precaution is to create an account for those you want to share your files with so that you can tell if/when they log in to your computer.

**NOTE**

**Sharing Files with Macs**

The AFS (Apple File Share) setting in the Options panel of the Sharing Preference enables other Mac OS X computers to connect with your Mac when File Sharing is enabled.

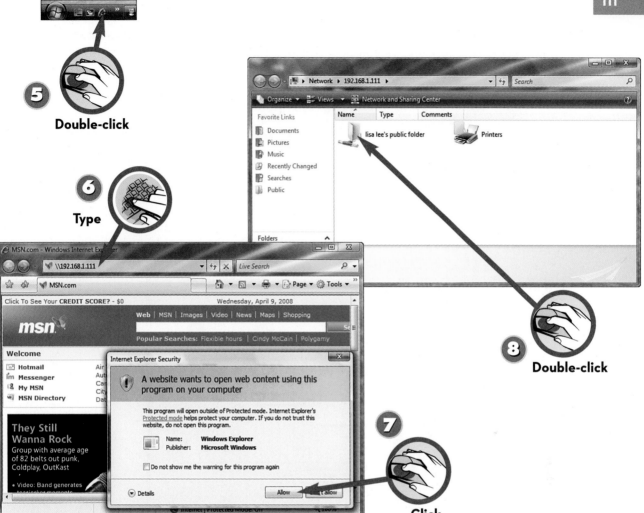

**5** Double-click

**6** Type

**7** Click

**8** Double-click

**5** On the Windows computer, open **Internet Explorer**.

**6** Type the IP address of the iMac and press **Enter**. Open the **Applications > Utilities> Network Utility** program and select the **Info** tab.

**7** Click the **Allow** button in the Internet Explorer Security panel.

**8** The Public folder on the Mac appears in Internet Explorer. Double-click it to open it.

*End*

**TIP**

**Networks and File Sizes**

Sharing files works great if you have a 2MB to 5MB file. Your Mac or Windows machine may slow down a little while the data is sent across the network.

**NOTE**

**Network and Large Files**

Larger files, especially on a slow network, may cause a computer to perform slowly or even crash. For best results, try to avoid sharing files larger than 10MB.

# CONNECTING TO A WINDOWS VISTA COMPUTER

Macs running Mac OS X Leopard can access files shared on Windows computers as well as on other Macs. This task shows you how to use a Max OS X Leopard machine to log in to a Windows computer that has enabled File Sharing.

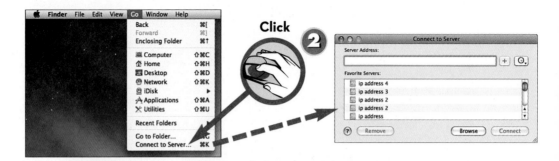

*Start*

**1** On the Windows computer, choose the **Turn on file sharing** option.

**2** On the Mac, choose **Connect to Server** from the Finder's **Go** menu.

*Continued*

**TIP**

**Alternative Names**

If the computer name doesn't work, try typing the TCP/IP address of the Windows computer in Step 3.

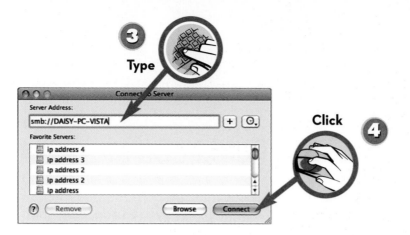

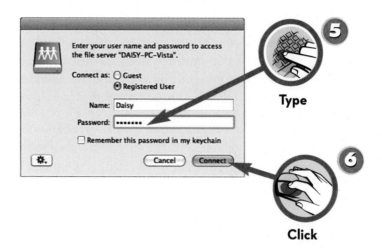

**3** On the Mac, type the name of the Windows Vista computer in the Connect to Server window.

**4** Click the **Connect** button.

**5** Type the name and password into the login window.

**6** Click the **Connect** button.

**NOTE**

**Test with a Windows Computer**

If your Mac is not able to connect to a Windows Vista computer, try to access it with a second Windows XP or Vista machine. If the Windows machine is successful, consider checking the network connection on the Mac.

## MANAGING AND SYNCING CONTACTS WITH ADDRESS BOOK

The Address Book is part of Mac OS X. It enables you to add, edit, and remove name, phone, email and address information for individuals, companies, and groups on your Mac. It also manages your Me card.

A Me card is created when you first log in to Mac OS X. The name you create for your user account is added to the Address Book as a Me card. You can add more people to the Address Book as individuals or groups. You can also print Address Book contacts (for example, if you want to print mailing labels for invitations or to let folks know your address has changed).

The contacts in Address Book can also be synced with an iPod or iPhone, enabling you to quickly access the phone number, email, or address when you're computer is not available. This task shows you how to add, edit, and sync contacts with Address Book.

# THE ADDRESS BOOK WORKSPACE

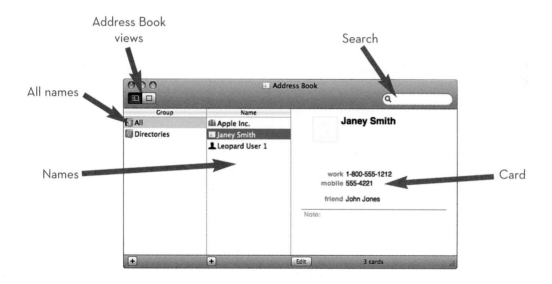

Address Book views

Search

All names

Names

Card

# ADDING A NAME

Address Book has a simple yet elegant feature set that enables you to add, modify, or remove Address Book fields easily. This task shows you how to add a new name to your Address Book.

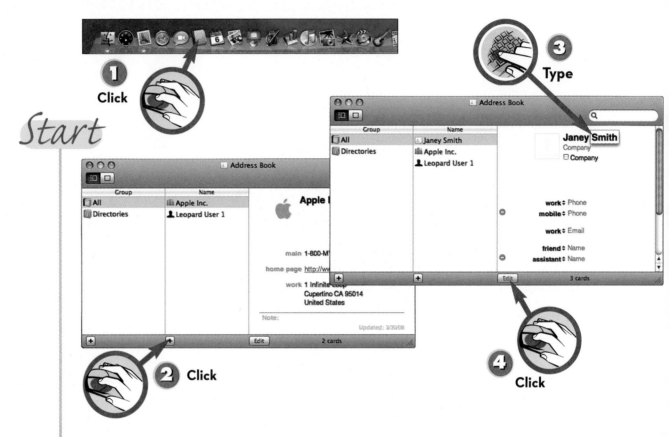

**1** Click

*Start*

**2** Click

**3** Type

**4** Click

**1** Click the **Address Book** icon on the Dock to open Address Book.

**2** Click the + (plus) button. The card window appears in the Address Book window.

**3** Type a first and last name. Type a company name also, if applicable.

**4** Click the **Edit** button to save your changes.

*End*

**TIP**
**Add to Your Address Book**
Have a bunch of addresses in Microsoft Outlook or Entourage? Import vCards from Microsoft Outlook or Entourage to Address Book. In Address Book, choose **File > Import > vCards** to open the Import sheet.

**NOTE**
**Create a vCard**
Select an individual or group from the Name list in Address Book. Drop the entry onto the desktop. A vCard with the addressee's name appears on the desktop.

# EDIT AN ADDRESS BOOK CARD

As time goes by, you, your associates, neighbors, family, and friends will inevitably move or change email addresses, cell phone numbers, and so on. Address Book can help you keep up with the changes so that you can be sure that you are always up-to-date. This task shows you how to edit an existing contact.

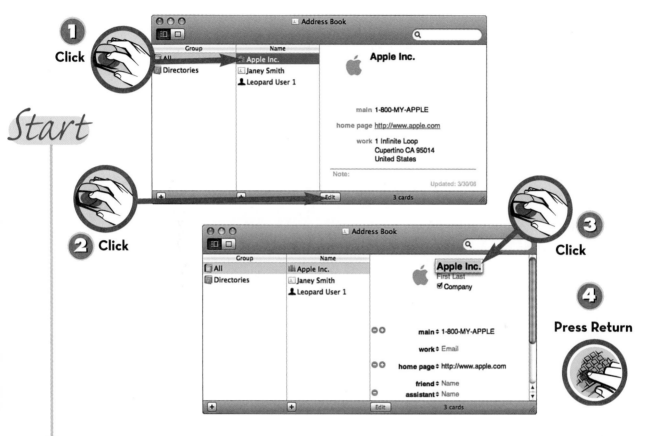

1. Select a contact from the Name column in Address Book.

2. Click the **Edit** button. Text in the First Name field is highlighted.

3. Select the field you want to edit, such as **Company Name**. Click to place the insertion point in the field and type to add text, or press **Delete** to remove text.

4. Press **Return** to end the editing of the field.

---

## TIP
### Address Book Views
The tasks in this chapter use the View Card and Column window view. An alternative view is the View Card Only mode; both views are available in the upper-left corner of the Address Book window.

## NOTE
### Keyboard Shortcuts
Press ⌘-] to navigate to the next card in the Name list. Press ⌘-[ to navigate to the previous card in Address Book. Press ⌘-L to turn Edit mode on and off in Address Book.

# ADDING A NEW FIELD

Address Book enables you to add multiple phone numbers, email addresses, and so on for the same contact. A green plus button appears beside fields that can show more than entry. This task shows you how to add a phone number to an Address Book card.

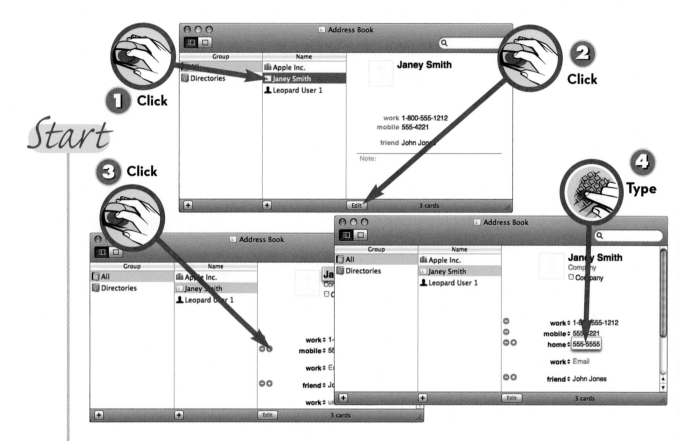

*Start*

**1** Select a name in Address Book

**2** Choose the **Edit** Button. The card changes to Edit mode.

**3** Click the green **+** button beside the Phone Number section in the card window. A new phone field appears.

**4** Type in the field. Press **Return** to save your changes.

*End*

---

**NOTE**

**More Address Book Fields**

Choose from a complete list of Address Book fields. Open the **Card > Add Field** menu in Address Book. Here you can insert fields for Phonetic First/Last Name, Prefix, Middle Name, Suffix, Nickname, Job Title, and more.

# REMOVING A FIELD

Removing fields is just as easy as adding them. You might need to remove a field to update information in a card, or to only show the minimum amount of information in a card. This task shows you how to remove a field from a card.

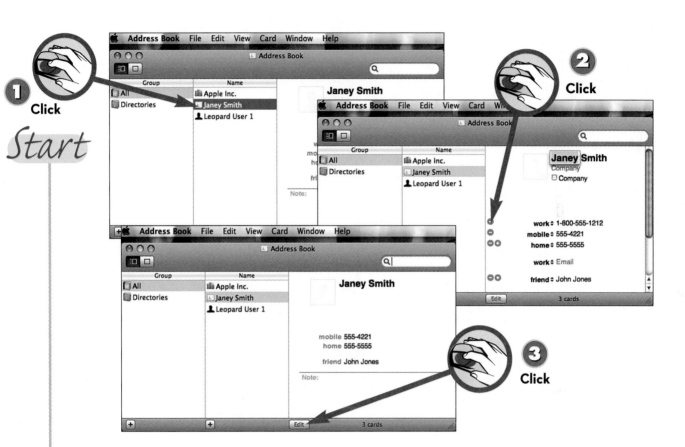

**Start**

**Click**

**Click**

**Click**

1. Select a name in Address Book.

2. Click the — (minus) button for the field you want to remove. The text in the corresponding field is cleared.

3. Click the **Edit** button again. The field no longer appears in the card.

**End**

**NOTE**

**Remove a Contact from Address Book**

Select a contact in the Name column in Address Book. Press **Delete** to remove the contact from Address Book.

**TIP**

**Restoring a Deleted Field**

Choose **Edit > Undo Edit Property** to restored a deleted field immediately after its been deleted.

# CREATING A GROUP

Each name in Address Book can be added to one or many groups. Groups enable you to organize names into groups to make it easier to do things such as send email to a group or invite a group to lunch. This task shows you how to create a new group.

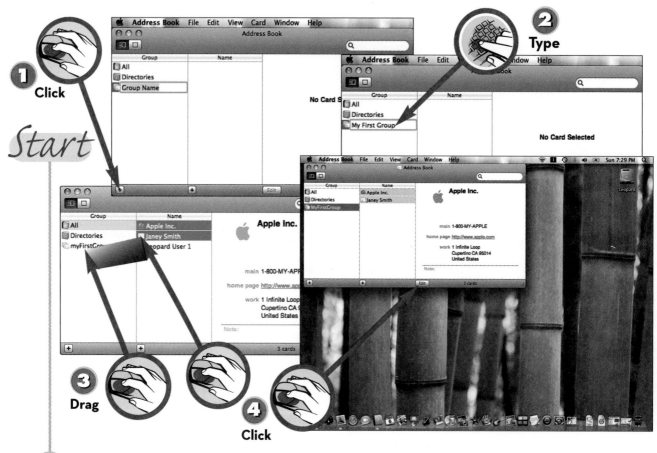

**Start**

**1** Click

**2** Type

**3** Drag

**4** Click

**1** Click the + (plus) button below the Group column of the Address Book window.

**2** Type a name for the group. Press **Return**.

**3** Drag names into the group.

**4** Click **Edit** to modify any individual's information.

*End*

**TIP**

**Sending Email to a Group**

Open Mail and create a new message. In the To field, type the name of the group in Address Book. Now you can send this email to a group of people!

**TIP**

**Search Address Book**

Select a group or set of names in Address Book. Type a word or words you want to search for in the Search field. Press **Return** to see whether there is any matching criteria.

# PRINTING A MAILING LIST WITH ADDRESS BOOK

Printing a list of labels for invitations or holiday greetings can be a chore if you have to print each page one by one. This task shows you how to print labels for a mailing list with Address Book.

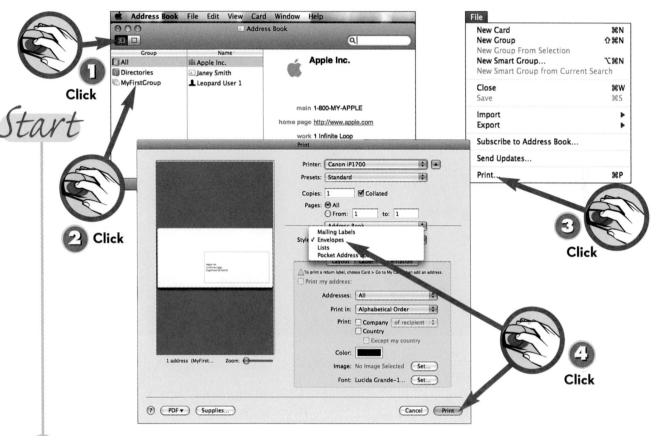

1. Click the **View Card and Column** view.

2. Select a group or more than one name in the Address Book window.

3. Choose the **File** > **Print** from the Address Book menu bar.

4. In the Print sheet, select the **Mailing Labels** from the Styles drop-down menu. Choose from Avery Standard, Avery A4, or DYMO from the Page drop-down menu or create a custom page. Click the **Print** button.

*End*

---

## TIP
### Print a Test Sheet First

Before you put the actual mailing label paper in the printer, print a sheet to regular paper. Place it over the mailing label paper and hold it under the light. See whether the printed text maps to the label borders on the mailing label paper.

# SYNCING CONTACTS WITH IPOD

iTunes enables you to share the same Address Book contacts on your Mac with the calendar on your iPod or iPhone. This task shows you how sync contacts with an iPod.

**Connect** ①

*Start*

② **Click**

① Connect the iPod to your Mac.

② iTunes opens. Select the iPod in the sidebar.

*Continued*

---

**TIP**

**Sync Back to the Mac**

If you add contacts on the iPhone or iPod Touch, the new contacts can also be added to your Mac when you sync with iTunes.

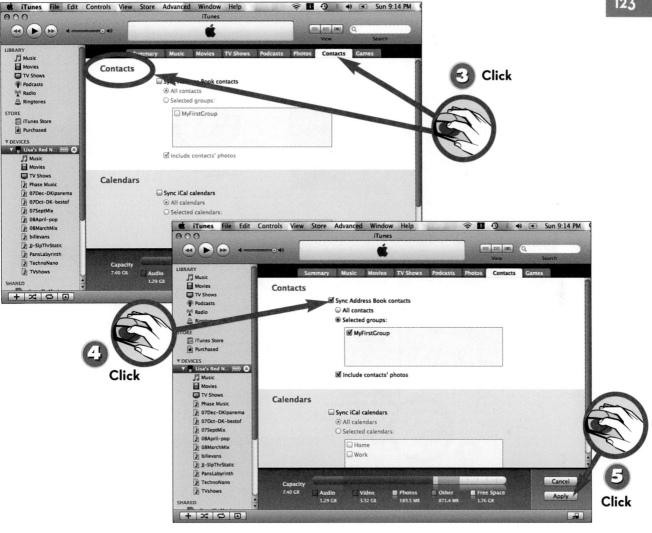

**3** Click the **Contacts** tab.

**4** Check the **Sync Address Book contents** check box.

**5** Click **Apply**. The Tunes status shows the sync progress to your iPod.

*End*

**TIP**

**Sync Calendar Events**

To find out how to sync your calendar to an iPod or iPhone, see Part 9, "Managing and Syncing Your Calendar with iCal."

# SYNCING NAMES WITH IPHONE

iTunes enables you to sync schedules to your iPod or iPhone. This task shows you how to set up iTunes to automatically sync a calendar to an iPhone.

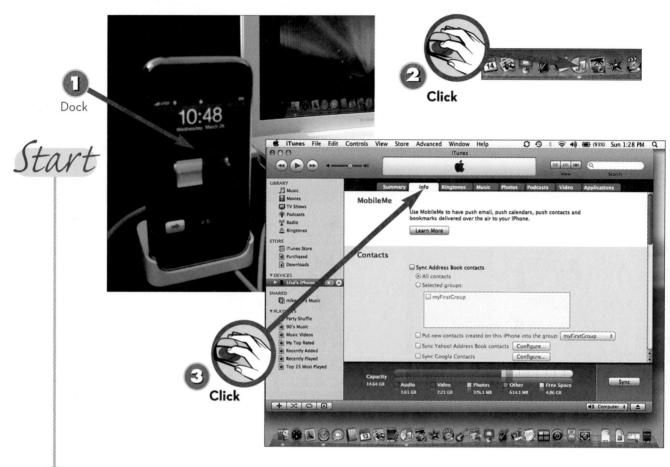

Dock

**2** Click

*Start*

**3** Click

**1** Connect the iPhone dock to your Mac and set the iPhone in it.

**2** iTunes opens. Select the iPhone from the sidebar.

**3** Click the **Info** tab.

*Continued*

**TIP**

**Secure Your Information**

Your iPhone and iPod Touch holds a lot of precious information about you and your friends. To protect your iPhone from the wrong hands, add a passcode. From the iPhone's Home screen, select **Settings** > **General** > **Passcode Lock** to assign a passcode and turn this feature on or off on your iPhone.

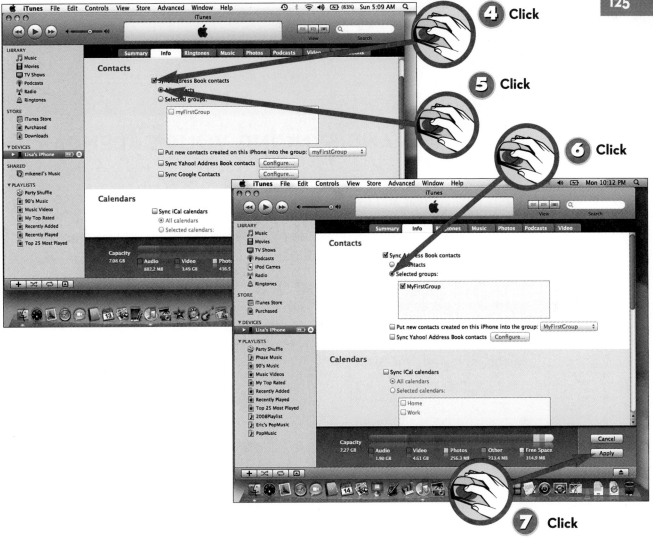

**4** Click

**5** Click

**6** Click

**7** Click

**4** Check the **Sync Address Book contacts** check box.

**5** Choose **All Contacts** to sync all the groups to your iPhone.

**6** Choose **Selected Groups** if you want to sync only some of your Address Book data.

**7** Click **Apply**. The Tunes status shows the sync progress to your iPhone.

*End*

**NOTE**

**Learn More About Devices**

To find out more about how to add devices to your Mac, go to Part 14, "Adding New Devices."

**TIP**

**Locating Contacts on iPod Touch and the iPhone**

On the iPhone, from the Home screen, select the **Phone** button. Then choose the **Contacts** button to view, add or delete contacts from your iPhone.

## 9

# MANAGING AND SYNCING YOUR CALENDAR WITH ICAL

iCal is the calendar and event-scheduling program installed with Mac OS X. iCal enables you to schedule one-time or recurring events in a calendar. You can create separate calendars for home, work, or whatever you like. You can also import calendar events from Entourage in Mac Office or export calendars.

Events in iCal can also be synced with the calendar on most iPods (shuffle and mini do not have this feature) and on iPhones, enabling you to quickly access your schedule when you're computer is not available. This task shows you how to add, edit, and sync events with iCal on your Mac with an iPod and iPhone.

# THE ICAL WORKSPACE

Go to today's Calendar view

Calendar view

Search

Calendar sidebar

Current time

Month view

View Shortcuts

Event

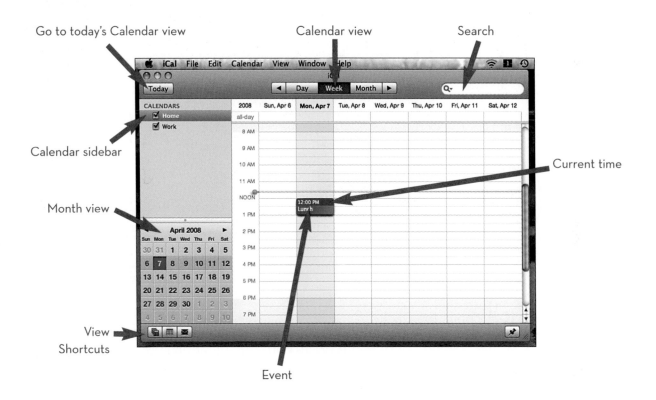

# ADDING AN EVENT

iCal is great for managing one or many calendars. iCal enables you to set a reminder, set an appointment, meet with someone, or manage your day. This task shows you how to create an event in iCal.

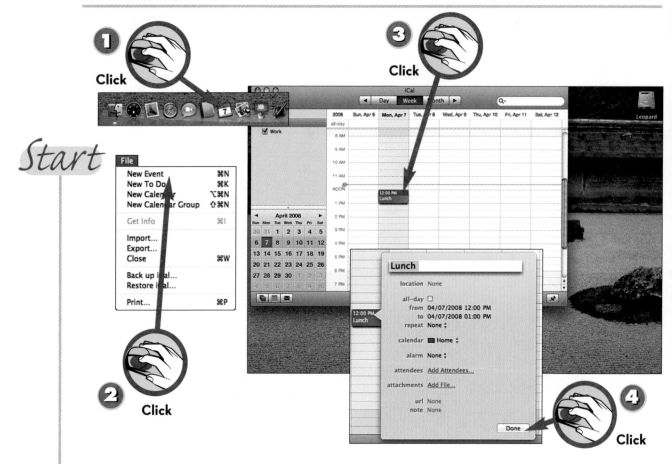

1. Select the **iCal** icon in the Dock.

2. Choose **File** > **New Event**. The event is created in a one-hour time slot at the current time in the calendar.

3. Select the event. Review or change the name, and set the dates and times in the **from** and **to** fields.

4. Click **Done**.

*Start*

*End*

---

**-TIP-**

**Creating an Event on an iPhone**

Click the **+** button in the calendar to add an event to Today.

**-TIP-**

**iCal Knows Today's Date**

Each time you open iCal or the calendar on iPhone or an iPod Touch, today's calendar will appear. Today's date will appear in iCal's icon in the dock, or on the iPhone's Home screen.

# EDITING AN EVENT

Often, the name or time for an event changes after you've set it up in your calendar. This task shows you how to edit the date and time and set the alarm for an existing task in iCal.

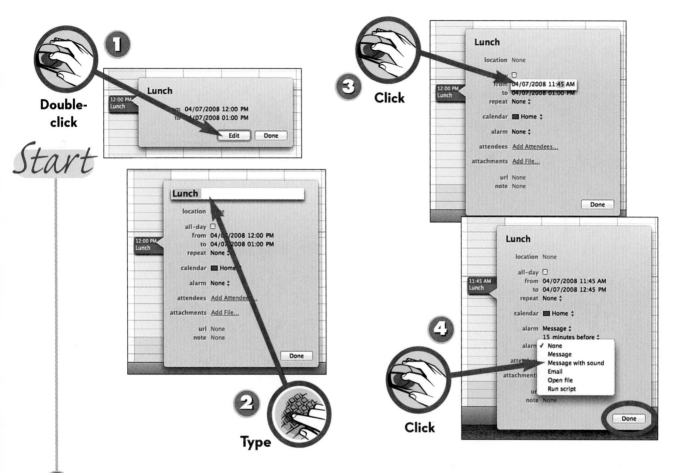

**Double-click**

**Start**

**Type**

**Click**

**Click**

**End**

1. Double-click the event and click the **Edit** button.

2. The name of the event is highlighted. Edit the name of the event if you like.

3. Change the date or time in the **from** and **to** fields.

4. Click in the **alarm** field to set the alarm. There are several options, including receiving an email. Click **Done** when you have finished.

**TIP**

**All-Day Events**

Check the all-day check box if you want an event to fill your workday or span several days. Events that are scheduled across multiple days will appear only on the first day in the calendar.

**NOTE**

**Editing Events on an iPhone**

Because the iPhone has a touch screen, it's a little more entertaining to change the times in an event. The from and to fields are spinning wheels in the iPhone calendar.

# CREATING A REPEATING EVENT

Some things happen more often than others, such as a weekly sporting event or a bimonthly meeting. So, instead of creating a new event on the calendar for that biweekly lunch date with Mom, create a repeating event. This task shows you how.

*Start*

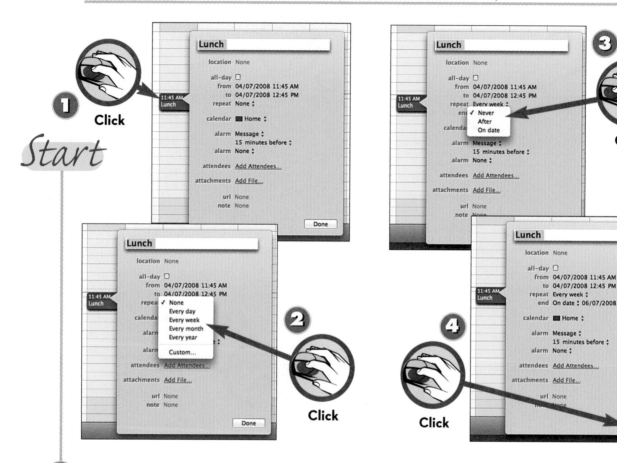

**Click**

**Click**

**Click**

**Click**

**1** Select an event on your calendar. Press ⌘-**E** to make the event editable when it opens.

**2** Select the frequency/interval from the **repeat** menu in the event pop up.

**3** Set the **end** date for the repeat event.

**4** Click the **Done** button to save your changes and close the event panel.

*End*

## TIP

### Import Events

iCal supports importing the: vCal, or Entourage calendar file formats. Choose **File** > **Import** to take the first steps toward populating your calendar.

## NOTE

### Deleting Repeating Events

You can delete one or all instances of a repeating event. Select the event in the calendar and press the Delete key. iCal ask whether you want to delete the one-time event or the repeating event. If you need to remove only one instance, delete the one-time event.

# CUSTOMIZING PREFERENCES

iCal has several preferences for customizing what you see in the main calendar window. This task shows you how to configure iCal preferences.

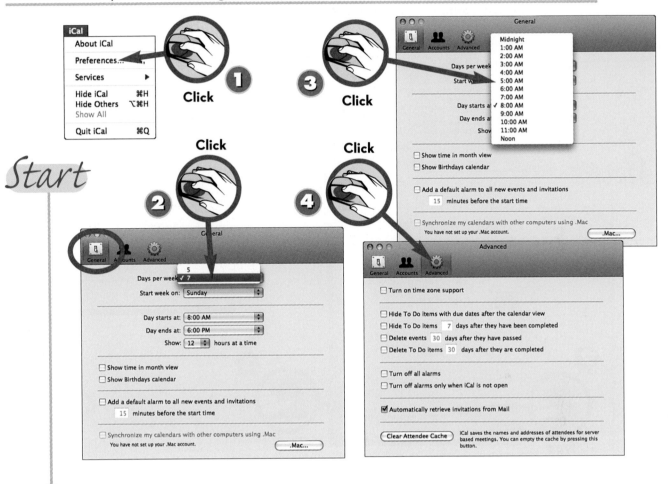

**Start**

**Click** ①

**Click** ②

**Click** ③

**Click** ④

**End**

① Choose **iCal** > **Preferences** to open the **Preferences** window.

② Choose the **General** panel, and then select the day view for your calendar from the **Days per week** drop-down list. You can choose a full 7-day week or, if you prefer, you can show only a 5-day workweek that starts any day of the week.

③ Set the hours available for events in the **Day starts at** and **Day ends at** drop-down lists.

④ Click the **Advanced** button on the toolbar to access additional options that customize the way iCal works. Close the **Preferences** window to return to iCal.

---

**NOTE**

**Day View Versus Month View**

The Month view is like the 10,000-foot level view of your schedule. A day-to-day view enables you to focus on the tasks at hand.

**NOTE**

**Mac OS X Preferences**

Advanced preferences in iCal can help keep your calendar organized, such as hiding completed To-Do items, retrieving invitations from Mail, and deleting past events. To find out more about preferences in Mac OS X, go to Part 3, "Customizing Mac OS X Leopard."

# ADDING A NOTE

Most events are recognizable by their title. Notes, however, can come in handy if you want to capture some thoughts that don't quite fit in the Title field. This task shows you how to add a note to an event.

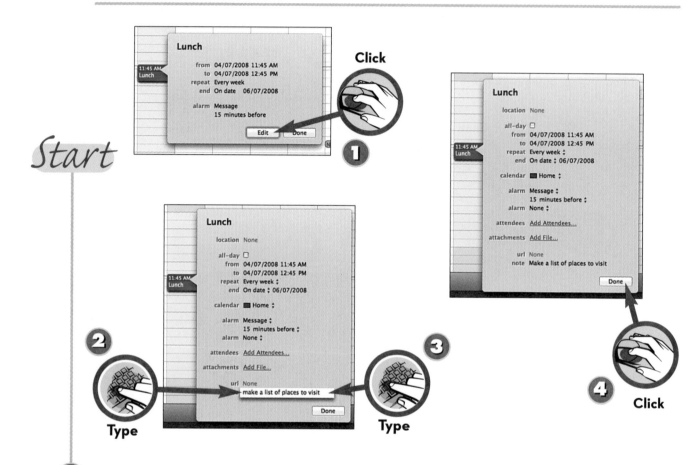

*Start*

**Click**

**Type**

**Type**

**Click**

*1* Select an event and click the **Edit** button.

*2* Place the insertion point in the **Notes** field. Type a note.

*3* Press **Return** to end editing the field.

*4* Click **Done** to save your changes and close the event panel.

*End*

**TIP**

### Abbreviations in Titles

One way to fit more details into an event title is to use abbreviations. This is where notes can help. Decrypt the abbreviations by pasting the de-abbreviated acronyms in a note.

# MOVING AN EVENT

There are two ways to move an event on a Mac. You can change the date in the Event pop-up panel, or you can just drag it to the day you want. If it is a repeating event, you'll be asked whether the change applies to the entire event or just the one instance that you moved.

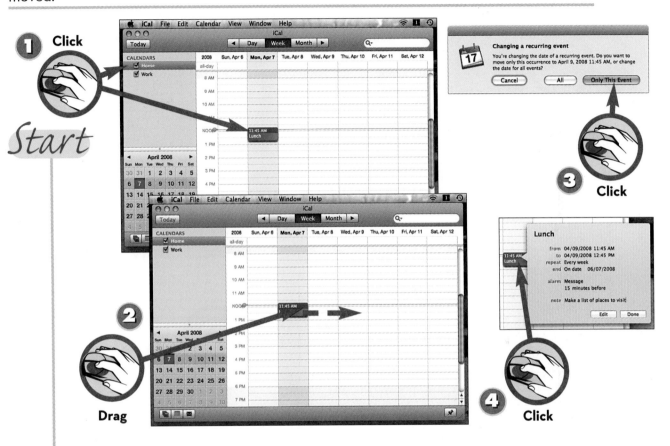

**① Click**

**Start**

**③ Click**

**② Drag**

**④ Click**

① Choose the calendar you want in iCal, and then select an event in that calendar.

② Drag it to another day.

③ If the event is repeating, choose **Only This Event** if you want one only instance of the event to change, or **All** if you want them all to change.

④ Select the event again to view the new date.

**End**

## TIP

### Rescheduling Events

Sometimes it's easier to create an entirely new event instead of modifying the original one. Keep the original until after the new event is created to make sure all the details and notes are preserved in the new event. Then select the original one and delete it.

# SYNCING EVENTS WITH AN IPOD

The calendar on the iPod can show similar calendar information that is on your Mac. This task shows you how to sync events from your Mac to an iPod. Before you start, connect your iPod Touch, Classic, or Nano to your Mac.

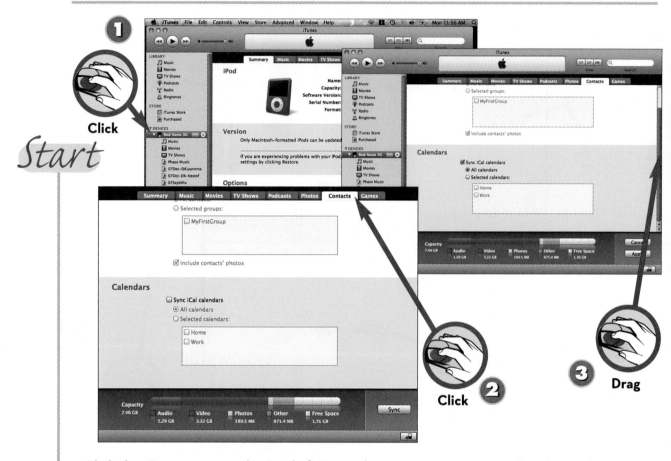

*Start*

**1** Click the **iTunes** icon on the Dock if iTunes doesn't open automatically. The iPod is selected.

**2** Click the **Contacts** tab.

**3** Scroll down to the **Calendar** section of the panel.

*Continued*

**TIP**
**Sync Back to the Mac**
If you add events on the iPhone or iPod Touch, you can also add the new events to your Mac the next time you sync with iTunes.

**NOTE**
**Deleting Events on an iPod**
Unfortunately, you cannot edit or delete events on any iPod other than the iPod Touch.

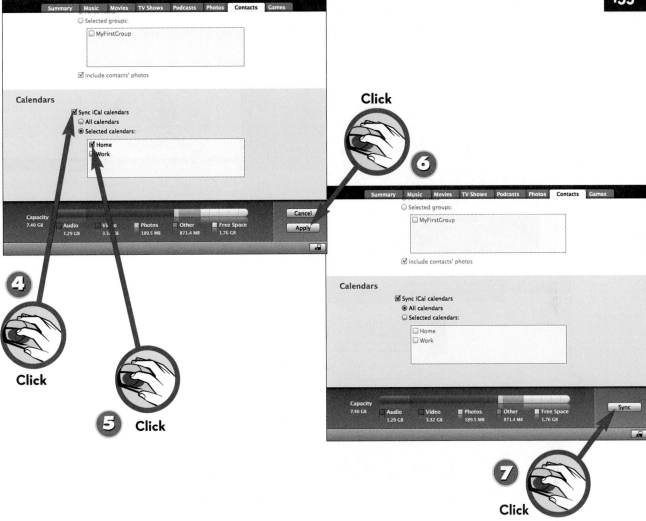

**Click**

**4**

**Click**

**5** **Click**

**6**

**Click**

**7**

**Click**

**4** Check the **Sync iCal calendars** check box.

**5** Choose the calendars you want to sync.

**6** Click **Apply** to save your changes.

**7** Click **Sync** to update your iPod. Eject the iPod and view the updated events in the calendar.

*End*

**TIP**

**Sync to Get the Latest Events**

If you make changes to your calendar on your Mac after updating your iPhone, iPod Touch, or iPod Classic or Nano, just click **Sync** and the latest events will be updated to your iPhone.

**NOTE**

**Learn More About iPhoto**

While you're waiting for the next event, take some time to smell the roses; look at some good or not-so-good photos in iPhoto. To learn how to sync photos from your Mac to an iPod or iPhone, go to Part 11, "Working with Digital Photos."

# SYNCING EVENTS WITH IPHONE

Syncing events to an iPhone works similarly to syncing events to an iPod. This task shows you how to send events to an iPhone.

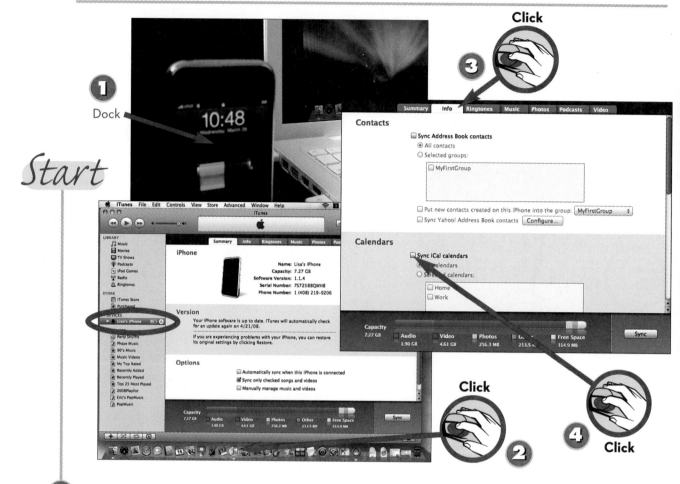

1. Dock the iPhone. (Make sure the dock is attached to the Mac.)

2. Open **iTunes**.

3. Click the **Info** tab.

4. Click the **Sync iCal calendars** check box in the Calendars area of the Info tab.

Continued

**TIP**

**Editing and Deleting Events**
Any changes you make to events on your iPhone, including deleting events, migrate to your Mac when you sync via iTunes.

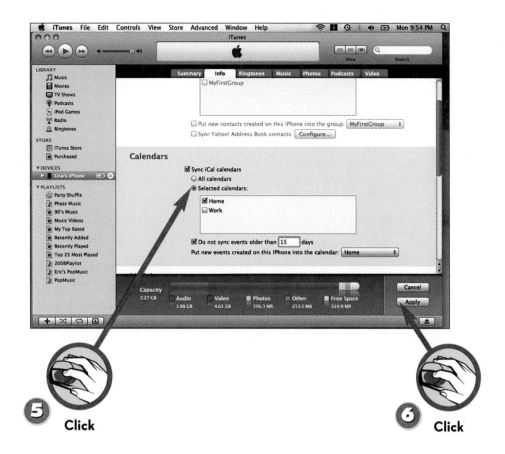

**5** Click

**6** Click

**5** Choose the calendars you want to sync.

**6** Click **Apply**. The calendar sync status appears at the top of the iTunes window.

*End*

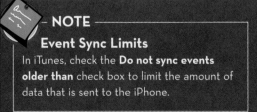

**NOTE**

**Event Sync Limits**

In iTunes, check the **Do not sync events older than** check box to limit the amount of data that is sent to the iPhone.

## 10

# PLAYING MUSIC AND MOVIES IN ITUNES

Organize, purchase, and play music and movies on your Mac, iPod or iPhone with iTunes. The iTunes store is the top-selling music retailer in the United States and iPods are Apple's best-selling music players. If you don't already have it installed on your computer, download iTunes from Apple's website. It's free!

iTunes enables you to do more than just organize, purchase and play music, you can also rip audio CDs and burn new CDs with Mac OS X and Windows computers. The workflow for using iTunes is to populate your Music, Movies, or Podcast libraries in iTunes, create playlists, pick the items you want to put on an iPod or iPhone, connect the iPod or iPhone to your Mac, and then synchronize music to the iPod or iPhone. iTunes can also sync contact, calendar, movies, and photos to the latest iPod Classic and Nano models, iPod Touch, and iPhones.

Music, movies, TV shows, podcasts, and music videos are available for purchase from the iTunes store. You can listen to preview clips of each song or movie before you buy, or rent a movie if you don't want to buy it. You can also add your own music to your iTunes Music library, and of course sync it with your iPod or iPhone. This chapter shows you how to make the most of iTunes.

# THE ITUNES WORKSPACE

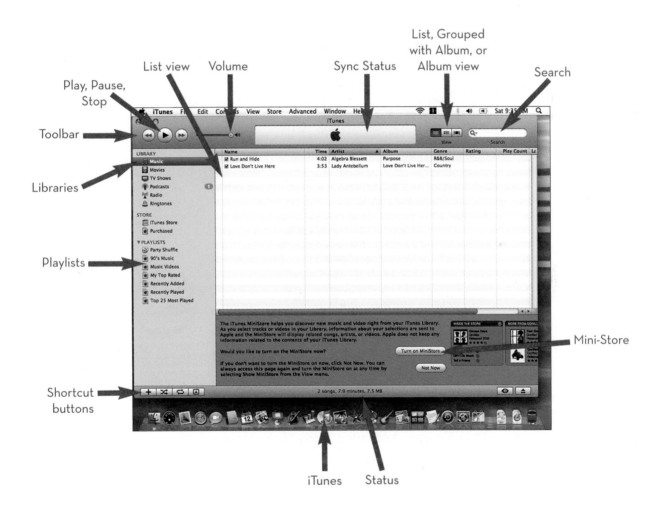

List view
Volume
Sync Status
List, Grouped with Album, or Album view
Search
Play, Pause, Stop
Toolbar
Libraries
Playlists
Mini-Store
Shortcut buttons
iTunes
Status

# CONFIGURING ITUNES IN OS X

The first time iTunes open, several screens appear asking you how you want to configure iTunes. You can also access these settings from the Preferences panel, or when it is first launched. This task walks through the first launch screens.

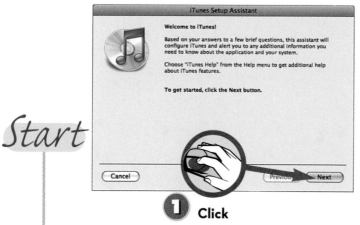

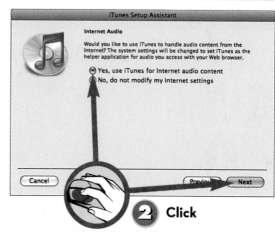

*Start*

**1 Click**

**2 Click**

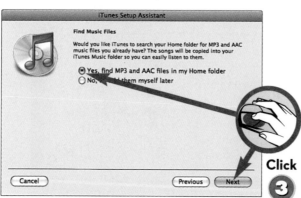

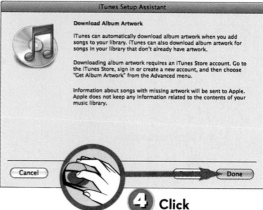

**Click 3**

**4 Click**

**1** Double click the iTunes icon in the dock. Follow the onscreen instructions and click **Next** to move to the next screen.

**2** Select the **Yes, use iTunes for Internet Audio content** option on the Internet Audio panel of the iTunes Setup Assistant. Click the **Next** button to move to the next step.

**3** Choose **Yes, find MP3 and AAC files in my Home folder** in the Find Music Files panel. Click the **Next** button. If you choose Yes, you may find it will take a while to complete if you have a lot of music on your hard drive.

**4** Click the **Done** button. The main iTunes window opens.

*End*

## TIP
### iTunes Requirements
iTunes 7 requires a Mac with PowerPC G3 processor or better, 256MB of memory, 32MB of video RAM, Mac OS X 10.3.9 or 10.4.9 or later (10.4.10 or later required for iPhone), QuickTime 6.5.2 or later, Combo SuperDrive, and a broadband/Internet connection.

## NOTE
### Playing Shared Music
Listen to others' music in iTunes. If other folks on your network are sharing music, a **Shared** section appears in the iTunes sidebar. Select a playlist from the shared machine and click **Play** to listen.

# PURCHASING A SONG OR MOVIE

You can add your music to your iTunes Music Library manually by ripping your audio CDs (compact discs). If you don't have a song or want to shop for music or movies, you can purchase a single song, album, TV show, or movie from the iTunes Store. This task shows you how to purchase a song.

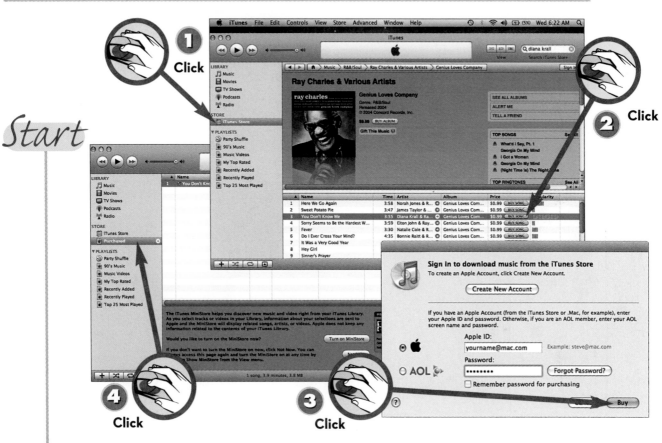

*Start*

**Click** ①

**Click** ②

**Click** ③

**Click** ④

*End*

① Choose the iTunes Store.

② Select **Music** and navigate to a song you want to purchase. Click the **Buy Song** button.

③ Type your login and password for your Apple ID or AOL account. Click the **Buy** button on the Confirmation dialog.

④ Wait for the song to download. Click **Purchased** in the iTunes sidebar. The song appears in the window list.

-TIP-
### Free Music and TV Shows
The Music and TV Show links are located on the left side of the **iTunes Store** home page. A free song is available as the single of the week from the **Music** home page. Free TV show downloads are available on the **TV Shows** home page.

-TIP-
### Learn How to Rip a CD
To find out how to convert your audio CDs into music in iTunes, go to "Ripping an Audio CD" later in this part.

# PLAYING MUSIC IN ITUNES

After you have music or movies in your iTunes libraries, you can watch them. This task shows you how to play a song in the Music Library.

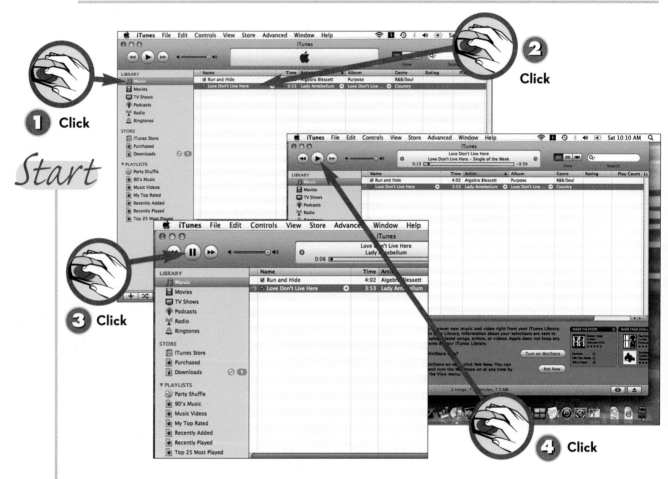

*Start*

**1** Click

**2** Click

**3** Click

**4** Click

**1** Select the **Music** library in the iTunes sidebar.

**2** Choose a song in the list.

**3** Click the **Play** button to play the selected song. You can also double click a song from the list view window to play it.

**4** Click the **Pause** button to stop playing music.

*End*

**TIP**

### Album Art

As you build your Music Library, you might notice some of the music doesn't show its album art. Try manually downloading it from iTunes. Choose Advanced > Get Album Art. The album art is downloaded if the song is recognized by the iTunes store. If that doesn't work, take a photo or copy/paste album art. Then Get Info on a song and paste it into the Album field of the Artwork panel. There's also a Dashboard widget available that searches for artwork online as each song plays in iTunes.

# PLAYING A MOVIE IN ITUNES

You can start watching a movie while its downloading or after it has been downloaded. This task shows you how to play a movie from your Movie library.

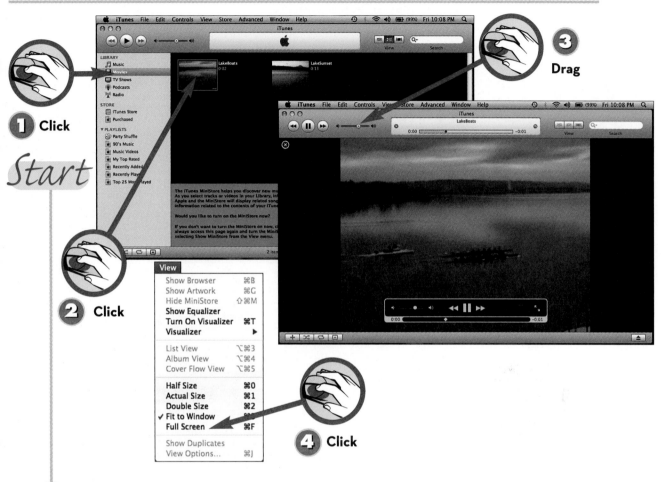

*Start*

**1 Click**

**2 Click**

**3 Drag**

**4 Click**

**View**

| | |
|---|---|
| Show Browser | ⌘B |
| Show Artwork | ⌘G |
| Hide MiniStore | ⇧⌘M |
| **Show Equalizer** | |
| **Turn On Visualizer** | ⌘T |
| **Visualizer** | ▶ |
| List View | ⌥⌘3 |
| Album View | ⌥⌘4 |
| Cover Flow View | ⌥⌘5 |
| **Half Size** | ⌘0 |
| **Actual Size** | ⌘1 |
| **Double Size** | ⌘2 |
| ✓ **Fit to Window** | |
| **Full Screen** | ⌘F |
| Show Duplicates | |
| View Options... | ⌘J |

1. Select the **Movie** library from the iTunes sidebar.

2. Click a movie. It starts playing in the iTunes window automatically.

3. Drag the **Volume** slider at the top of the window or in the to adjust the volume level of the movie.

4. Select the **View** > **Full Screen** menu to view the move without the iTunes window.

*End*

**NOTE**

**Keyboard Shortcuts**

Press ⌘-**F** to view the movie in full screen. Press ⌘-**3** to maximize the size of the movie on your computer screen.

**TIP**

**Movie Rentals**

Not sure which movie to buy? Rent a movie. Visit **Movie Rentals** in the iTunes Store to see what's available.

# PLAYING A PODCAST

Podcasts were originally created by iPod fans who wanted to listen to news, learn a language, or be informed or entertained by their peers. Podcasts can be audio-only or video. This task shows you how to play an audio podcast.

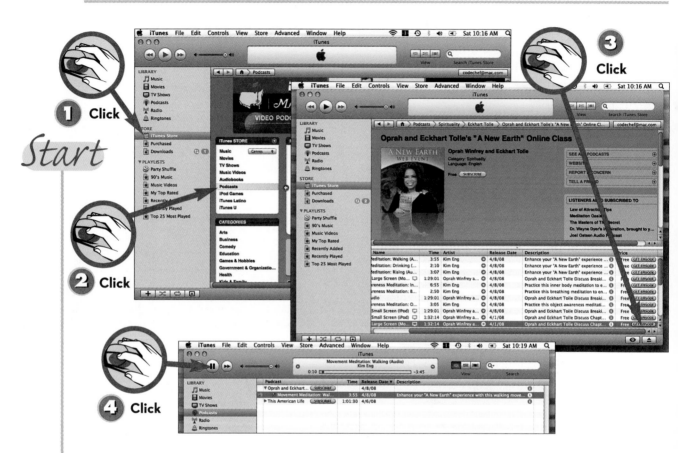

*Start*

**1** Click

**2** Click

**3** Click

**4** Click

**1** Choose the **iTunes Store** in the sidebar.

**2** Click the **Top Podcasts** link in the store.

**3** Click the **Get Episode** button. Wait for the file to download.

**4** Select the file from the Podcasts Library from the iTunes sidebar and then click the **Play** button. Click the **Subscribe** button to subscribe to the latest podcasts from your Podcast library. To view the latest episodes, Control-click the podcast and choose **Update Podcast**.

*End*

## TIP
### More Free Downloads
Podcasts are free downloads available from the iTunes Store. Select the **iPodcast** link in the iTunes Store to see what's available.

## NOTE
### Audio Versus Video
Podcasts come in audio or video formats. The video files can be considerably larger than the audio files. If you notice your iPod or hard drive filling up, consider backing up and removing the video podcasts from your Mac's internal drive.

# CREATING AN ITUNES PLAYLIST

Playlists enable you to organize your music for playback on your iPod or iPhone or for burning to a CD. This task shows you how to create a new playlist.

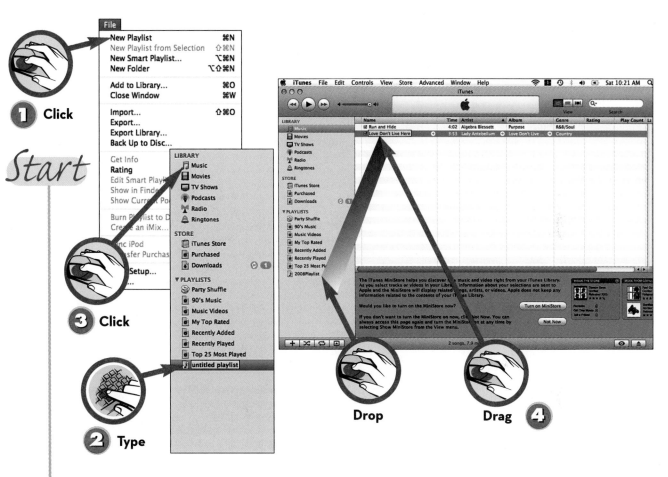

**Start**

**1 Click**

**3 Click**

**2 Type**

**Drop**

**Drag 4**

1. Select **File** > **New Playlist** from the menu bar.

2. Type a name for the playlist. Press **Return**.

3. Select the **Music** library from the iTunes sidebar.

4. Drag music files to the new playlist. Alternatively, select the files you want to add to a playlist and choose the **File** > **New Playlist** menu or press ⌘-Shift-N to create the new playlist with the selected songs.

*End*

**TIP**
**Smart Playlists**
iTunes includes several *smart playlists*, which autopopulate with songs that fit the criteria of the smart list. You can use those provided with iTunes or create your own. Visit smartplaylists.com to find out more about creating you own custom smart playlists

**NOTE**
**Play on the Go**
On the iPod, you can create an On the Go playlist by holding down the center of the click wheel when selecting a song. The song is added to the On the Go playlist. When you sync, this playlist is created in iTunes.

# REMOVING SONGS FROM A PLAYLIST

Playlists can contain as many songs as you like. You can add or remove songs as you please. This task shows you how to remove a song from a playlist.

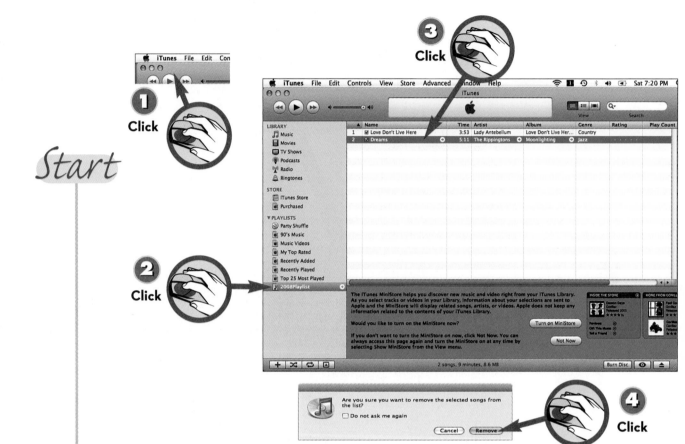

*Start*

**Click**

**Click**

**Click**

**Click**

1. Click the **iTunes** icon on the Dock to open it.

2. Select a playlist from the iTunes sidebar.

3. Select a song in the playlist.

4. Press the **Delete** key. Click **Remove**.

*End*

-TIP-
**Removing Songs from Your Mac**
To find out how to remove music or movies from your Mac, go to "Removing Music and Movies from your Mac," later in this part.

-NOTE-
**Undo Removing Music from Your Library**
Change your mind about deleting that song? Immediately after deleting the song yet after a deletion, you can undo the remove. choose **Edit > Undo** to bring it back into the Music library or playlist.

# RIPPING AN AUDIO CD

Another way to bring music into iTunes is to rip it—that is, convert the audio files on the audio CD into digital music in your Music library. This task shows you how to rip an audio CD.

**Insert**

**1**

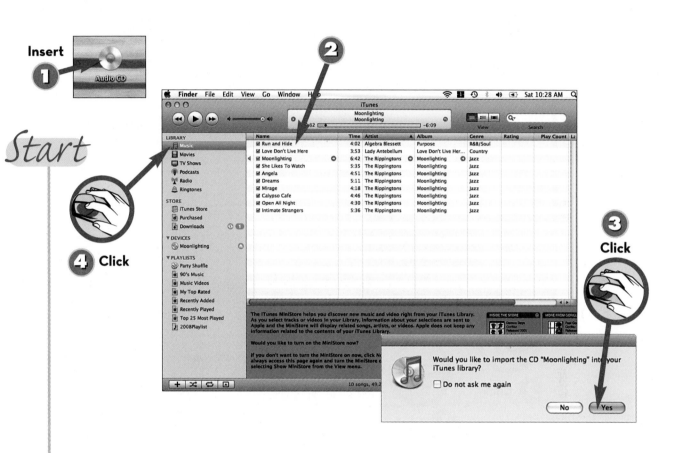

*Start*

**4** Click

**2**

**3** Click

**1** Insert an audio CD. iTunes opens automatically.

**2** iTunes opens automatically and displays the contents of the audio CD.

**3** An alert appears asking if you want to import the CD. Click the **Yes** button and wait for iTunes to rip your music.

**4** The songs appear in your Music library.

*End*

## TIP
### Copy Protection and Audio CDs
Some audio CDs have special copy protection. Most work with the Mac. But if you are not able to open an audio CD, it may not be compatible with the CD or DVD drive on your Mac.

## NOTE
### Rate Your Songs
Each song in the iTunes library can have a rating. Ratings can be used to determine how frequently shuffled songs are played, or to help you search for your favorite songs. Drag the cursor in the Rating column for any song in the Music library to add its rating.

# BURNING AN AUDIO CD IN ITUNES

If you have a favorite playlist that you want to listen to on a CD player, you can burn the music to one or more CDs. This task shows you how to burn a CD.

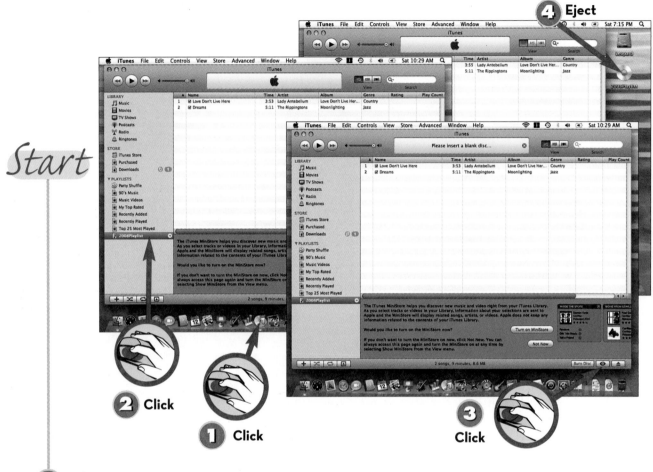

*Start*

*End*

1. Click the **iTunes** icon on the Dock to open iTunes.

2. Select a playlist from the sidebar.

3. Click the **Burn Disc** button. Insert a CD

4. When the burn process finishes, the CD appears on the desktop. Select the CD and drag it to the Eject (Trash) icon in the dock to remove it from your Mac.

**TIP**

**Fitting a Playlist on a CD**

iTunes enables you to create an audio CD of a selected playlist, or more than one audio CD if the playlist is too large to fit on one CD. The number of CDs varies depending on how many songs are chosen in the playlist.

# PURCHASING A TV SERIES

From the iTunes Store, you can purchase one song or one TV show, or an album or TV season. If you're not sure whether you want to buy a season, you can buy one or two shows (or songs). This task shows you how to buy a TV season. Purchasing an album is similar.

**Start**

**2 Click**

**1 Click**

**3 Click**

**4 Click**

1. Select the **iTunes Store** link in the iTunes sidebar.

2. Click the **TV Shows** link.

3. Choose a TV series.

4. Click the **Buy Season** button. Purchase the movie/series and wait for the show or shows to download.

*End*

---

**NOTE**

**Sync the Most Recent Shows**

You can manually manage your movies and TV shows on your iPod or iPhone or have iTunes automatically sync all unwatched (or a subset of the most recently unwatched) shows. Connect an iPod or iPhone to your Mac. Go to the Music, Movies, TV or Podcast tab and choose one of the **Most Recent** options from the pop up menu.

# DISABLING AUTO-SYNCING WITH AN IPOD OR IPHONE

When you connect an iPod or iPhone to any Mac, iTunes automatically syncs the data configured for the device. To avoid deleting some or all of the content on your iPod or iPhone, turn off the auto-sync setting in Preferences. This task shows you how.

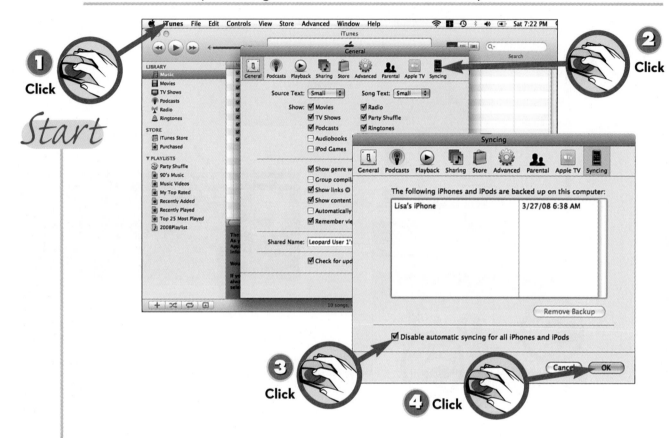

*Start*

1 Choose **iTunes** > **Preferences**.

2 Click the **Syncing** button.

3 Check the **Disable automatic syncing for all iPhones and iPods** check box.

4 Click **OK**. Close the Preferences window to save your changes.

*End*

## NOTE

### Changing the Date and Time on an iPod

Automatic syncing does not occur when the Disable automatic syncing for all iPhones and iPods option is checked. However, any time an iPod Touch, Classic, or Nano is connected to a Mac, the date and time information on the Mac is synchronized to the iPod. This can be helpful if you're traveling with your iPod and want it to show the local time.

# MANUALLY SYNCING WITH AN IPOD

One of the benefits of manually configuring your iPod is that you can add music to it from other computers. This task shows you how to manually sync music with an iPod.

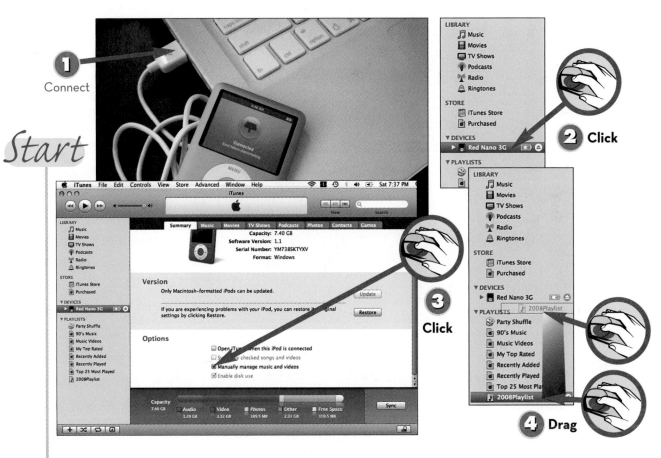

1. Connect the iPod to your Mac iTunes automatically opens.

2. Select the iPod in the iTunes sidebar.

3. In the Summary page, check **Manually manage music and videos**.

4. Drag playlists, songs, TV shows, podcasts or movies to the iPod.

**NOTE**

**Automatically Sync**

To find out how to disable automatic syncing, go to the "Disabling Auto-Syncing with an iPod or iPhone" task in this chapter.

# PERMANENTLY REMOVING MUSIC AND MOVIES

Permanently removing a duplicate song, or any music or movies, from your Mac is similar to removing it from iTunes. However, this time it is permanent. This task shows you how to remove a file from your computer.

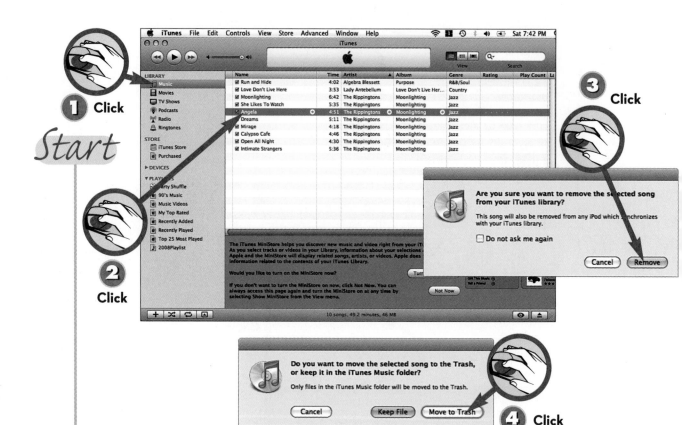

*Start*

**1** Select the **Music** library.

**2** Select a song you want to delete.

**3** Press the **Delete** key on the keyboard. A dialog appears asking you to confirm the deletion. Click the **Remove** button.

**4** A second dialog appears allowing you to keep or remove the file from your iTunes folder. Choose the **Move to Trash** button.

*End*

**-NOTE-**

### Songs That Won't Play

If audio files are deleted or moved to a different location in the iTunes folder, an alert appears when you try to play the song. Navigate to the file's new location to fix the error in iTunes.

# TRANSFERRING PURCHASES

You can copy music and movies from your iPod to your iTunes libraries on a Mac—that would be a different Mac than the one you originally synced from. This task shows you how to transfer music from an iPod to a Mac.

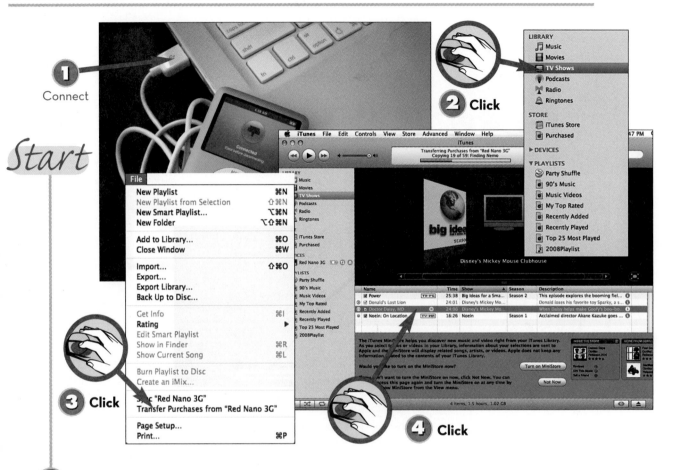

**Start**

**1** Connect

**2** Click

**3** Click

**4** Click

**1** Connect the custom iPod connector to your iPod. Connect the USB cable to your Mac.

**2** Select a library in iTunes (preferably the library where the transferred files will appear).

**3** Choose **File** > **Transfer Purchases** from the iTunes menu bar. Wait for the music or movies to sync to your Mac.

**4** View or play the transferred files.

**End**

 **TIP**

**Look for Duplicates**
If you transfer purchases onto a machine that already has some of the music or movies on your iPod, the iTunes library will show two files with the same name. Delete any duplicate files using the steps in the "Permanently Removing Music and Movies" task earlier in this part.

# AUTHORIZING A COMPUTER

If you have transferred music or movies from your iPod to iTunes, before you can play them you must authorize the computer. This task shows you how authorize a Mac using a .Mac account.

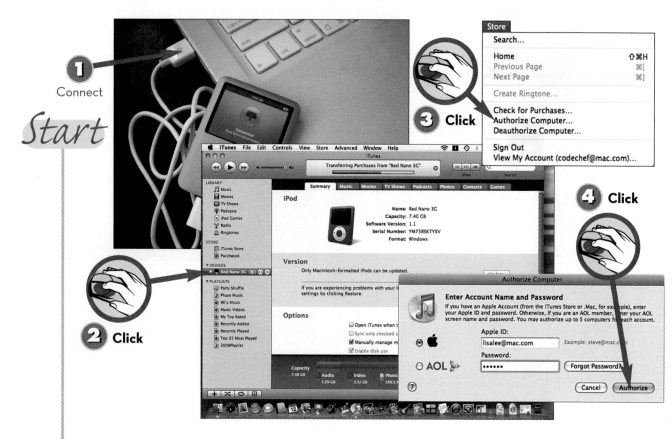

**(1)** Connect your iPod to your Mac. iTunes opens.

**(2)** Select the iPod in the iTunes sidebar.

**(3)** Choose **Store** > **Authorize Computer**.

**(4)** Log in to your .Mac or AOL account and click **Authorize**.

---

**TIP**

**When Is Authorization Needed?**

Any free or purchased music, TV shows, or movies require authorization before you can sync them to an iPod or play them on your Mac.

# BACKING UP MUSIC AND MOVIES

It is possible to have more music and movies than your hard drive can hold. iTunes has a backup setting that enables you to back up all or part of your library to DVD or CDs. This task shows you how.

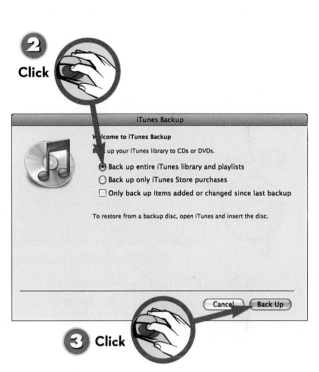

**1** In iTunes, choose **File** > **Back Up to Disk**.

**2** Choose a backup option from the iTunes Backup panel.

**3** Click the **Back Up** button. Insert a CD or DVD and wait for the backup to complete.

*End*

**TIP**
### What Is a Backup?
A backup is a copy of a file or folder of files. If you are working on critical documents, be sure to create a backup to prevent losing all the work you've done. If something happens to your work in progress, you can restore the last backup and proceed from there instead of starting from scratch.

# EXPORTING A PLAYLIST

You can share your playlists with others or with other computers. Sharing a playlist is a two-step process. First export the list, and then import it. This task shows you how to export a playlist.

*Start*

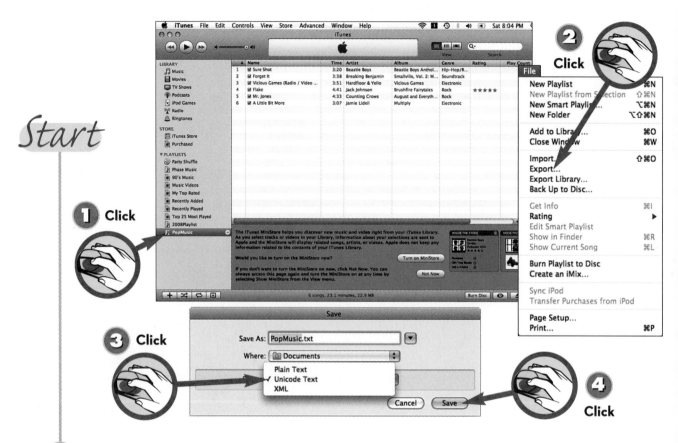

**Click**

**Click**

**Click**

**Click**

① Select an iTunes playlist.

② Choose the **File** > **Export**.

③ Select a file format from the **Format** drop-down list.

④ Click the **Save** button.

*End*

---

**TIP**

**Exporting a Library**

Exporting a library enables you to generate a complete list of all the music, movie, and TV files you have on your Mac. Select a library from the sidebar. Choose **File** > **Export a Library** and select a file format (XML).

**NOTE**

**Choosing an Export Format**

When exporting a playlist, you can choose from three different file formats: XML, Unicode Text, or plain text. Try exporting the list as XML.

# IMPORTING A PLAYLIST

This task shows you how to import a playlist. If you are using the same machine for both the export and import, first rename the playlist you have in iTunes, and then follow the steps in this task.

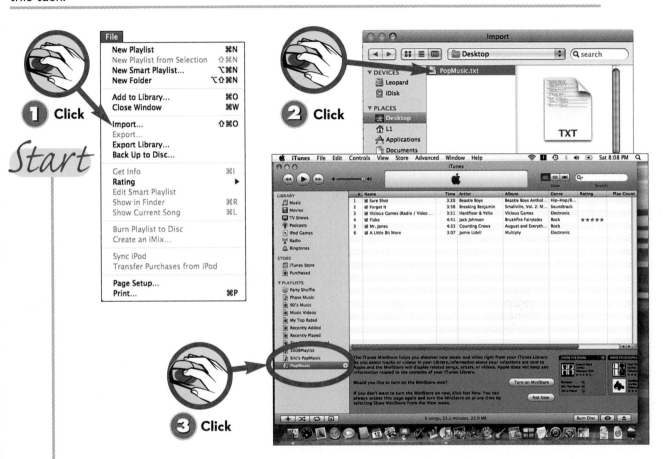

*Start*

**1** Click

**2** Click

**3** Click

**1** Select **File** > **Import**.

**2** Navigate to the exported playlist and select it.

**3** View the playlist in iTunes.

*End*

## TIP

### Importing Music for the Playlists

Importing a playlist places the names of the songs into iTunes, but you also need to add audio files themselves to iTunes. Copy them to your local drive, and then drop them into the Music Library window. When copying purchased media, you must authorize the machine before you can play or sync.

## 11

## WORKING WITH DIGITAL PHOTOS

iPhoto helps you organize photos similarly to the way iTunes helps you organize your music and movies. You can download photos from your digital camera into iPhoto, organize photos into albums, change the order of photos, zoom into one, or view a group of photos in the main window. In addition, several photo-editing tools enable you to enhance your photos. Don't forget all these photos can be synced to iPods or iPhones.

If you have imported photos to iPhoto you can view pictures as events, all photos, last imported photos, or in albums. When you open iPhoto, the default view shows Events. An event can group photos by folder or by a date or range of dates. Dragging the cursor over the event icon shows the photos associated with that event.

This part introduces you to the iPhoto workspace and shows you how to import and delete photos and create an album. After you have the pictures in iPhoto, you can remove red-eye, retouch, rotate, and so on. The tasks at the end of this chapter show you how to import photos from a digital camera, export photos out of iPhoto, and sync them to your iPod.

# THE IPHOTO WORKSPACE

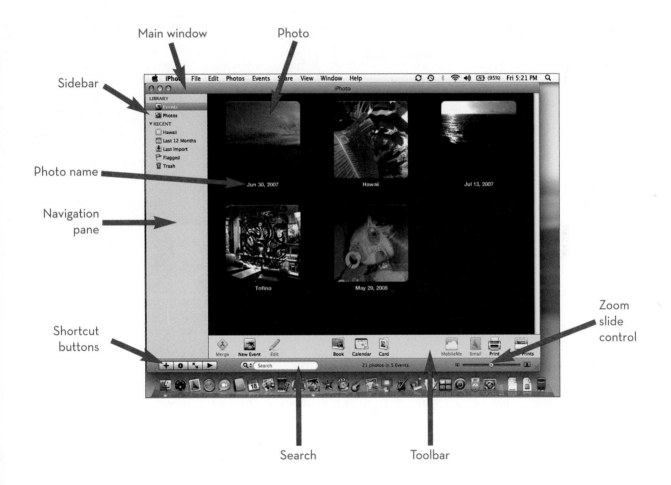

Main window

Photo

Sidebar

Photo name

Navigation pane

Shortcut buttons

Zoom slide control

Search

Toolbar

# NAVIGATING PHOTOS

Digital cameras are incredibly popular today. So popular, in fact, that it can be difficult to manage all your digital photos. iPhoto enables you to view several photos simultaneously or one at a time. This task shows you how to navigate photos in the iPhoto workspace.

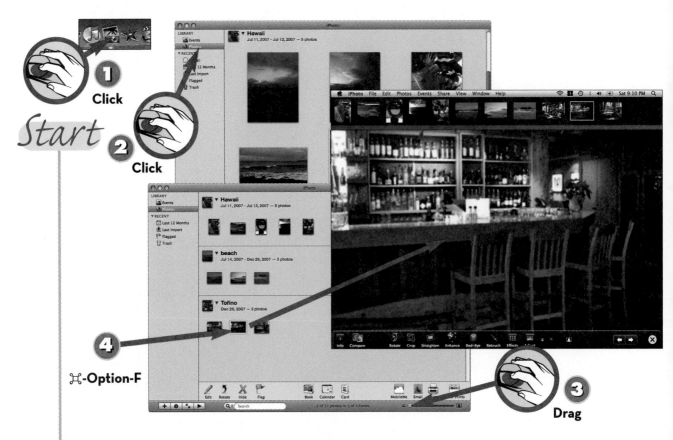

Start

**1** Click

**2** Click

**3** Drag

**4** ⌘-Option-F

**1** Click the **iPhoto** icon on the Dock to open iPhoto.

**2** Select **Photos** from the sidebar.

**3** Drag the slider. The number of photos increases as the slider moves to the left and decreases as the slider moves to the right.

**4** Choose a photo. Press ⌘-**Option-F** or select **View** > **Full Screen**. The workspace changes to full-screen mode. Press the **Esc** key to exist Full Screen mode.

*Continued*

**NOTE**

**Toolbar Buttons**

Notice the Rotate, Crop, Straighten, Enhance, Red-Eye, Retouch, Effects, and Adjust buttons on the toolbar at the bottom of the iPhoto screen.

**TIP**

**iPhoto Requirements**

iPhoto, part of iLife, requires a Mac with PowerPC G4 processor or Intel processor, 512MB of memory, 1GB of memory recommended, 32MB of video RAM, 3GB of available disk space, DVD drive for installation, Mac OS X 10.4.9 or later, and QuickTime 7.2 or later.

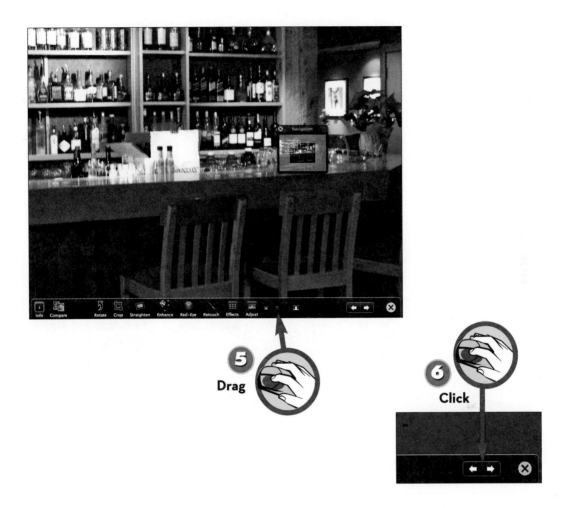

**Drag**

**Click**

(5) Drag the **Zoom** slider control to zoom in on a photo.

(6) View photos by clicking the **Previous** or **Next** buttons or pressing the left-and right-arrow keys.

*End*

**TIP**

**Sort Events**

Choose the **View** > **Sort Events** menu to change the sort order of the images that appear in each event thumbnail in the iPhoto window. Choose from one of the following sort options: By Date, By keyword, By Title, By Rating, Manually. You can also sort images in Ascending or Descending order.

# IMPORTING PHOTOS ON YOUR HARD DRIVE INTO IPHOTO

Before you can view or edit photos in iPhoto, you must import them from your hard drive or from a digital camera. Imported files appear in the Last Import view in the sidebar. You can also view photos from the Event or Photo views, or in an album view. This task shows you how to import photos stored on your hard drive into the iPhoto workspace. You'll learn how to import from a camera later in this Part.

**Start**

**Click** 1

**Click** 1

**Click** 3

**Click** 2

**Click** 4

1. Open iPhoto from the Dock. Click the **Yes** button if you want to use iPhoto to sync with your digital camera. If you're not sure you want to start up iPhoto every time you plug in your camera, click the **Decide Later** button.

2. Choose **File** > **Import to Library**.

3. Select the folder you want to import. Choose **File** > **Import to Library**.

4. Choose **Last Import** to view the files.

*End*

---

**TIP**

**USB Versus USB**

You can connect a USB cable to the camera and to your Mac to download images. A second method is to remove the storage card from the camera and insert it into a USB card reader connected to your Mac's USB port. Alternatively, some media, such as SD media, can be inserted into a USB port.

**NOTE**

**Importing Images Shortcut**

Drop one or several picture files or folders onto the iPhoto window to quickly add them to the iPhoto library.

# CREATING AN ALBUM

Photos can fit into one or many categories. Creating an album in iPhoto can help you organize your photos as you like. This task shows you how to create an album.

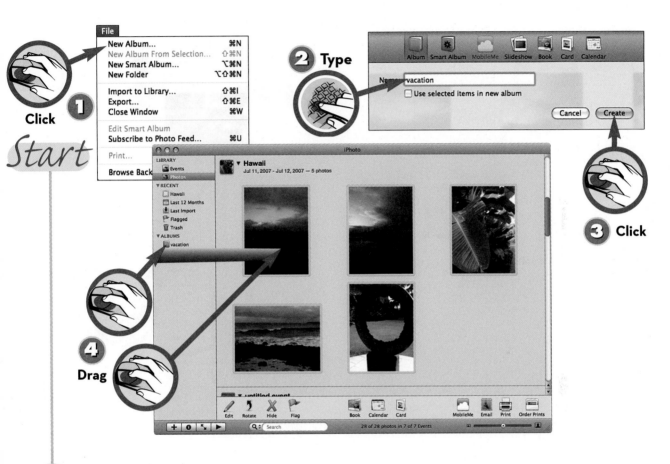

Click **1**

Start

**2** Type

**3** Click

**4** Drag

**1** Select **File** > **New Album**.

**2** Type the name of the album.

**3** Click the **Create** button. The album appears in the sidebar.

**4** Drag photos from the main window into the album to add them to the album. As an alternative, choose the **File > New Album** menu.

End

**NOTE**

**Sidebar Ordering of Albums**

Albums in the iPhoto sidebar can be organized as you like. Drag and drop an album to move it to the top or bottom of the list, or anywhere in-between.

**TIP**

**Naming an Album**

Selecting photos in iPhoto works the same as selecting files in a Finder window. Press **Shift** to choose a continuous group of photos or ⌘-**click** to pick specific photos, and then drag them to an album.

# DELETING PHOTOS FROM AN ALBUM

Organizing is a relatively simple task. You can create and delete albums to group pictures any way you like. For the albums you keep, you can change the order the pictures appear in the album. As you work with each album, you may decide to remove some. This task shows you how to remove a photo from an album.

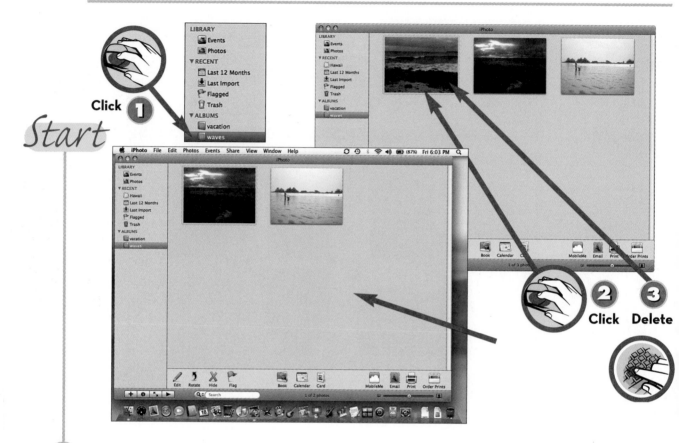

**Click 1**

*Start*

**Click 2** **Delete 3**

1. Select an album from the iPhoto sidebar.

2. Select a photo.

3. Press the **Delete** key. The photo is removed from the main window.

*End*

**TIP**

**Backing Up Your Photos**

Check the **Save a copy to the iPod** check box to back up photos you sync to your iPod.

**NOTE**

**Undo Deleting a Photo**

Choose the **Edit** > **Undo** menu command or press cmd-z after deleting a photo and voilà! It's back in the album and appears in the iPhoto window. You must do this immediately after you delete a photo from an album.

# REMOVING RED-EYE IN A PHOTO

When the flash on a camera goes off, especially when the subject of the photo isn't well lit, the light from the flash bounces off the subject's retina. The result is what most folks call "red-eye." This task shows you how to correct red-eye using the Red Eye tool in iPhoto.

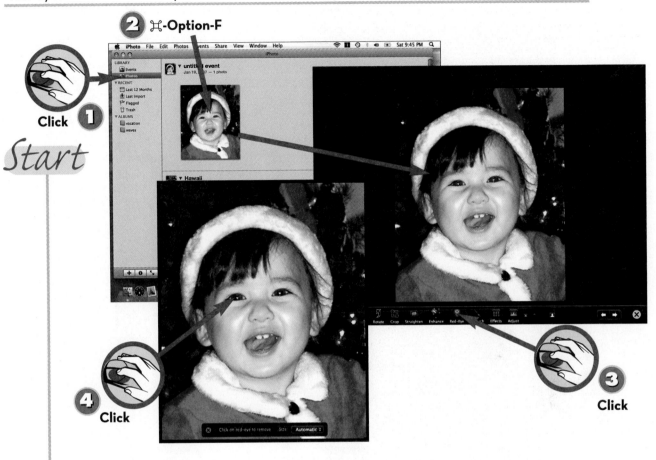

Start

End

1 Select a photo.

2 Press ⌘-**Option-F** to switch to full-screen mode, or choose **View** > **Full Screen**.

3 Click the **Red Eye** button on the toolbar.

4 Place the cursor over the red eye, and then click the photo to apply the Red Eye tool.

## TIP
### Removing Red Colors
The Red Eye tool can change any red color to mix with its surrounding colors. To experiment with the Red Eye tool, open a photo with lots of red colors and apply the Red Eye tool to different red colors in the photo.

# RETOUCH A PHOTO

The Retouch tool enables you to remove blemishes and artifacts from photos. It may work better with some photos than others. Generally, retouching a photo takes a lot of time and patience, taking many small steps to gradually transition one element in a photo to blend with everything around it. This task shows you how to remove a flower bush from a photo with a single click using the Retouch tool.

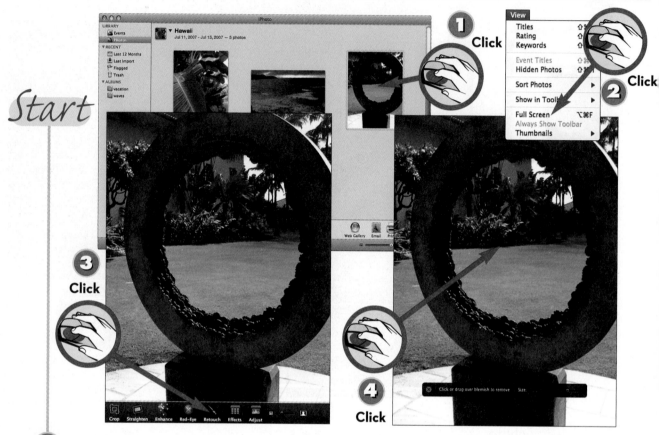

**1** Select a photo.

**2** Choose **View** > **Full Screen**. iPhoto is in full-screen mode.

**3** Click the **Retouch** button on the toolbar

**4** Click the photo to apply it. Click the **Apply** button to save your changes.

**NOTE**

## Full Screen Mode Tip

If you don't see buttons at the bottom of the screen after entering Full Screen mode, don't worry. You must move the cursor to the bottom of the screen to show the photo editing tools.

# ROTATING A PHOTO

Photos can be in portrait or landscape mode when captured on a camera. Portrait photos may need to be rotated to be viewed in iPhoto. This task shows you how to rotate a photo.

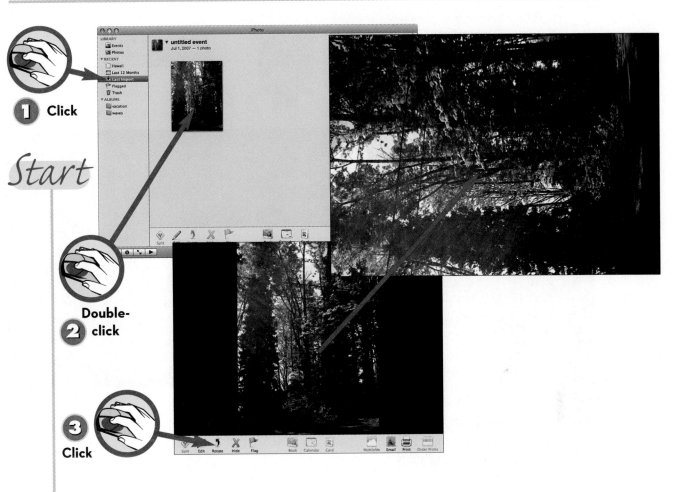

*Start*

**1** Click

**2** Double-click

**3** Click

**1** Select photos or an album.

**2** Double-click a photo.

**3** Click the **Rotate** button on the toolbar.

**4** The photo is rotated counterclockwise.

*End*

**NOTE**

**Rotate Shortcuts**

Press ⌘-**R** to rotate the picture counter clockwise. Press ⌘-**Option-R** to rotate the picture clockwise. You can also choose the **Photos** > **Rotate Clockwise**, or **Photos** > **Rotate Counter Clockwise** menu commands to rotate a picture.

# CROPPING A PHOTO

The Crop tool in iPhoto enables you to define a portion of a photo and exclude the outer border. This task shows you how to apply the drop tool to a photo.

**Start**

**1** Click

**2** Click

**3** Drag

**4** Click

1. Select a photo. Choose **View** > **Full Screen** or press ⌘-**Option-F**.

2. Click the **Crop** button on the toolbar.

3. Drag the cursor to define the portion of the photo you want to preserve. Any part of the photo outside of the selected area will be removed.

4. After the selection area has been defined, you can drag to continue to modify the crop area. When you're ready to crop the image, click the **Apply** button.

**End**

NOTE

**Desktop Photos**

Most monitors and desktops work best with photos that have landscape orientation. Cropping a portrait photo enables you to view the subject's face without worrying about the desktop clipping the top and the bottom of a too-tall photo.

# EXPORTING PHOTOS

The Export settings in iPhoto enable you to save files in their current format or as a TIFF, JPEG, or PNG. This task shows you how to export files in their current format.

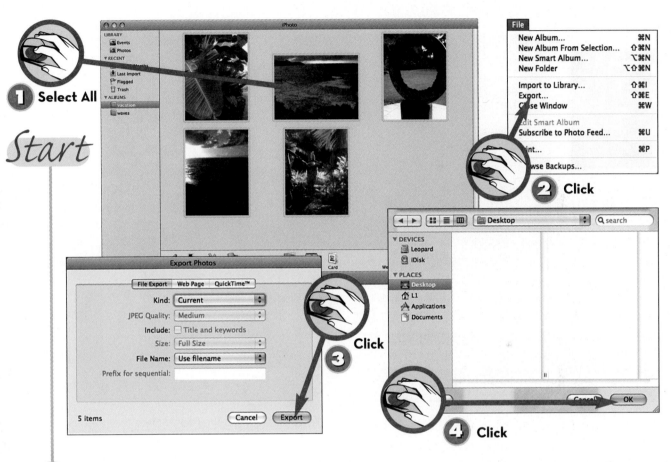

**Start**

**End**

1. Select an album in the sidebar and drag to select photos or choose **Edit** > **Select All**.

2. Choose **File** > **Export**.

3. The default setting is to export photos in their current file format. Click the **Export** button.

4. Select a location for the files on your hard drive, and then click the **OK** button.

## TIP

### Exporting Files

The selected files are exported to the location you pick. If you want to keep them all together, create a new folder before exporting them.

## NOTE

### Export to a Web Page

iPhoto can put those photos on a web page. Choose **File** > **Export**. Select the **Web Page** tab in the Export Photos dialog. Then customize any settings. Click the **Export** button. Drag the HTML file into a Safari window to view the photos.

# IMPORTING PHOTOS FROM A CAMERA

iPhoto offers two ways to import photos from a digital camera into the iPhoto workspace. You can view any files on the camera before downloading, and then download all files or selected files. This task shows you how to download selected files.

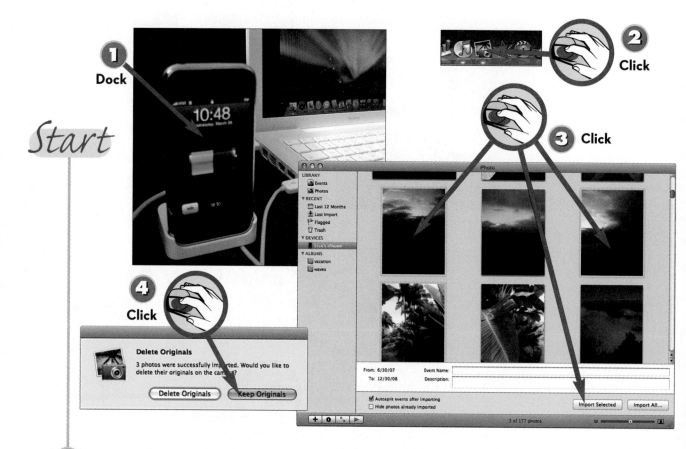

*Start*

**Dock**

**Click** ②

**Click** ③

**Click** ④

**Delete Originals**
3 photos were successfully imported. Would you like to delete their originals on the camera?

Delete Originals    Keep Originals

**1** Connect your camera or phone to your Mac.

**2** Click the **iPhoto** icon in the dock to open it.

**3** Select the photos you want to import. Click the **Import Selected** button.

**4** Wait for the pictures to appear in the main window. Click **Keep Originals** to keep the photos on your camera or phone.

*End*

**TIP**

**SD Media for USB**

Perhaps your camera uses SD media cards. If so, you can find 1GB and 2GB cards that fold in half and fit into a USB slot. This is probably the fastest way to access photos on your desktop.

# SYNCING PHOTOS TO IPOD AND IPHONE

When you have your albums and photos where you want them, you can sync them to an iPod or iPhone. Syncing photos to your iPod or iPhone enables you to view them on your iPod or iPhone when your not sitting in front of your computer. This task shows you how to sync all your photos to an iPod.

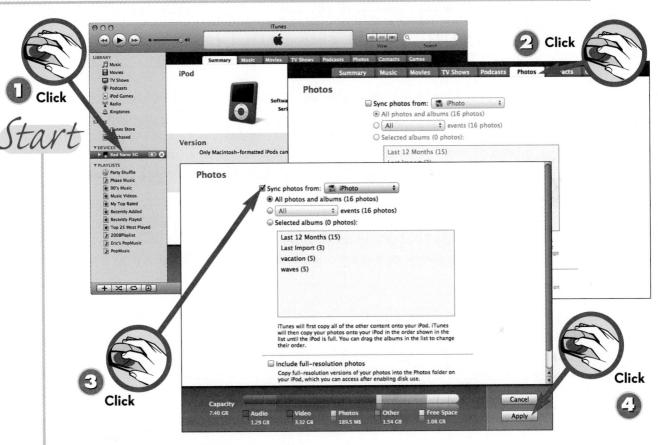

1. Dock the iPod and then select it in iTunes.

2. Choose the **Photos** tab.

3. Select the **Sync** check box.

4. Click the **Apply** button.

*End*

---

### NOTE

**Sync Menu Command**

Select an iPod and choose **File** > **Sync** to sync iTunes with an iPod.

### TIP

**Media Browser**

Photos and albums in iPhoto and Aperture are available in applications such as iWeb, Pages, Numbers, and Keynote, in each of those programs' Media Browser windows. Click the **Media Browser** button on the application's toolbar. Select **iPhoto** to access your photos. Just drag and drop the photo into a document.

## 12

## WORKING WITH THE BUILT-IN CAMERA AND PHOTO BOOTH

MacBooks, iMacs, and MacBook Pros all have built-in cameras. The camera is centered at the top of the monitor. When you set up your account with your new Mac, you may have noticed the built-in camera enables you to create a photo of yourself for the login screen. Photo Booth is another application that takes advantage of the built-in camera. Photo Booth enables you to capture photos or movies with the built-in camera.

The tasks in this part introduce you to the Photo Booth work space. Learn how to capture photos and movies, Delete any you don't want to keep, play them in a slideshow or export one or all to iChat or iPhoto.

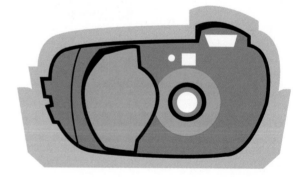

# THE PHOTO BOOTH WORKSPACE

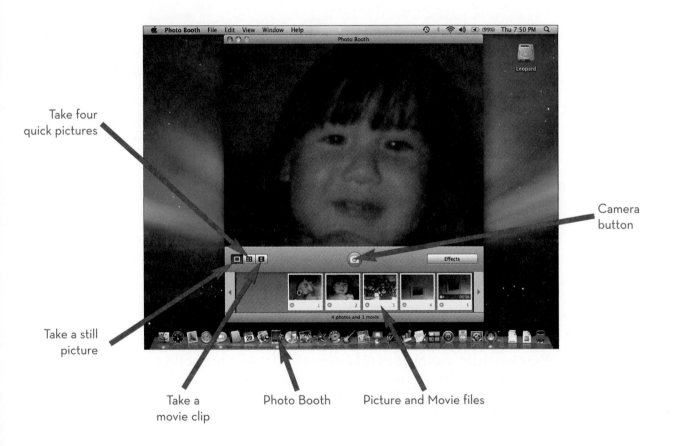

Take four
quick pictures

Camera
button

Take a still
picture

Take a
movie clip

Photo Booth

Picture and Movie files

# TAKING A STILL PICTURE

The built-in camera in the MacBooks, iMacs, and MacBook Pros enables Photo Booth to capture still pictures (photos) and video. This task shows you how to capture photos.

Start

End

1. Open **Photo Booth**. The Still Picture button is selected by default.

2. Pose for the camera. Click the **Camera** button to take a snapshot. A timer will count down to zero; Photo Booth then takes the picture.

3. View the photos by clicking the one you want to view at the bottom of the main window. Click the **Camera** button to exit picture viewing and return to viewing the live camera in the Photo Booth window.

## TIP

### Stay in Focus

For the clearest photos, try to pose for 1 to 2 seconds before pressing the Camera button in Photo Booth.

## NOTE

### Four Quick Pictures

Click the **Four Quick Pictures** button and then click the **Camera** button in the Photo Booth window to capture four photos in quick succession. All four photos appear in the thumbnail at the bottom of the Photo Booth window. All four photos appear in a grid. Select any photo to zoom into it and view it as single image.

# MAKING A MOVIE CLIP

Movies can capture subtle nuances that escape the single-frame photo. This task shows you how to capture a movie with Photo Booth.

*Start*

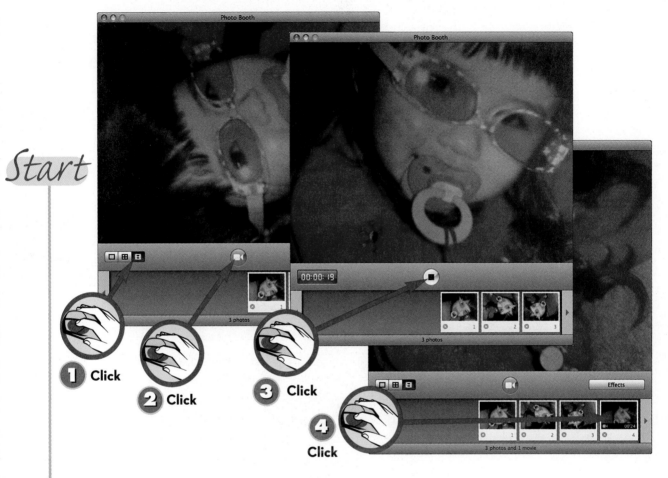

**1** Click

**2** Click

**3** Click

**4** Click

**1** Click the **Movie Clip** button.

**2** Click the **Camera** button to start recording.

**3** Wait 15 to 30 seconds or a few minutes as Photo Booth records the movie. You can wave to the camera or say "hi" for this movie clip if you like. Then click the **Stop** button.

**4** The movie appears in the main window. Select it and to play the movie. Click the **Camera** button to switch to exit viewing the movie clip.

*End*

**NOTE**

**Movie Playback**

When you capture a movie in Photo Booth, you can play it back by selecting it. Unlike iTunes, you cannot stop, pause, rewind, or fast forward the movie; you can only play it.

# DELETING A PHOTO

As you capture photos, you may choose to remove one or more at some point. This task shows you how to delete a photo.

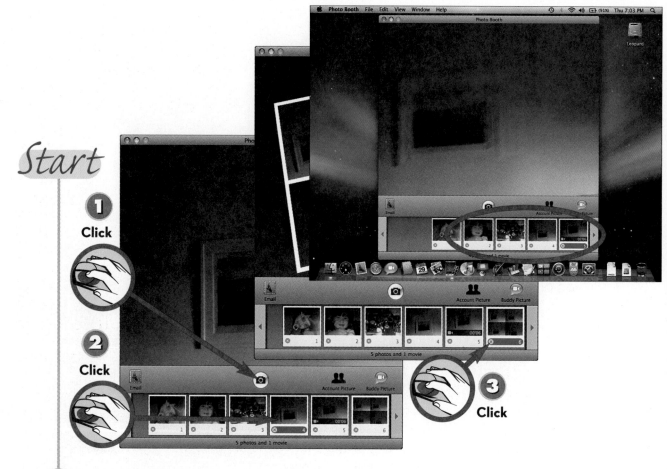

**Start**

**1** Click

**2** Click

**3** Click

**1** Capture photos.

**2** Select a photo.

**3** Click the **x** (delete) button to delete the image from Photo Booth.

**End**

**NOTE**

**Navigating Movies and Photos**

After you have selected a photo or movie at the bottom of the Photo Booth window, press the left- or right-arrow keys on your keyboard to select the different media files. Or, click the arrow buttons on each end of the photo sorter.

# VIEWING PHOTOS AS A SLIDESHOW

Working with photos in the main window is fine, but the desktop background can be distracting. If you prefer, you can view the photos full screen as a slideshow.

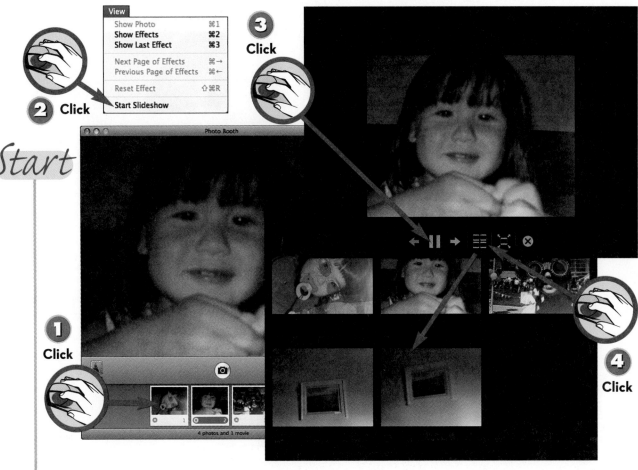

*Start*

1. Open **Photo Booth** and view your photos.

2. Choose **View** > **Start Slideshow**.

3. Click the **Play/Pause** button to start the slideshow. Click it again to stop the slideshow. Click the **Fit to Screen** button to grow the picture size to fit on your screen. Click the **Close** (X) button to stop the slideshow.

4. Click the **Index Sheet** button to view all photos in the slideshow.

*End*

**TIP**

**Movie and Photo Dimensions**

Photo Booth captures photos and movies in 640 × 480 pixels. This is roughly equivalent to a 1-megapixel image. This is great if you want to share files online or print 4 × 6 or 5 × 7 inch photos.

# EXPORTING A PHOTO TO IPHOTO

If iPhoto is installed, Photo Booth works seamlessly with it. After the photo is in iPhoto, you can add it to an album, and then sync it to an iPod Classic, Nano, or Touch or iPhone using iTunes. This task shows you how to export a Photo Booth still picture into iPhoto.

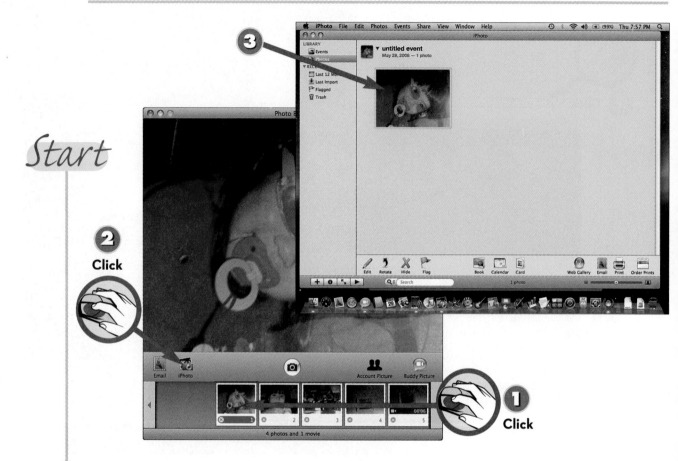

*Start*

**2** Click

**1** Click

*End*

**1** Click a photo you've taken in Photo Booth.

**2** Click the **iPhoto** button

**3** View the photo in the iPhoto main window To find out more about iPhoto, go to Part 11, "Working with Digital Photos."

 **TIP**
**Send to Mail**
In step 3, click the **Mail** button to import the photo into an email message.

 **TIP**
**Export to Finder**
To export a photo or movie from Photo Booth, just select it in the Photo Booth window, and then drag it to the desktop. The photo (.jpg) or movie (.mov) file appears on your desktop.

# CREATING A BUDDY PICTURE

iChat is included with Mac OS X. It enables you to exchange text messages and files over a network connection. This task shows you how to import a Photo Booth image as your iChat icon with Bonjour.

**1** Select a photo in Photo Booth.

**2** Click the **Buddy Picture** button in the Photo Booth window.

**3** The picture appears in the Buddy Picture window. Drag the slider control to adjust the scale of the image.

**4** When you are ready to save the picture in iChat, click the **Set** button. iChat opens and shows the Photo Booth image in the Bonjour List window.

*End*

**TIP**

**Learn More About iChat**

To find out more about how to use iChat, go to Part 13, "Chatting and Sharing Files with iChat."

179

## 13

# CHATTING AND SHARING FILES WITH ICHAT

Chatting online is the digital equivalent of hanging out and chatting with your neighbor. Chatting online involves exchanging text messages, files, images, and more over the Internet. You can also chat with video if your Mac has a built-in or connected third-party camera.

To chat, you must first set up an AOL IM, MobileMe, or Gmail account. Then, add as many buddies as you like. Chatting can be encrypted or unencrypted. Bonjour is yet another way to chat with your local network neighbors without having to set up an account first. You can view your buddies' status and share your status. The tasks in this chapter show you how to create an iChat account, log in, chat, change your online status, exchange files with a friend, and customize your status.

# THE ICHAT WORKSPACE

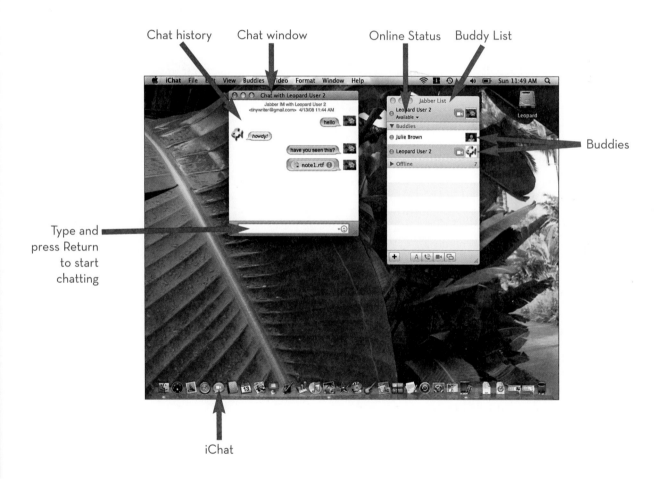

Chat history

Chat window

Online Status

Buddy List

Buddies

Type and press Return to start chatting

iChat

# SETTING UP YOUR MOBILEME ACCOUNT

Before you can add a buddy or chat with any of your buddies via MobileMe, you need to set up your iChat account information. First, you need to set up a MobileMe account. Then follow the steps in this task to add that account to iChat.

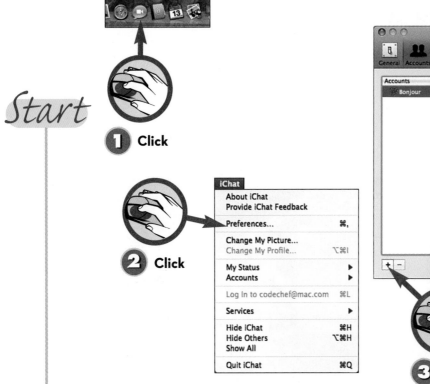

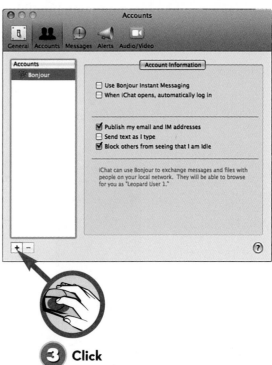

**1** Open **iChat** by clicking its icon on the Dock.

**2** Select **iChat** > **Preferences**. The Preferences window opens.

**3** Click the **+** (plus) button.

*Continued*

**TIP**

**Setting Up a MobileMe Account**

Be sure to review and agree to the cost of a MobileMe account before signing up to use it. To find out how to setup your MobileMe account, go to the "Configuring MobileMe" task in Part 7.

**TIP**

**Bonjour and iChat**

Chat with others on your local network. To find out more, go to the "Starting a Bonjour Chat" task, later in this chapter.

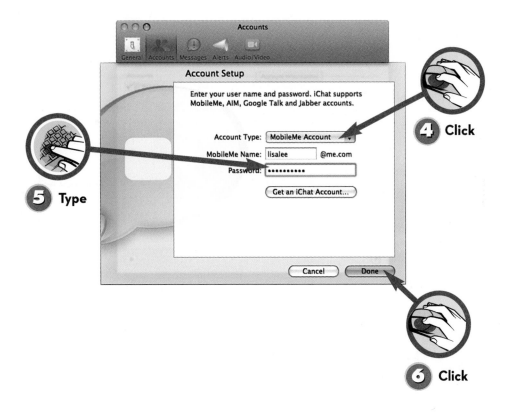

**4** Select **MobileMe Account** from the Account Type menu.

**5** Type your login information for the MobileMe account.

**6** Click the **Done** button to create the account. Select the account from the iChat Preferences window or from the Window menu. The Buddy List window for the selected account opens.

*End*

**TIP**

**iChat Security**

For ultimate security, check **Encryption** in preferences to connect to someone else with encrypted iChat. Encryption is only available with **MobileMe** accounts configured in iChat.

# SETTING UP A GOOGLE TALK ACCOUNT

Google offers free chat and email accounts. You can chat with any Gmail or Google Talk users using iChat. This task shows you how to set up the Google Talk account in iChat preferences.

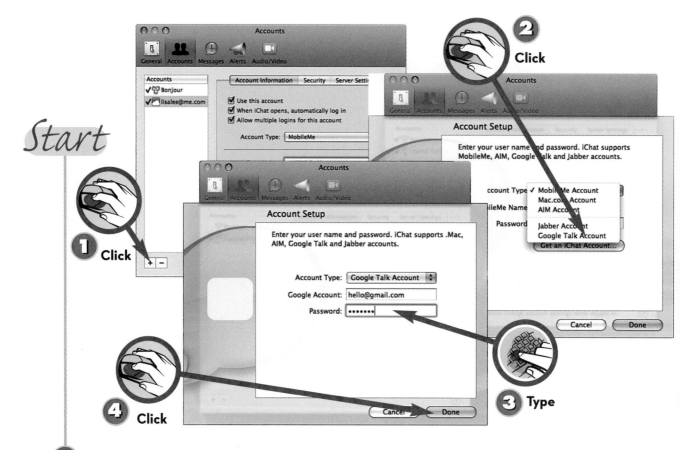

**Start**

**1 Click**

**2 Click**

**3 Type**

**4 Click**

**End**

**1** Choose **iChat** > **Preferences**. Click the **+** (plus) button to create a new account.

**2** Select **Google Talk Account** from the Account Type menu.

**3** Type your account info.

**4** Click the **Done** button to create the account. A Jabber List window opens when the Google account is selected from the Window menu.

---

**TIP**
### What Is Google Talk?
Google is best known for speedy Internet search on the web. Mail and chat are also available. To find out more, visit google.com.

**NOTE**
### iChat Preferences
Configure iChat to log in to a specific account. In the iChat Preferences window (opened from **iChat** > **Preferences**), click the **Accounts** button. Select an account. Check the **When iChat opens, automatically log in** check box.

# ADDING A BUDDY

Add as many buddies as you like to each of your iChat accounts. Buddies are friends who also have MobileMe, Google Talk, or AIM accounts and chat online. This task shows you how to add a buddy to a Google Talk account from the Jabber List window.

**Type**

**Click**

*Start*

**Click**

**Click**

1. Open iChat. Log in to your Google account.

2. Choose the Google account from the **Window** menu and click the + (plus) button in the **Jabber List** window. Choose the **Add Buddy** menu item from the Plus button's drop down menu.

3. Type the Gmail address for your buddy, and your buddy's first and last name.

4. Click the **Add** button. The person appears in your Jabber List window.

*End*

# CHATTING WITH A BUDDY

The heart and soul of iChat is chatting—sending and receiving text messages with your buddies. This task shows you how to start a chat session with a buddy.

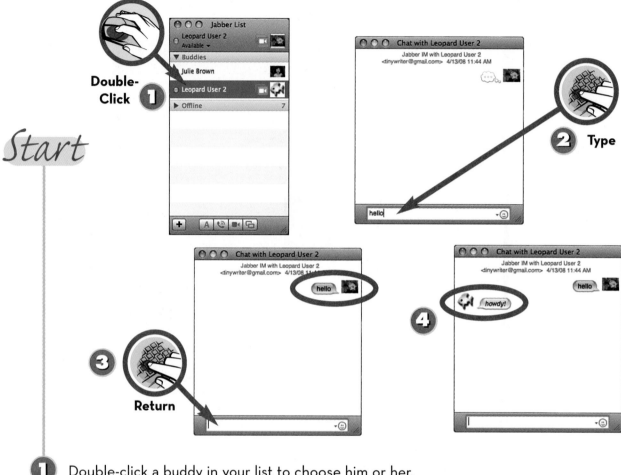

**Start**

**Double-Click** 1

2 **Type**

3 **Return**

4

1 Double-click a buddy in your list to choose him or her.

2 Type in the chat window.

3 Press **Return**. The text message appears in the chat window.

4 Wait for your buddy to reply. Read your buddy's message in the chat window.

*End*

**TIP**

### Video Chat

If a video camera icon displays next to your buddy's iChat icon, select it to video chat. Video in iChat enables you to see your buddy while you chat online!

# CHANGING YOUR ONLINE STATUS

One of the more common things you'll do in iChat is change your status. Letting your buddies know when you're available or away enables your buddies to know when they can start a chat session with you. Choose the Away status allows a buddy to start a chat session. The next time you return to your computer you can reply to your buddy without having to look for them online. This task shows you how to change your iChat status.

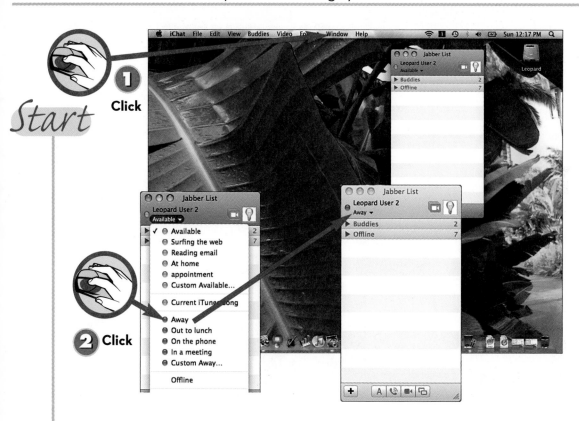

**1** Choose a Buddy or Jabber List from the Window menu .

**2** Choose a different status from the menu.

**3** View the new status in the Buddy or Jabber List window.

*End*

### TIP
**Custom status**
To find out how to create a custom status message, go to the task titled "Customizing Your Status."

### TIP
**Emoticons in Chat Status**
If you want to add a little color or smiley face to your status, type **:-)** to show a smiley face in your status. Alternatively, choose a smiley face from the drop down menu in the text edit field of the chat session window.

# SHARING FILES

File sharing is available in iChat. You can send files to your buddies while chatting. This can come in handy if you don't have the Mail program set up or simply want to share information without losing track of your conversation. This task shows you how to send a file to a buddy.

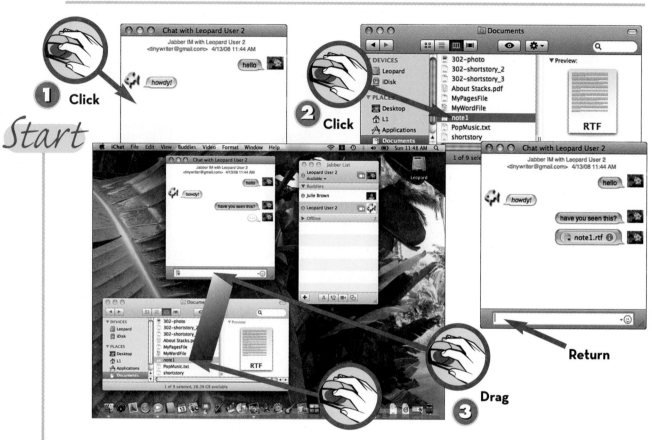

**Start**

① **Click**

② **Click**

③ **Drag**

**Return**

---

① Exchange a few chat messages with a friend.

② Choose a file you want to share.

③ Drag the file from the Finder window and drop it in the text field of the chat window.

④ Press **Return**. Wait for your buddy to download the file.

*End*

---

**TIP**
### Share Small Files
When you share a file over iChat, try to keep the file size to a minimum. Smaller files transfer quickly over the network.

**NOTE**
### More About Sharing Files
When sharing files, keep in mind that to view it the person receiving the file must have an application that can read the file.

# SHARING IMAGES IN ICHAT

Images can say more than words. iChat enables you to share images. This is similar to the way you share files. This task shows you how to share an image.

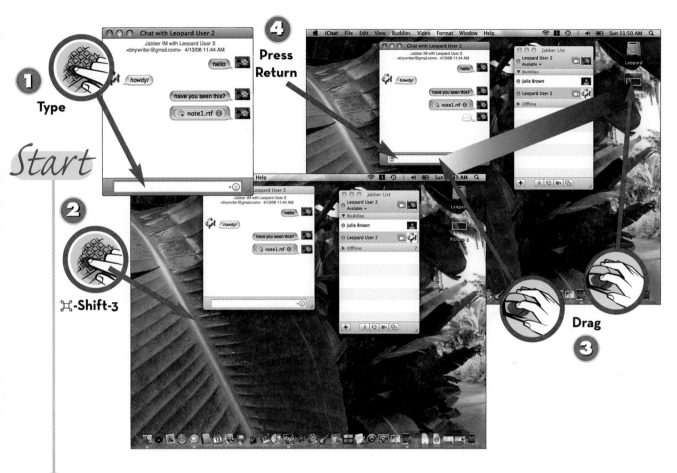

**1** Type

**2** ⌘-Shift-3

**Start**

**4** Press Return

**3** Drag

**End**

**1** Exchange a few chat messages with a buddy.

**2** Press the ⌘-**Shift-3** keys to create a screenshot of your desktop.

**3** Drop the image in the text edit field of the iChat window.

**4** Press **Return.** The image file appears in your chat window.

---

**TIP**
**Learn More About iPhoto**
To find out more about how to work with digital images, go to Part 11, "Working with Digital Photos."

**NOTE**
**Image File Formats**
For best results, share .jpg, .png, .tif, or .gif files over iChat. Safari and the Preview app can open these image files.

# CUSTOMIZING YOUR ICHAT ICON

Your iChat icon appears in your chat window. It also appears in all your buddy windows. There are several preinstalled images to choose from, or you can create your own. This task shows how to make your own icon.

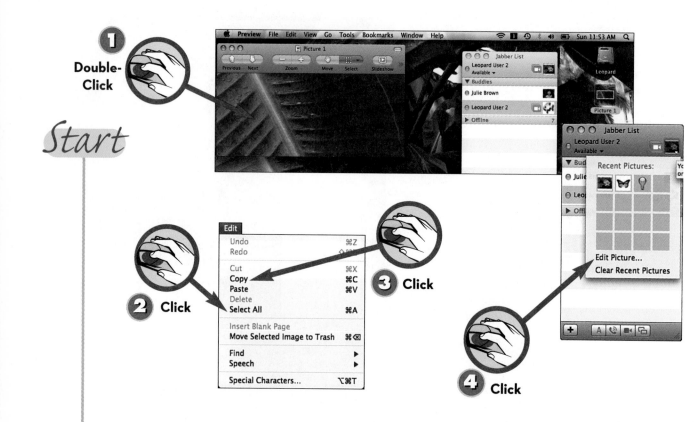

**Double-Click** ①

*Start*

② **Click**

③ **Click**

④ **Click**

① Drop an image on the Preview program in the Dock.

② Choose **Edit** > **Select All**.

③ Choose **Edit** > **Copy**.

④ Click your chat icon. Choose **Edit Picture** from the shortcut menu.

*Continued*

**TIP**

**Learn More About Preview**

To find out more about how to view images with the Preview app, go to the Viewing Photos in Preview task in Part 4, "Installing and Using Applications."

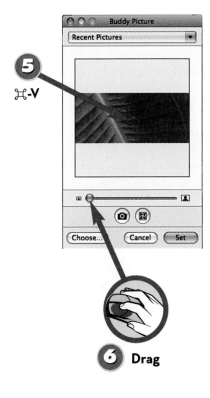

**5**
**⌘-V**

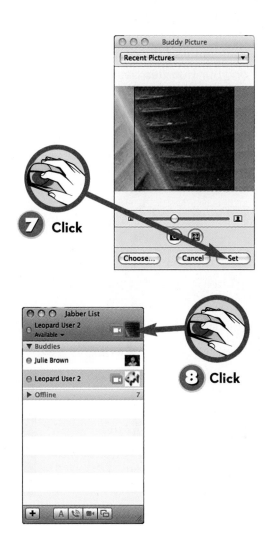

**7** Click

**6** Drag

**8** Click

**5** Press ⌘-**V** to paste the image into the Buddy Picture window.

**6** Drag the slider to adjust the zoom level of the image.

**7** Click the **Set** button to save your changes.

**8** View your new iChat icon in the chat window.

*End*

—TIP—
**Change Your iChat Icon in One Step**
A faster way to customize your iChat icon it to just drop the image on the iChat icon in the Buddy, Jabber, or Bonjour List window.

—TIP—
**Keyboard Shortcuts**
Press ⌘-**L** to log in to or out of an iChat account.

# SHARING SCREENS

iChat enables you to share your desktop with another Mac OS X Leopard user on the same network. When you share your screen with a buddy, your desktop appears in a second window on your buddies desktop. Your buddy can switch between desktops, or end the sharing session. This task shows you how to share your desktop screen with another Mac running Mac OS X Leopard.

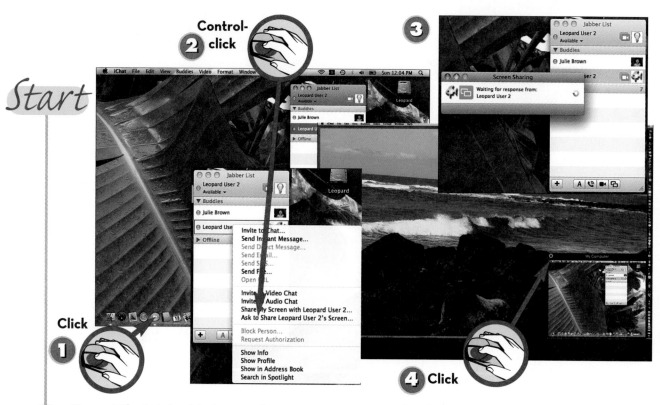

**1** Open **iChat**. A buddy list window opens automatically. If not, select a buddy list from the Window menu.

**2** Control-click a buddy in the chat window list and select **Ask to Share *Buddy's Screen***. Conversely, choose Share My Screen from the menu if you want to share your Mac desktop with a buddy.

**3** Wait for your buddy to confirm your request.

**4** View your buddy's desktop screen. Click on the My Computer window to make it the larger window on your desktop. Click the **Close** box on the My Computer window to end the screen sharing session.

*End*

-TIP-
**Sharing Security**
When you share a screen with a friend, that buddy has complete access to your computer. Be sure you have made a backup of any security-sensitive documents before sharing your desktop with a buddy.

# SAVING A CHAT SESSION

As you chat, or even after you've chatted for a bit, you might want to capture the information shared. This task shows you how to save a chat session as a file.

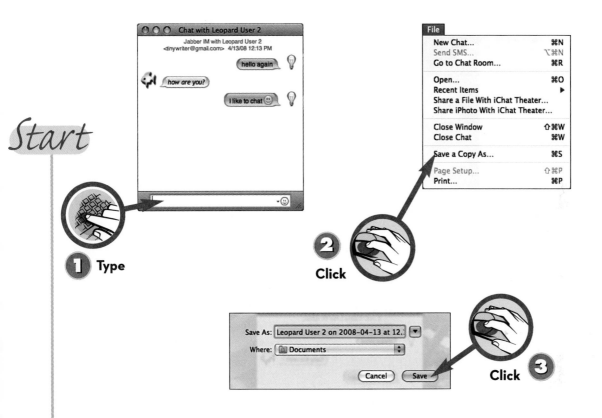

Start

**1** Type

**2** Click

**3** Click

**1** Choose a buddy and start a chat. Exchange a few messages.

**2** Select **File** > **Save a Copy As**.

**3** Click the **Save** button.

End

# CUSTOMIZING YOUR STATUS

You can customize the Available or Away status to show any message you like, including emoticons. This task shows you how to create a custom status message.

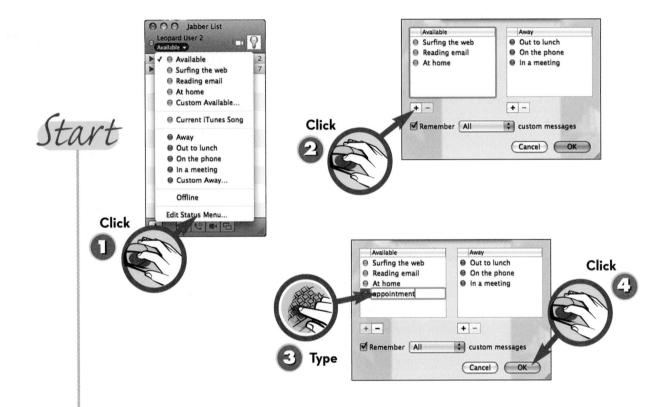

*Start*

**Click** **①**

**Click** **②**

**Type** **③**

**Click** **④**

*End*

**①** Choose the status menu and select **Edit Status Menu**.

**②** Click the **+** (plus) button.

**③** Type your status message.

**④** Click the **OK** button. You can now select your new status from the menu.

**NOTE**

**Window Menu**

Can't find a chat window? Open the **Window** menu to view all iChat windows.

**TIP**

**View Menu**

Customize the picture, audio, and video status of your buddies from the View menu. Here you can turn each setting on or off.

# STARTING A BONJOUR CHAT

Bonjour enables you to chat with other people in your immediate network without setting up an account. For example if you are connected to your home network, you can chat with others connected to the network in your home. But you won't see anyone on the Internet, or outside your home network. This task shows you how to get started with Bonjour.

*Start*

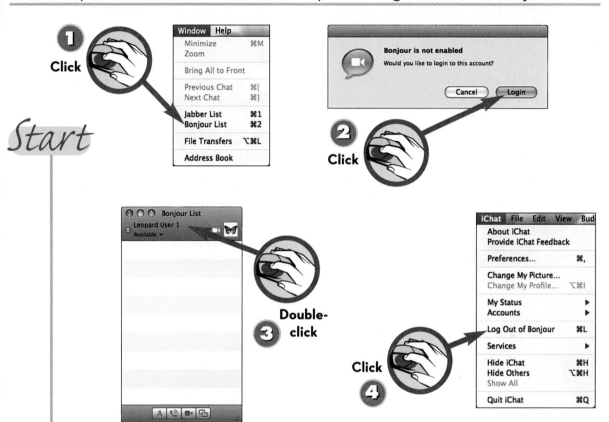

**1** Choose **Window** > **Bonjour List**.

**2** The first time Bonjour opens, an alert appears. Click the **Login** button in the alert dialog.

**3** The **Bonjour List** window opens. Click to select the window. Double-click a buddy's name to start a chat.

**4** Choose **iChat** > **Log out of Bonjour** to close the Bonjour connection.

*End*

**NOTE**

**When to Use Bonjour instead of Jabber or MobileMe Accounts**

Jabber and Buddy List windows offer encrypted iChat. In order to enable encryption, check the SSL (for Jabber accounts) or encryption (for MobileMe accounts) check boxes in the iChat preferences window for the corresponding account.

## ADDING NEW DEVICES

Macs are hubs for digital devices. iPods, iPhones, and mobile phones connect to the Mac's USB port to sync and share files. You can also connect speakers, wireless keyboards, mice, and other Bluetooth, USB, or FireWire devices to your Mac. External hard drives, including iPods that are configured as hard drives, enable you to copy files to an external device, or make your files more mobile by syncing them to an iPod or iPhone.

The tasks in this chapter show you how to connect and remove hard drives, add a printer, and connect to another Mac. Learn how to set up an Apple TV connection, FTP connection, and use an iPod as a hard drive. Finally, extend your Mac by connecting it to an external TV, wireless keyboard or mouse, mobile phone, or Time Capsule drive.

# A DISK DRIVE OVERVIEW

Internal drive

External drive

Audio CD

iPod hard drive

# CONNECTING A HARD DRIVE

You can connect several kinds of hard drives to your Mac: FireWire, USB, or over a network. You can also use an iPod as an external drive. This task shows you how to connect an external drive to a MacBook running Mac OS X Leopard.

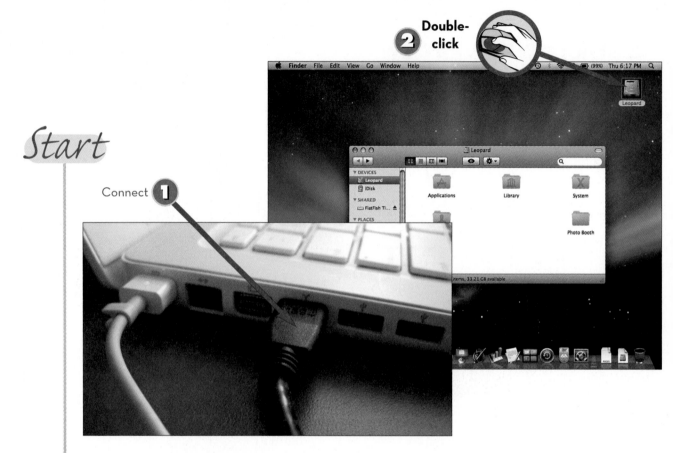

*Start*

Connect **1**

Double-click **2**

**1** Connect the hard drive to your Mac.

**2** Wait for the drive to appear on the desktop. Double-click the hard drive icon to open it. Navigate its files and folders in a Finder window.

*End*

**NOTE**

**Partitioning Drives**

Your Mac ships with a hard drive with one partition. You can divide it into two or more partitions, but this requires reformatting the drive and deleting all current data on the drive. After formatting the drive with partitions, each one appears as a separate volume on your desktop. To find out more about how to partition a drive, go to "Formatting a Hard Drive," in Part 17.

# REMOVING A HARD DRIVE

When you've finished copying files or using files on the external hard drive, you can disconnect it from your Mac. Before you pull the plug, first eject the drive from Mac OS X. This task shows you how to properly eject a drive.

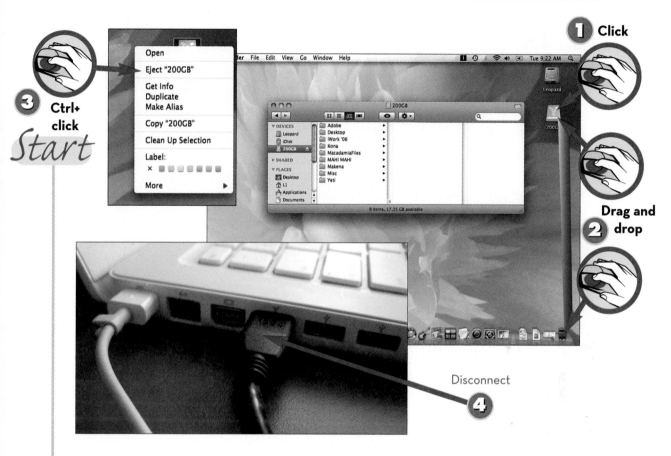

 *Start*

**3** Ctrl+ click

**1** Click

**2** Drag and drop

Disconnect **4**

1. Click to select the hard drive on your desktop.

2. Drag the hard drive icon to the Eject icon on the Dock. The Trash icon changes to the Eject icon while you are dragging the hard drive.

3. Alternatively, **Ctrl-click** the drive and select Eject to remove the drive from your desktop. Wait for the icon to be removed from the desktop.

4. Disconnect the drive from your Mac.

*End*

**TIP**

**Eject Shortcut**
**Control-click** the drive on your desktop and choose **Eject** from the shortcut menu to remove the drive in one step.

**NOTE**

**Disconnecting a Cable**
If you accidentally disconnect the USB or FireWire cable from the Mac while a drive is connected, Mac OS X shows an alert indicating the drive was disconnected improperly and the data may have been lost.

# ADDING A PRINTER

With all those files on your Mac, sure you can share files electronically. Printing comes in handy when you need to share with folks who don't have computers. This task shows you how to connect and print to a USB printer whose driver is included with Mac OS X Leopard.

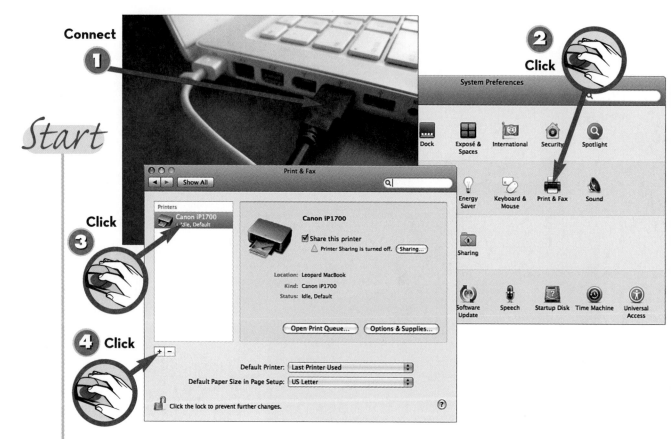

1. After installing the printer driver software for your printer on Mac OS X Leopard, connect one end of the USB cable to the printer and the other end to the Mac.

2. In System Preferences, click the **Print & Fax** button.

3. The printer appears in the window list. If you only have one printer set up with the Mac, it is the default printer. If you have more than one printer, you can select one from the list.

4. Click the + (plus) button to add a printer. A window opens with Default selected. A list of networked printers or any printers connected to your Mac's USB or FireWire ports appears in this window list.

Continued

-TIP-

**Printer Drivers and Mac OS X Leopard**

Mac OS X Leopard includes drivers for many HP, Brother, Canon, and other popular printer brands. If you're not sure if your printer is supported by Leopard. Connect it to your Mac and see whether it appears in the Printer Name list in step 5. If it does not, visit the Printer manufacturer's website to download a Mac OS X Leopard-compatible drive.

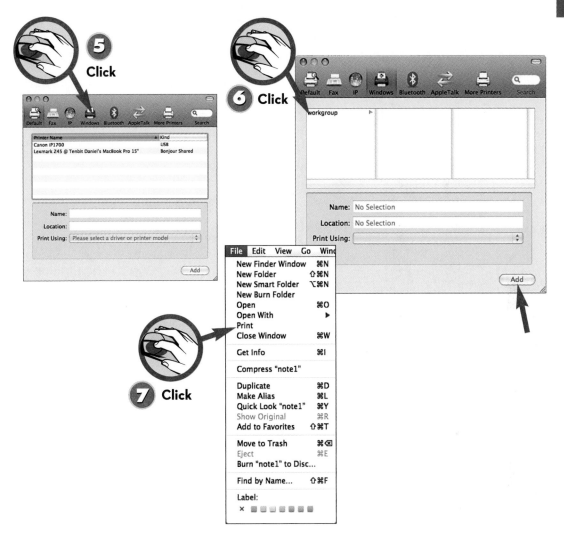

**5** Select a printer from the **Default** list and click the **Add** button to add it to the Printers list in the Print & Fax window. The buttons at the top of the window enable you to view or select Fax, IP, Bluetooth, AppleTalk, or other types of printers. If your Mac is connected to a network with Windows printers, choose the **Windows** button.

**6** Select the Windows workgroup name ( in this example the default name, workgroup is shown). Choose a printer from the list and click the **Add** button. In this example, there aren't any Windows printers available on the network.

**7** Open a **Finder** window, and select a document to print. Choose **File** > **Print**. The document prints to the default printer.

*End*

**TIP**

**Selecting a Printer in an Application**

The list of printers that appear in the Printers list in the **System Preferences > Print & Fax** screen also appear when you print a document from an application, such as Text Edit. Open a document and choose **File > Print**. Click the Printers drop-down menu to view and choose a printer. Click the **Print** button to send the document to the selected printer.

# CONNECTING TO ANOTHER MAC

Macs can connect to other Macs or Windows machines that have File Sharing on. This task shows you how to connect to another Mac that has File Sharing activated in the System Preferences > Sharing window.

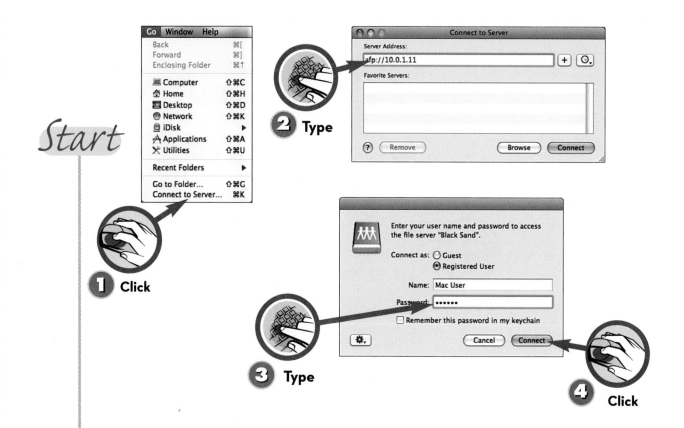

*Start*

**1 Click**

**2 Type**

**3 Type**

**4 Click**

*End*

**1** Choose **Go** > **Connect to Server**.

**2** Type the IP address of the other Mac and press **Return**. (The IP address can be located by going to **System Preferences** and choosing the **Network** panel in the **TCP/IP** tab).

**3** Type a username and password to log in to the Mac.

**4** Click the **Connect** button.

---

**TIP**

**Connect to a Windows Machine**
To find out how to connect to a Windows Vista machine, go to Part 7, "Setting Up a Wireless Home Network."

**NOTE**

**Disconnecting from a Mac**
When you connect to another Mac, the computer will appear under the Shared list of a Finder window sidebar. To remove the Mac from your desktop, click the **Eject** button next to the computer's name in the sidebar.

# CONNECTING TO AN APPLE TV

Apple TV enables you to view and purchase movies and music from the iTunes Store through your TV rather than your Mac. This task shows you how to access shared music and movies on your Mac via an Apple TV.

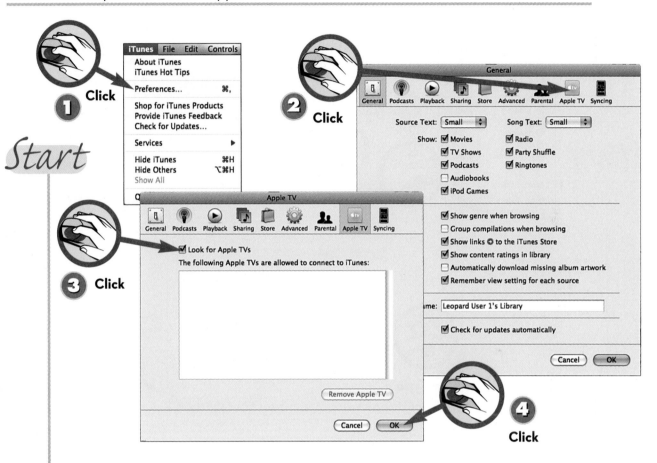

1. In iTunes, select **iTunes** > **Preferences**.

2. Click the **Apple TV** button in the Preferences window.

3. Check the **Look for Apple TVs** check box. Wait for your Apple TV to appear in the window.

4. Click the **OK** button.

**TIP**

**Apple TV and iPods**

If you want to watch a movie or view your photos on a big TV screen occasionally, you can connect an iPod or iPhone to the video input jack on a TV. If you want a more permanent setup, you can connect an Apple TV to the television and upload movies, photos, and music to it.

# CONNECTING TO A COMPUTER VIA FTP

FTP (File Transfer Protocol) is one of the file-sharing options in the System Preferences > Sharing window. It enables you to share files with other users on the Internet. This task shows you how to connect to another computer that has file sharing and FTP turned on.

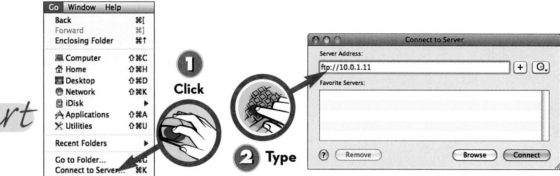

1 Choose **Go** > **Connect to Server**.

2 Type the IP address or URL for the computer to which you want to connect and press **Return**.

3 Type the username and password.

4 Click the **OK** button.

*End*

-TIP-
**Keyboard Shortcut**
Press ⌘-**K** to open the Connect to Server window.

# USING AN IPOD AS A HARD DRIVE

When an iPod is connected to a Mac, you can configure the iPod to work as a hard drive with iTunes. In the Summary page, check the **Enable disk use** check box to enable this setting. The next time you connect your iPod to a Mac, the iPod appears on your desktop. Now you can store files on it, too! This task shows you how to connect and access the iPod as a hard drive.

Connect ① Double-click ② Control-click ④ Click ③

Start

End

1 Connect the iPod dock to the Mac and place the iPod in the dock.

2 Double-click the iPod's icon on the desktop to see its contents in a Finder window.

3 Copy files to or from your computer.

4 **Control-click** the iPod and select **Eject** from the menu to remove the iPod from the desktop.

**TIP**
**iPod Drive Format**
If you want to use your iPod as a hard drive on a Mac and PC, format it on a Windows machine. The DOS file format enables the iPod to store files on a Mac and Windows machine, and also sync and play any files on either machine.

# CONNECTING A TV AS A SECOND MONITOR

Every Mac has an external monitor port that enables you to connect it to an external monitor or television. The second display can mirror your desktop or become a second desktop. This task shows you how to connect a MacBook to a TV.

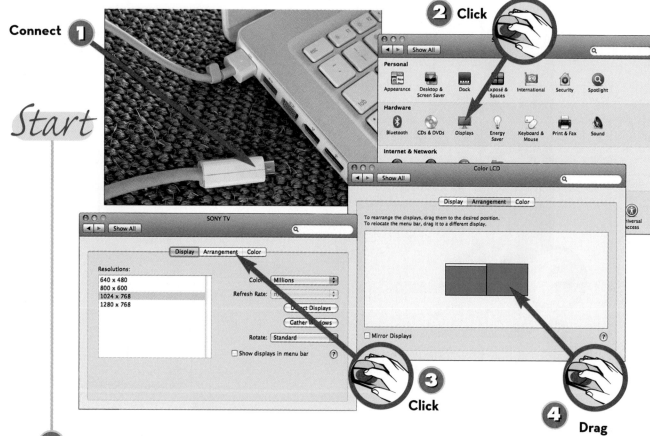

Connect **①**

**②** Click

Start

**③** Click

**④** Drag

**①** Connect the TV monitor cable to the Mac.

**②** Open **System Preferences** from the Dock and click the **Displays** button.

**③** Click the **Arrangement** button.

**④** Drag each screen to create your monitor configuration. Drag the menu bar to the monitor you want the main application windows to open into.

End

**TIP**

**Monitors and Remotes**

Use the Mac's remote when its connected to a TV to navigate the media files on your computer. To find out more about how to use Apple Remote, go to the "Using Front Row to Surf Your Music, Movies and Photos" task in Part 4, "Installing and Using Applications."

# CONNECTING A WIRELESS KEYBOARD

Apple's wireless keyboard enables you to connect a keyboard to a desktop or MacBook over a Bluetooth connection. It is similar to the MacBook keyboard. But it lacks a number pad, and there are only 12 function keys. This task shows you how to connect a wireless keyboard to your Mac.

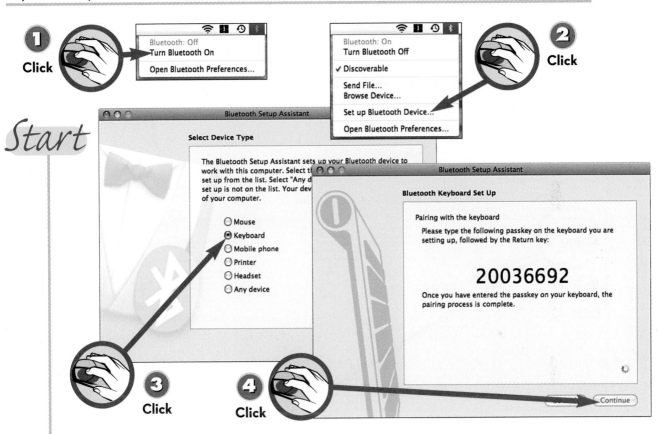

**Start**

**1** Click

**2** Click

**3** Click

**4** Click

**1** In the Bluetooth menu, choose **Turn Bluetooth On**.

**2** Choose **Bluetooth** > **Set up Bluetooth Device**.

**3** Choose **Keyboard**. Hold the keyboard within 5 inches of the Mac screen and click **Continue**.

**4** Type the number to pair the keyboard with your Mac. Click the **Continue** button to return to the desktop.

**End**

**TIP**

**Wireless Keyboard Benefits**
One of the benefits of using a wireless keyboard is that you can place it at a different level than your laptop. This is great if you're working on your computer for long periods of time and want to optimize screen viewing and posture while working on your laptop.

# CONNECTING A WIRELESS MOUSE

If you have a wireless keyboard, you may have a wireless mouse. A wireless mouse enables you to move your mouse freely without having to connect a cable to your Mac. This task shows you how to connect a wireless Bluetooth mouse to your Mac.

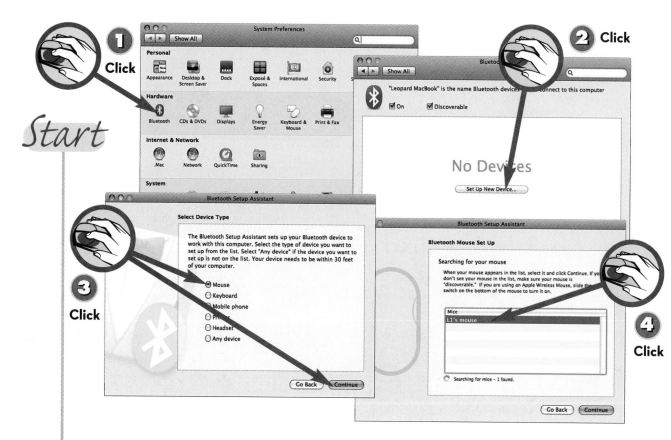

Start

End

1. Open **System Preferences** from the Dock and click the **Bluetooth** button. Turn Bluetooth **On**.

2. Click the **Set Up a New Device** button.

3. Power on the mouse and hold it a few inches from your Mac. Click **Mouse**, and then click **Continue**.

4. When your mouse appears in the list, click **Continue** to finish the pairing process.

## TIP

### Preserve Battery Live

The wireless keyboard and mouse can put itself to sleep when not in use. You can also power them off to prolong battery life. On the mouse, slide the white plastic lid until it covers the red IR light; press the power button on the keyboard. To turn it back on, slide the lid down, and then click the mouse button.

# SELECTING A TIME CAPSULE DRIVE

Time Capsule is a hybrid product. It combines an Apple Extreme Base Station, for wireless networking, with a built-in hard drive. You can use Time Capsule to back up files on your Macs running Leopard, and then restore files with Time Machine. This task shows you how to configure Time Machine with the Time Capsule's hard drive.

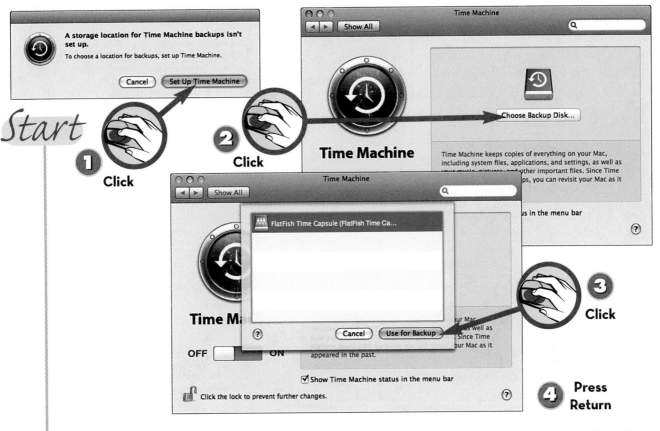

*Start*

**①** Click

**②** Click

Time Machine

**③** Click

**④** Press Return

**①** Open **Time Machine** from the Dock. If this is the first time it is opening, click the **Set Up Time Machine** button. The Time Machine system preferences window opens.

**②** Click the **Choose Backup Disk** button in the Time Machine window. A list of available drives appears.

**③** Select the Time Capsule device. Click the **Use for Backup** button.

**④** Type the password and press **Return** to add the Time Capsule drive to Time Machine.

*End*

**TIP**
**Restoring Files with Time Machine**
To find out how to restore a file or folder with Time Machine, go to "Restoring Files with Time Machine" in Part 17, "Taking Care of Your Mac."

**TIP**
**Find Out More About Time Capsule**
To find out more about how to set up Time Capsule, go to "Configuring Time Capsule" in Part 7, "Setting Up a Wireless Home Network."

# CONNECTING TO A MOBILE PHONE

Bluetooth file sharing enables you to access photos and movies stored on a cell phone that supports Bluetooth. This task shows you how to connect your Mac to a cell phone.

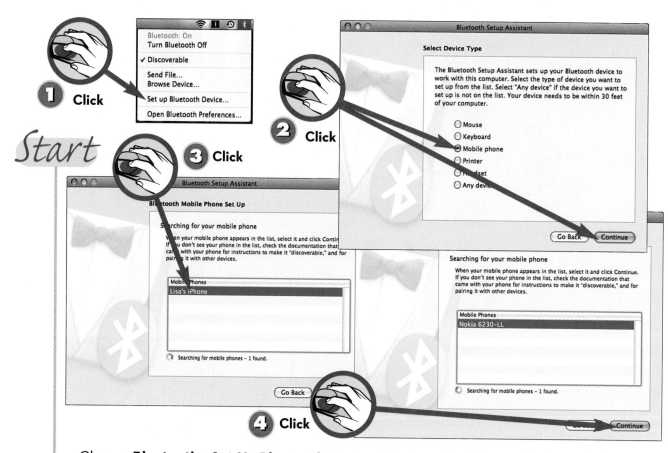

**1** Choose **Bluetooth > Set Up Bluetooth Device**. (To show the Bluetooth menu in the menu bar, check the Show Bluetooth status in the menu bar check box in the System Preferences > Bluetooth window.)

**2** Click the **Mobile Phone** radio button and click **Continue**.

**3** Select your mobile phone from the list. Read the onscreen instructions.

**4** Click the **Continue** button. The Bluetooth Mobile Phone Set Up window appears.

Continued

-TIP-

**Active Bluetooth Devices**
Select the **Bluetooth** menu from the menu bar to view a list of devices paired with your Mac. Devices that are boldface are actively connected to your Mac.

-NOTE-

**Disconnecting the Bluetooth Device**
To turn off the Bluetooth connection, select **Open Bluetooth Preferences** from the Bluetooth menu. Select a device from the list on the left. Select the **Action** menu and choose **Disconnect**. The two devices disconnect from each other.

**5** Type on the cell phone

**6** Click

**7** Click

**5** Type the number into your cell phone and click **Continue** on the Mac to pair the phone with the Mac.

**6** Review the settings. Make any changes you desire. Click the **Continue** button.

**7** Click the **Quit** button to complete setup.

*End*

**TIP**

**Browse Mobile Phones**

To view detailed information about any Bluetooth enabled mobile phones, select **Browse Device** from the Bluetooth menu. Select the mobile phone and navigate files on the phone.

## 15

## RUNNING WINDOWS ON YOUR MAC

Macs run software on Intel processors—the same processors used to run Windows. To run Windows on a Mac, you need Boot Camp, which is an application that is part of your Mac OS X Leopard software. Boot Camp enables you to run Windows on a separate drive partition on your Mac.

The process for configuring Boot Camp involves adding a Boot Camp partition to your internal hard drive. Then you install Windows on it. Windows Vista is the star of this chapter, but as an alternative you can install Windows XP.

The tasks in this chapter focus on running Boot Camp and setting up your Mac to run Windows. You'll learn how to create the Boot Camp partition, install Windows Vista, and add Mac driver software. Tasks also include how to install applications, customize the desktop on the Windows partition, and sync an iPod with iTunes on Vista.

# WINDOWS VISTA DESKTOP

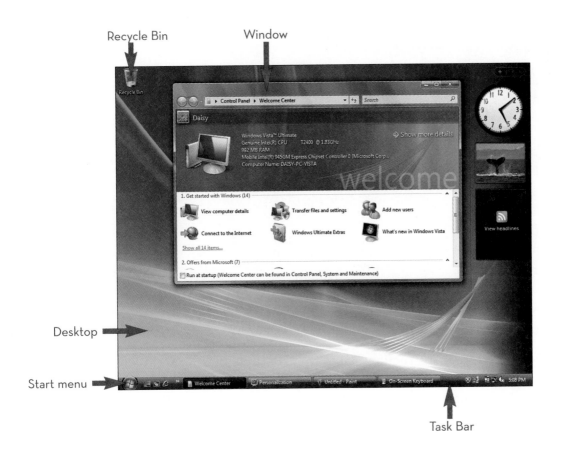

Recycle Bin

Window

Desktop

Start menu

Task Bar

# INSTALLING WINDOWS WITH BOOT CAMP

Boot Camp is an application that enables you to format a hard drive or partition to make it Windows compatible and install Windows XP or Vista. This task shows you how to install Windows Vista Ultimate Edition.

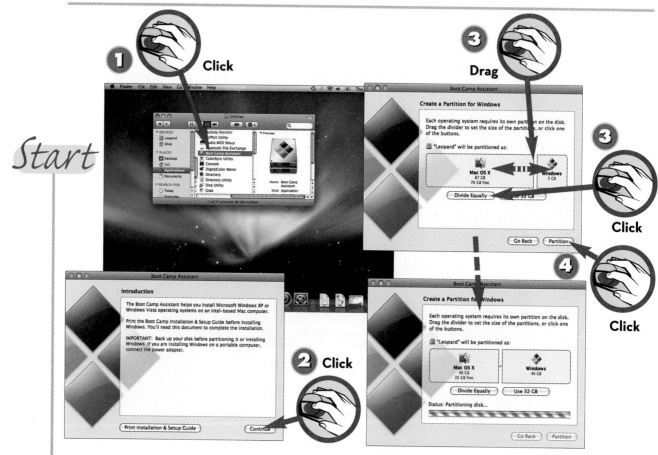

1. Open the Boot Camp Assistant application by opening the Application folder and clicking its icon in the Utilities folder.

2. Follow the onscreen instructions. Click the **Continue** button.

3. Adjust the size of the partitions by dragging the middle area between the Leopard and Windows graphics in the Boot Camp window. Click the **Divide Equally** button if you want to make both partitions equal in size.

4. Click the **Partition** button.

*Continued*

---

## TIP
### Keyboard Differences
One of the first things you might notice is that the Mac keyboard, especially on a laptop, is missing keys traditionally found on a PC keyboard. For example, the print screen button. In Windows, select the **On Screen** keyboard located in the **Start > Accessories > Ease of Access** menu to access those options.

## NOTE
### External USB Keyboard
If you're running Windows on a MacBook, an alternative to using the onscreen keyboard is to connect an external USB keyboard.

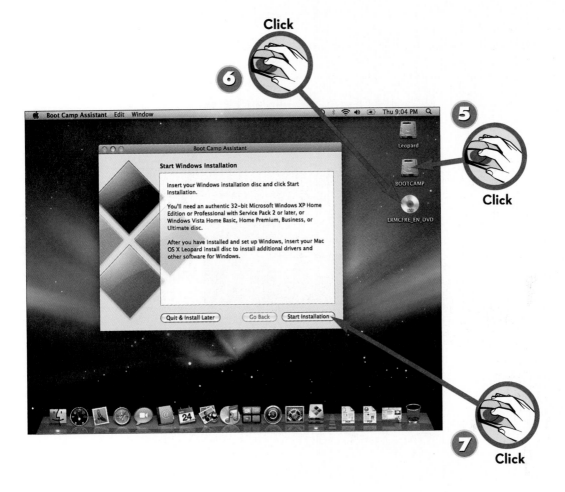

**5**    Wait for the format to complete. The Boot Camp partition appears on the desktop

**6**    Insert the Windows DVD.

**7**    Click the **Start Installation** button. Follow the onscreen instructions to install Windows on the Boot Camp partition.

*Continued*

### NOTE
#### More About Vista
For more information on how to use Vista, check out *Easy Microsoft Windows Vista* from Que Publishing (www.quepublishing.com).

### NOTE
#### Formatting an NTFS Partition for Windows
During the Windows install, one of the screens asks you to select the partition to install Windows on. Select the Boot Camp partition. Then click the **Advanced** link in the Windows Vista installer. Click the **Format** link. Then click **Next**. Complete the Windows install. Restart the machine.

**8** **Option**

**11** **Click**

**8** After the Windows installation is complete, you can boot into either OS by holding down the **Option** key while the computer powers up. Select the Leopard partition.

**9** Open the **System Preferences > Startup Disk** window. Choose the Windows partition icon in the Startup Disk panel.

**10** Click the **Restart** button. Wait for your Mac to restart.

**11** Wait for the Windows desktop to appear. Insert the Leopard DVD into the DVD drive. Open the **Computer** folder from the **Start** menu. Select the DVD drive from the Explorer window.

*Continued*

---

**NOTE**

**Virtual Windows**

An alternative to Boot Camp is to run Windows software on Mac OS X using virtualization software. Although configuration won't provide the same software performance as running the software in Boot Camp, you won't have to restart the Mac to run Windows software.

**NOTE**

**Virtualization Software for the Mac**

To find out more about running Windows in a virtual partition on your Mac, visit the websites for Parallels (parallels.com) and VMWare (vmware.com).

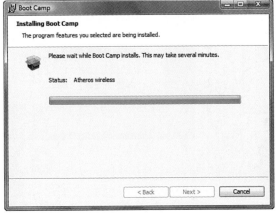

**Click**

**Click**

12 When the DVD is selected in step 11, Boot Camp starts. Read the onscreen instructions. Click the **Next** button.

13 Wait for the drivers to install.

14 Click the **Finish** button. Restart your Mac. Windows Vista now has all its drivers installed.

*End*

**NOTE**

**Windows Can Sleep**

Like Mac OS X, Windows Vista can be put to sleep, which is the equivalent to putting your Mac to sleep in Mac OS X. In Windows Vista, select the right arrow button at the bottom of the **Start** menu and select **Sleep** to put your Computer to sleep.

**NOTE**

**Switching to Mac OS X**

To shut down Windows, click the power button located on the Start menu. Choose **Shut Down** to exit Windows. When the Mac restarts, hold down the **Option** key and select the Leopard partition to return to Mac OS X.

# CUSTOMIZING YOUR WINDOWS DESKTOP

Windows enables you to assign a photo or image as a desktop picture. This task shows you how.

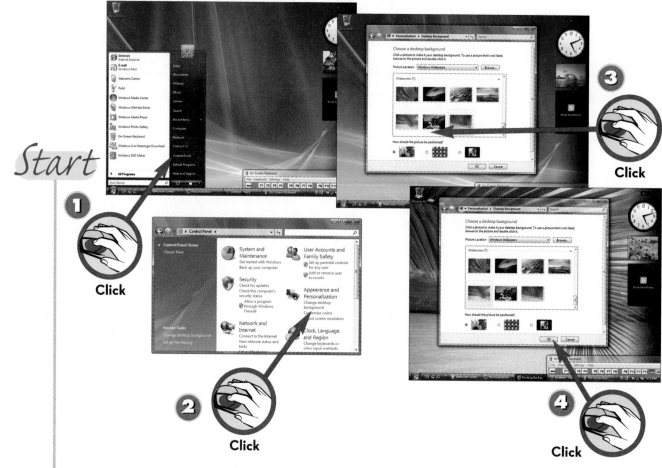

*Start*

**Click**

**Click**

**Click**

**Click**

**Click**

*End*

1. Click **Start** > **Control Panel** to open the Windows Control Panel. This is the equivalent of the System Preferences on the Mac.

2. Click **Change desktop background**.

3. Select a picture for your desktop.

4. Click **OK**.

---

**TIP**

**Images and the Pictures Folder**

Windows suggests saving photos and images to the Pictures folder. If you have photos in your Pictures folder, navigate to this folder to select one of your own photos as a desktop picture.

**NOTE**

**Sharing Mac Files with Windows**

To find out how to access files on a Mac with a Windows machine, go to "Sharing Files with a Windows Machine," found in Part 7, "Setting Up a Wireless Home Network."

# INSTALLING ITUNES

Apple's iTunes is free for Mac and Windows. Download it from http://apple.com/itunes. Unlike Mac OS X, iTunes is not preinstalled with Windows. This task shows you how to install it.

*Start*

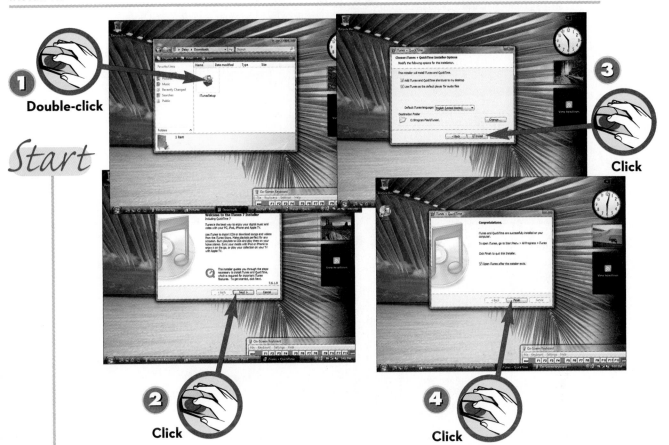

**1** Double-click

**3** Click

**2** Click

**4** Click

**①** Download the iTunes installer from the Apple website. Go to the folder you saved it to and double-click the installer to start it.

**②** Follow the onscreen instructions. Click **Next**.

**③** Follow the onscreen instructions for the license and customization options, clicking Next to move through each step. When finished, click **Install**.

**④** Click **Finish**. iTunes opens. Review the user agreement and accept the agreement if you agree with its terns.

*End*

## TIP
### Free Music and the iTunes Store
If you don't have any music in iTunes, go to the iTunes Store via the Store item in the Source pane. There are free music and TV show downloads available. You can use these files to test syncing and playing music and movies on your iPod.

## NOTE
### Transferring Purchases
To find out how to transfer music and movies on your iPod to a different machines, go to Part 10, "Playing Music and Movies in iTunes."

# ADDING AND PLAYING MUSIC IN ITUNES

Now that iTunes is up and running, you can populate it with music and movie files. This task shows you how to add a music file to your iTunes Music library.

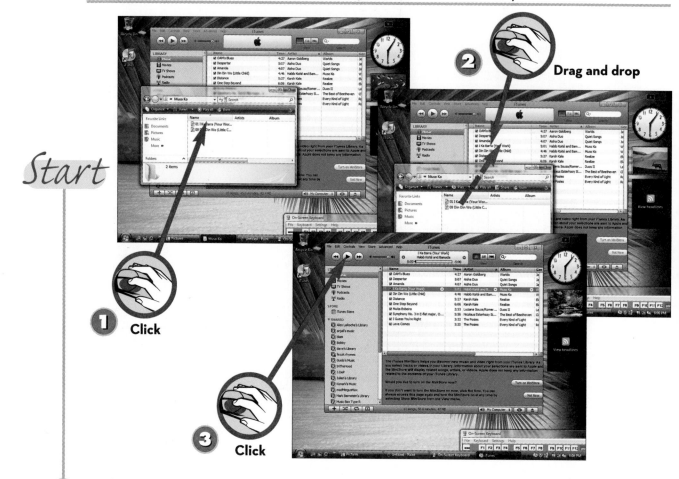

*Start*

**Drag and drop**

**①** **Click**

**②**

**③** **Click**

*End*

**①** With iTunes open, use Windows Explorer to locate a music file you've saved to your hard drive. You can also insert an audio CD or rip an audio CD to add music to your iTunes library.

**②** Drag it from the Explorer window and drop it into the iTunes window.

**③** Select it, and then click the **Play** button.

---

 **TIP**

**Configuring iTunes**

When you first open iTunes, several screens appear asking how you want iTunes configured. If you're not sure what to pick, select the manual setting. You can change settings later.

 **TIP**

**Syncing with Different Machines**

After you have your music and movies organized in iTunes, you can sync playlists and other media to an iPod. If you chose to auto-sync, you must use the same computer to update the iPod. If you use a different computer, all the automatically synced files will be removed.

# SYNCING YOUR IPOD

Syncing an iPod with Windows is similar to syncing an iPod with a Mac. Plug in one end of the USB cable to the Mac and the other end to the iPod. Open iTunes and, if you have already selected or updated playlists, just click **Sync**.

**1** Connect

*Start*

**3** Click

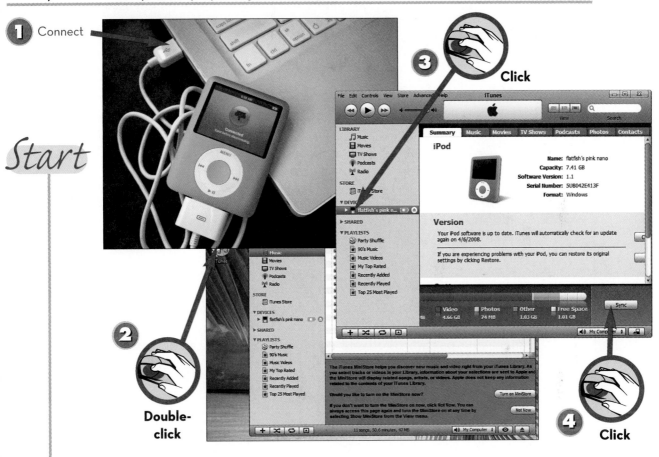

**2** Double-click

**4** Click

*End*

**1** Connect the iPod to the custom iPod connector. Connect the USB connector at the other end of the cable to your Mac.

**2** Double-click the **iTunes** icon on the Windows desktop to open iTunes.

**3** Select your iPod in the Devices list in the iTunes Source pane.

**4** Click **Sync**.

 **TIP**
**Reformatting an iPod**
iPods can be formatted with a DOS or Mac file system. Formatting an iPod with iTunes for Windows enables you to use your iPod to store files for Mac OS and Windows. If you choose to switch formats, all files will be deleted from the iPod. Back them up before formatting.

 **TIP**
**Syncing and Your iPod with Windows**
Syncing your iPod to any Windows computer, even if you don't add or remove anything, updates the clock and location on your iPod with the settings of that computer.

## 16

## PROTECTING YOUR COMPUTER

Computer security is a hot topic. Spam, identify theft, data theft, viruses, and worms are part of today's computer life on the Internet. Security on the Mac can be divided into two main areas: the software on the computer (Mac OS or Windows), and your software settings and personal data. This chapter provides some tasks that help you improve security with both areas.

You can download software security updates for Mac OS and Windows from Apple and Microsoft websites. They're also available when you choose the Apple > Software Update menu. Install the security updates to apply them to your computer.

To prevent unwanted visitors from accessing your computer, you can adjust some Safari software settings. In addition to changing your software settings, don't share your personal information in an email or chat session. Don't tell others your password for your computer login. You can optimize some Safari settings for security. The tasks in this chapter show you some basic ways to improve the security of your computer.

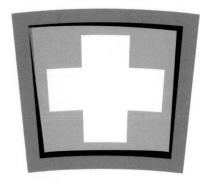

# ACTIVITY MONITOR OVERVIEW

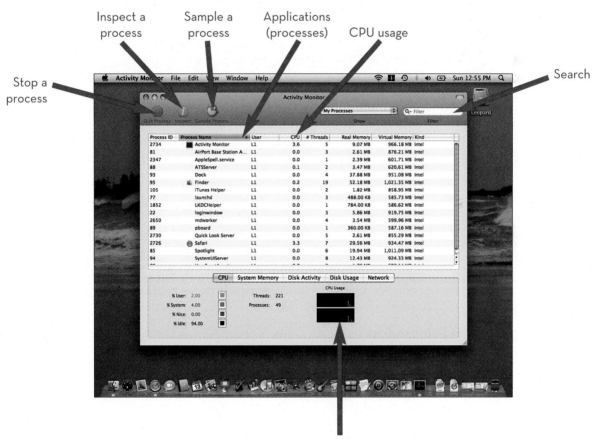

Inspect a process

Sample a process

Applications (processes)

CPU usage

Stop a process

Search

Processors and CPU usage

# CHANGING YOUR PASSWORD

Passwords don't provide a guarantee that your computer will be safe. However, it does slow down most folks from gaining access to your desktop and files. This task shows you how to change your password.

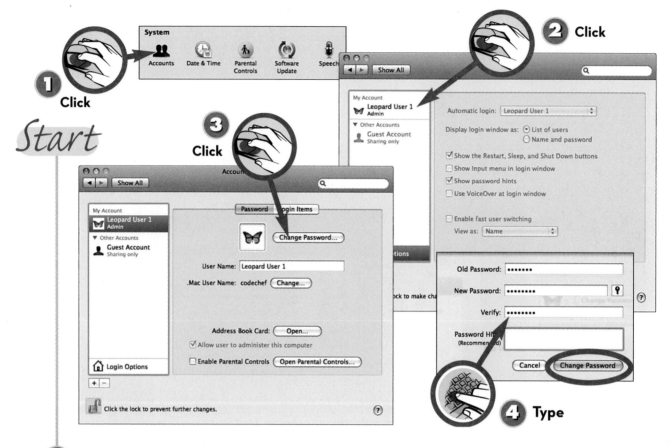

**1** Open **System Preferences** using its Dock icon and click the **Accounts** button.

**2** Click an account that you want to secure with a password.

**3** Click the **Change Password** button.

**4** Type the old password. Then type the new password twice and click the **Change Password** button.

**TIP**

**Secure Passwords**

Try to avoid using the same letter or number for your password (such as 111111 or aaaaaa). Also, try not to use a word from the dictionary. Instead, combine numbers and words to create a password. Another option is to elect the password assistant on the change password screen. It can provide some useful options for creating your password.

# CREATING ACCOUNTS

Add accounts to your Mac if you want to share your computer with multiple users.
Generally, there are four types of accounts: administrator, power user/debugger, standard
user, and guest. This task shows you how to create a standard user account.

*Start*

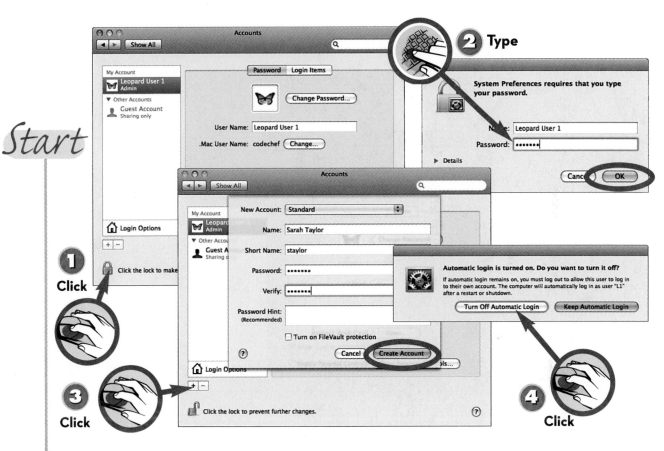

Click **1**

Click **3**

**2** Type

**4** Click

**1** In the **Accounts** preferences panel, click the padlock icon.

**2** Type the name and password for the administrator account. Click **OK**.

**3** Click the + (plus) button in the Accounts window. Type a login name and password, and
then click the **Create Account** button.

**4** Click the **Turn Off Automatic Login** button.

*End*

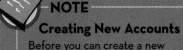

**NOTE**

**Creating New Accounts**

Before you can create a new
account, Mac OS X requires the
administrator login and password.

# REMOVING USER ACCOUNTS

Adding user accounts enables users to customize their Mac OS X environment as they please. When you no longer need an account, it's best to remove it so that no unauthorized users gain access to your Mac. This task shows you how to remove a user account.

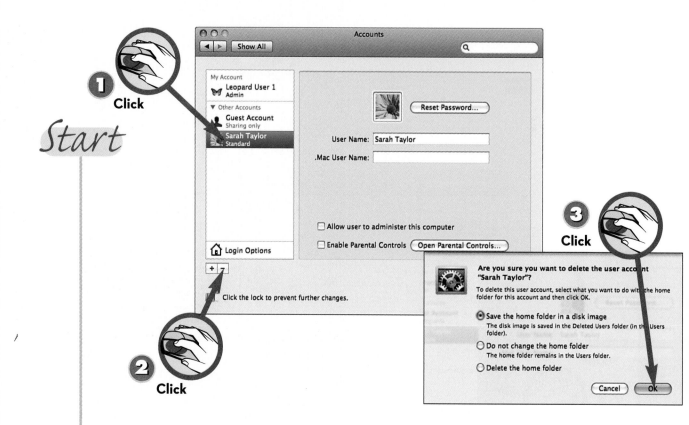

_Start_

**1** Click

**2** Click

**3** Click

_End_

**1** In the Accounts preferences window, choose an account from the list

**2** Click the – (minus) button in the Accounts window.

**3** Choose a radio button to select how you want to delete the account. Then click **OK**.

---

**TIP**

**When to Remove an Account**

Consider removing accounts created for guests, friends or family if they are no longer using your Mac.

**NOTE**

Preserving Account Data One way to preserve your account information is to create a back up. You can use Time Machine to back up and restore all the information on your Mac, including your account data. Go to Part 17, "Taking Care of Your Mac."

# DISABLING AUTOMATICALLY OPENING FILES IN SAFARI

There are many settings in Safari. When a web page loads in the browser, the web server can send a number of files to your computer. This task shows you how to disable Safari's "safe file download" setting. Disabling this setting can help reduce the number of files that make it onto your computer.

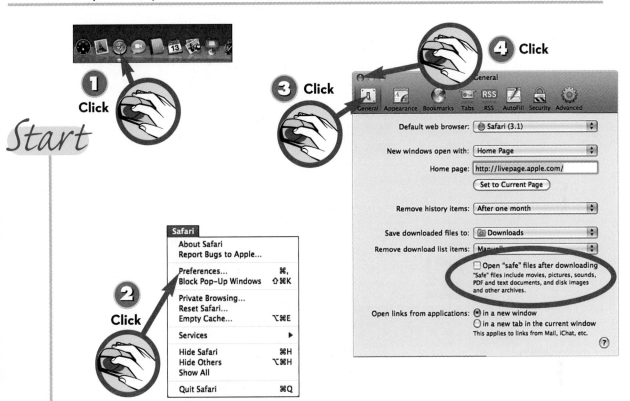

*Start*

*End*

1. Click the **Safari** icon on the Dock to open it.

2. Choose **Safari** > **Preferences**.

3. Click the **General** button. Then, uncheck the **Open "safe" files after downloading** check box.

4. Click the **Close** button on the Preferences window to save your changes. Quit Safari and reopen it to apply the changes.

 **TIP**
### Things to Avoid on the Internet
Avoid email and websites asking your for your personal information or account numbers. In addition, avoid websites with IP addresses rather than URLs (names).

 **NOTE**
### Keyboard Shortcuts
Press ⌘-, to open the Preferences window in Safari. This shortcut also works with Finder and most applications with preferences.

# BLOCKING POP-UP WINDOWS IN SAFARI

Some websites open pop-up windows when you visit them. Pop-up windows can be empty or contain advertisements or other content. When these windows open, they can distract you from viewing the web page you are visiting. This task shows you how to prevent them from appearing in Safari.

*Start*

**2** Click

**1** Click

**1** Open Safari.

**2** Select **Safari** > **Block Pop-Up Windows**. A check mark appears beside the menu item when blocking pop-up windows is active.

*End*

**NOTE**
**Enable Pop-Ups When Needed**
When downloading files or surfing the web, some web pages might require you to unblock pop-ups to complete a transaction or navigate the website.

**TIP**
**Not All Pop-Up Windows Are Blocked**
Some websites may bypass the Block Pop-Up security feature. If one or two small windows with ads appears while you're surfing, just close them to dismiss them.

# LOCKING AND UNLOCKING THE KEYCHAIN

The Keychain Access application enables you to view or edit any passwords and other security-related files that you have saved on your computer. If you really want to optimize Mac OS X for security, don't store any login or password information in your Keychain. This task shows you how to unlock the Keychain.

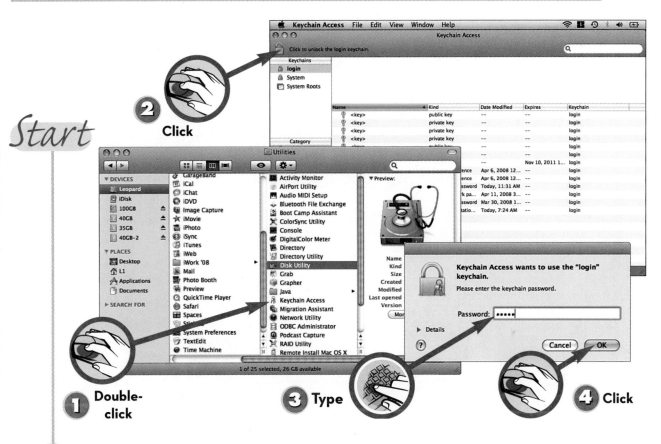

**Start**

**2** Click

**1** Double-click

**3** Type

**4** Click

**1** Open the **Applications** > **Utilities** > **Keychain Access program**.

**2** Click the **Lock** icon in the Keychain window.

**3** Type your password.

**4** Click **OK**.

*End*

---

**TIP**

### When Not to Save Your Passwords

If you're logging in to a web page, server, or computer from someone else's machine, don't save your password. Keeping it off the Keychain can help preserve the security of your personal information.

**NOTE**

### Keep the Keychain Locked

Keep the Keychain locked if you want to minimize access to its contents. If you have automatic login configured on your Mac, someone else may be able to view your account and password settings when you're not using the computer.

# DELETING SELECTED COOKIES IN SAFARI

They might sound tasty, but these cookies are files that may be downloaded while navigating or interacting with a website. Cookies can store different kinds of information, so you might not want to delete them all. This task shows you how to delete selected cookies from your Mac.

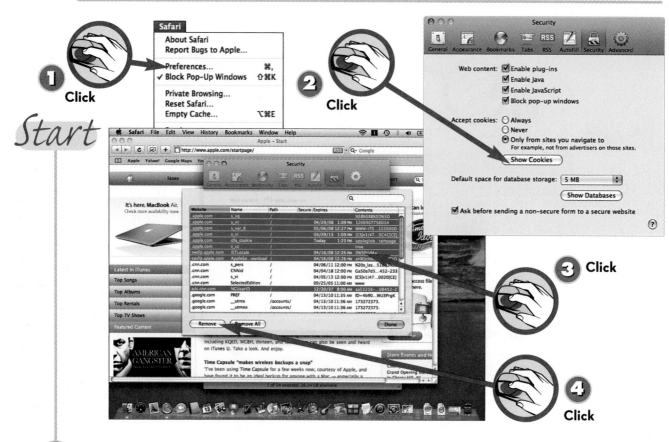

**Start**

In Safari, select **Safari** > **Preferences**.

Click the **Show Cookies** button.

Click to select the cookies you want to remove (or ⌘-**click** to select multiple cookies at one time).

Click the **Remove** button.

*End*

**NOTE**

**What Are Cookies?**

Cookies are files transferred from a web server to your machine. A cookie can work with other files to track information related to pages you surf on a website. Cookie behavior varies from site to site. For example, one site might store your login information in a cookie, another might track which pages you visit.

# CLEARING SAFARI'S CACHE

If you spend a lot of time on some web pages, over time the performance of the that particular web page may grow slower, or Safari may become unstable. One thing that might help reset Safari (without resetting everything) is to clear the browser cache. This task shows you how.

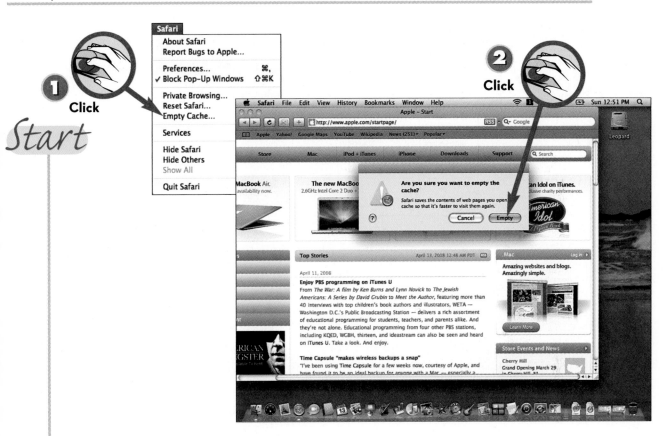

*Start*

**1** Click

**2** Click

**1** In Safari, select **Safari** > **Empty Cache**.

**2** Click the **Empty** button.

*End*

---

## NOTE

### Surfing on the iPhone

Although Safari runs on the iPhone, you cannot clear the cache or remove cookies. The best way to reset Safari on an iPhone is to disconnect from the wireless and cell networks. Then power off the iPhone.

## TIP

### What Is a Cache?

The cache stores temporary items, such as images, that load when you visit a web page for the first time.

# REMOVING ALL COOKIES

Removing all cookies is a rare occurrence. But if you want to clear all web page settings in Safari for any pages you may have visited or logged in to, clearing all cookies can remove most of this kind of data. This task shows you how to remove all cookies from Safari.

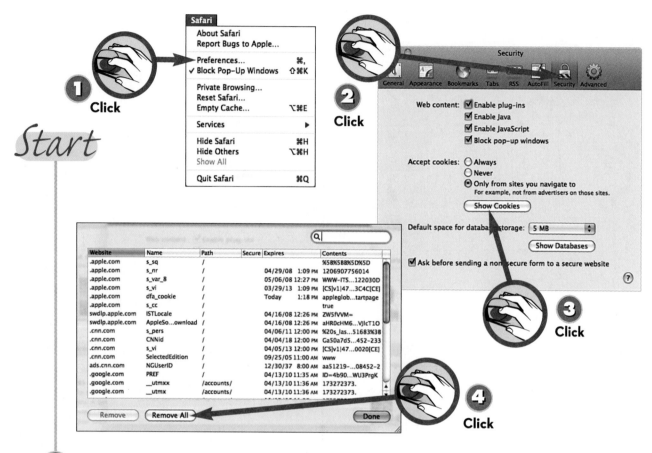

**Start**

**Click**

**Click**

**Click**

**Click**

1. In Safari, choose **Safari** > **Preferences**.

2. Click the **Security** button.

3. Click the **Show Cookies** button.

4. Click the **Remove All** button to clear all cookies. Quit Safari and reopen it. Any page for which you saved custom settings, such as login credentials, will no longer contain those settings.

*End*

**TIP**
**Reset Safari**
To return Safari to its original settings, choose **Safari** > **Reset Safari**.

**TIP**
**File Space and Cookies**
If you visit a lot of websites and notice your hard drive is filling up, be sure you have any information you need from Safari, such as account login and password information, and then clear all cookies. This can free up some disk space.

# VIEWING ACTIVE APPLICATIONS

You can view all software processes running on your computer from the Activity Monitor window. Activity Monitor also shows each processor and its activity level. This can be helpful if you want to see if application is not responding or busy. This task navigates some the Activity Monitor window and shows you how to see what's going on with your Mac.

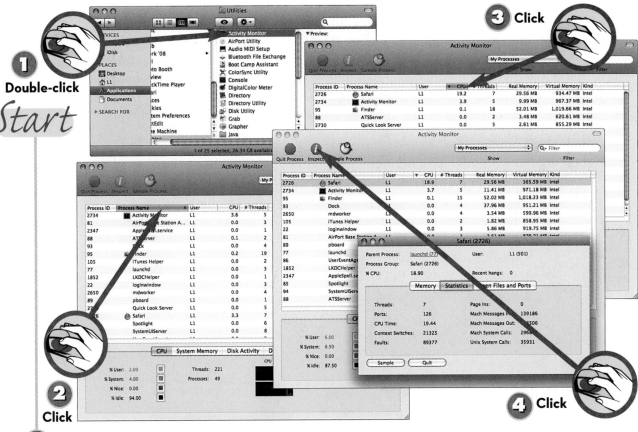

**Double-click**

**Start**

**③ Click**

**① ② Click**

**④ Click**

**End**

1. Open the **Activity Monitor** program in the Applications > Utilities folder.

2. Click the **Process** column to sort the threads by process.

3. Select the **CPU** column to sort by processes that are utilizing the CPUs.

4. Choose a process in the list. Then click the **Inspect** button to view details about a selected process.

## NOTE

**Keyboard Shortcut**

An alternative to pressing ⌘-**Option-Esc** to kill application processes is to select the process in the Activity Monitor and click the **Quit Process** button. When you kill an application process, any unsaved data is permanently lost.

## 17

## TAKING CARE OF YOUR MAC

You don't have to do a whole lot of cleaning or maintenance to keep your Mac hardware looking and working great. The case, keyboard, mouse, and monitor should be handled with care when you're carrying or using them. Maintaining your Mac is similar to maintaining other computers. Back up your files regularly. Keep track of any odd behavior such as slow performance or unexpected shutdowns.

The tasks in this chapter cover a relatively broad set of topics. First you learn how to back up and restore files with Time Machine. Followed by a task on how to back up your files manually. Next, the Disk Utility program is featured. You can use it to check and repair the file system on your hard drive. It can also check permissions and reformat a hard drive to work with Mac or Windows. Finally, the last set of tasks show you how to download software updates, install one manually, reset an iPod, and send in a crash report.

# EXPLORING TIME MACHINE

Finder window

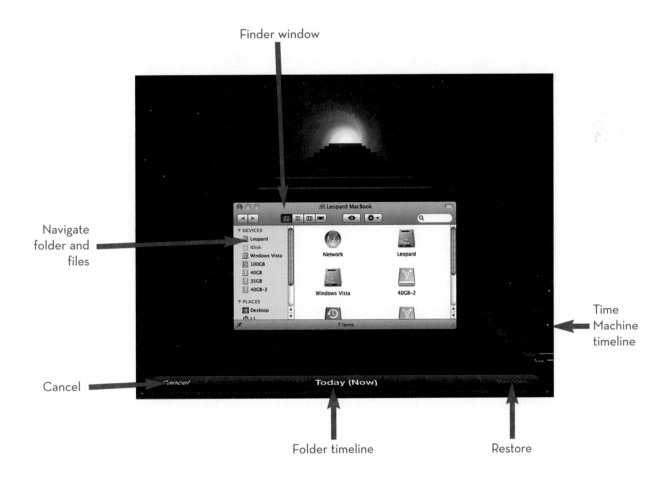

Navigate folder and files

Time Machine timeline

Cancel

Today (Now)

Folder timeline

Restore

# BACKING UP FILES WITH TIME MACHINE

Time Machine is the backup application included with Mac OS X Leopard. To create a Time Machine backup, you must first connect an external drive or Time Capsule to your Mac. Each time a drive is connected to your Mac, Mac OS X Leopard shows an alert asking if you want to use the drive to backup with Time Machine. Click the **Use as Backup Disk** button. Time Machine opens.

Connect an external drive to the Mac. Click Cancel if the Time Machine alert appears. Choose **System Preferences > Time Machine** to open the Time Machine Preferences window. Click the **Choose Backup Disk** button. A sheet appears showing the connected external drives on your Mac.

Select the drive you want to use and click the **Use for backup** button. Time Machine starts; the switch is On. The next scheduled backup time appears beside **Next Backup** in the Time Machine window.

Click the **Options** button. The Do Not Backup sheet opens. View the list of hard drives included in the backup. Select any drives you want to remove from the backup.

Click the **Done** button to save your changes in the Do Not Backup sheet.

---

**NOTE**
**Setting Up Time Capsule**
To find out how to set up Time Capsule with Time Machine, go to Part 7, "Setting up a Wireless Home Network." This task shows you how to manually set up Time Machine with an external hard drive to start backing up your internal hard drive.

**NOTE**
**Excluding Drives**
Choose the Options button to deselect any partitions or drives you do not want to include in the backup.

# RESTORING FILES WITH TIME MACHINE

Time Machine creates a backup of every file and folder on your hard drive. You can restore an earlier version of a file or folder and replace or preserve the existing file. This task shows you how to restore a file from Time Machine.

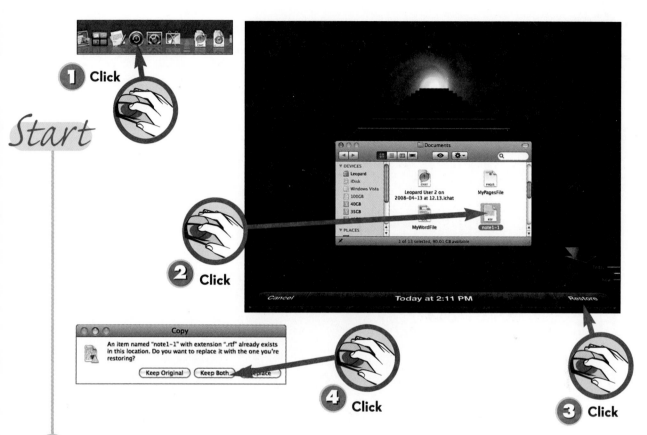

**Start**

**1** Click

**2** Click

**3** Click

**4** Click

Today at 2:11 PM

Cancel

Restore

**Copy**

An item named "note1-1" with extension ".rtf" already exists in this location. Do you want to replace it with the one you're restoring?

Keep Original | Keep Both | Replace

---

**1** Open **Time Machine** from the Dock.

**2** Navigate backward in the timeline. Select a file in the Finder window. If an older version of the file is available, the **Move Backward** arrow to the right of the window will be active. Click the Move Backward arrow to access older versions of the file or folder. Conversely, click the Forward arrow to view more recent versions of a file or folder.

**3** Click the **Restore** button.

**4** Click the **Keep Both** button.

**End**

---

**NOTE**

### Preparing the Time Machine Hard Drive

Be sure to clear enough room on the external hard drive before starting Time Machine if you plan to restore lots of files or files that occupy a lot of disk space.

**NOTE**

### Frequency of Backups

Time Machine backs up files hourly up to 24 hours. Daily backups are stored for the current month. Weekly backups are stored until the disk is full.

# BACKING UP FILES TO A DVD

You can manually back up a file in a few different ways. Copy it to an external hard drive, send it in email to yourself, or copy the file to a server. This task shows you how to back up and burn files to a DVD.

*Start*

**1** Insert a DVD. Click **OK** when the dialog opens.

**2** The DVD icon appears on your desktop. Double-click it on the desktop to open it.

**3** Open a folder on your hard drive. Drag files from any Finder window to the DVD icon or to one of its Finder windows. Mac OS X creates an alias for any files or folders added to the DVD.

**4** Choose **File > Burn to Disc**.

*End*

**TIP**

### Manual Backup Benefits

Convenience is the biggest benefit for manually backing up your files. Back up the files that are important to you as frequently or infrequently as you like. This process optimizes disk space, minimizes the time to restore files, and requires no special software.

# USING DISK UTILITY TO CHECK THE HARD DRIVE

The Disk Utility program provides many valuable features. The disk verification feature can help you find and repair problems with your hard drive's file system. This task shows you how to verify the files on a hard drive.

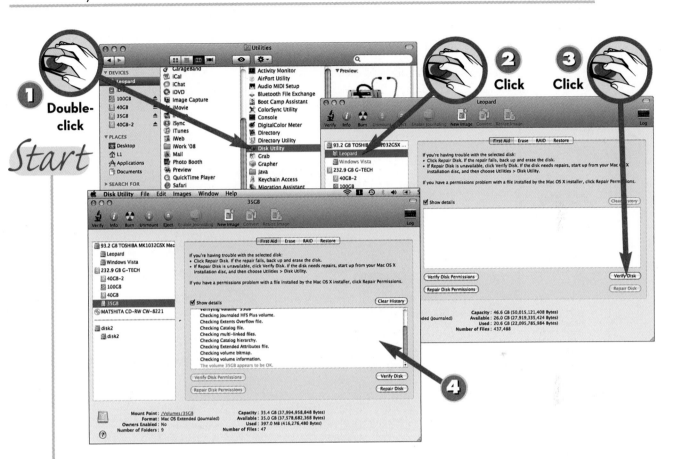

**Start**

**1** Double-click

**2** Click

**3** Click

**4**

**1** Choose **Applications** > **Utilities** > **Disk Utility**.

**2** Select the hard drive on the left list in the Disk Utility window.

**3** Click the **Verify the Disk** button. If the drive reports error during verification, back up the drive before repairing the errors. Choose the **Repair** button to repair the drive. If the repair fails the drive may become damaged and the data on the drive lost.

**4** View the results.

*End*

**TIP**
**More About Disk Repair**
In most cases, it's alright to repair any errors Disk Utility finds. However, if you want to be extra careful, you can purchase a third-party disk utility, such as Disk Warrior, and see whether it identifies the same errors on your drive before you repair anything.

# REPAIRING PERMISSIONS

Repairing permissions is another handy feature in Disk Utility. It enables you to verify permissions files on your Mac and repair them, too! This task shows you how to verify permissions on a Mac.

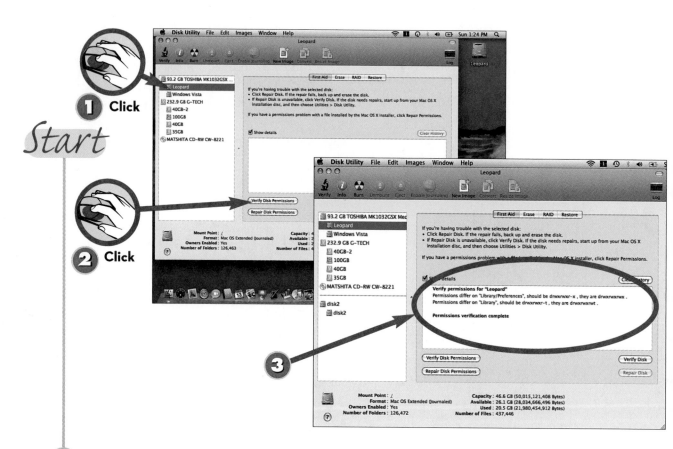

**1** Select the drive or a partition in the Disk Utility window.

**2** Click the **Verify Disk Permissions** button.

**3** View the results.

*Start*

*End*

-NOTE-

**Disk Permissions and the Boot Disk**

If you're not sure which disk to select to check permissions, choose the drive that contains Mac OS X. The OS X icon appears when a drive or partition is selected from the sidebar.

# CHECKING FOR SOFTWARE UPDATES

Software Updates contain bug fixes and security updates for Mac OS X and Apple's applications such as iLife, iWork, and so on. They are available for download from Apple's Web site. This task shows you how to review and install software updates for your Apple software with a Mac connected to the Internet.

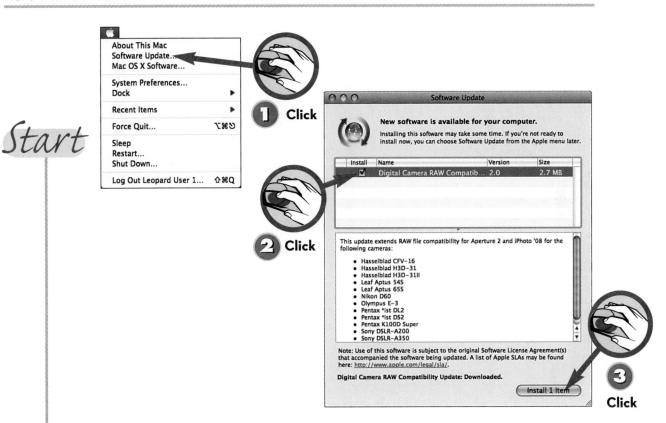

1. Click the **Apple** menu and choose **Software Update**. Review the software updates.

2. Select an update to view details about it. Check the update's check box to select it for download. Uncheck an update to ignore it.

3. Click the **Install** button.

## TIP
### Learn More About Mac OS X
To find out more about how to work with applications go to Part 4, "Installing and Using Applications."

## NOTE
### Update Third-Party Software
Software updates offered in Mac OX provide updates for any Apple software installed on your Mac. If you have third-party software installed, be sure to visit the product's website, such as Microsoft.com/macoffice, for the latest updates.

# MANUALLY INSTALLING SOFTWARE UPDATES

Apple offers software updates over the Internet periodically. You can also download them from Apple's website and install them manually. This task shows you how to install a Leopard update manually.

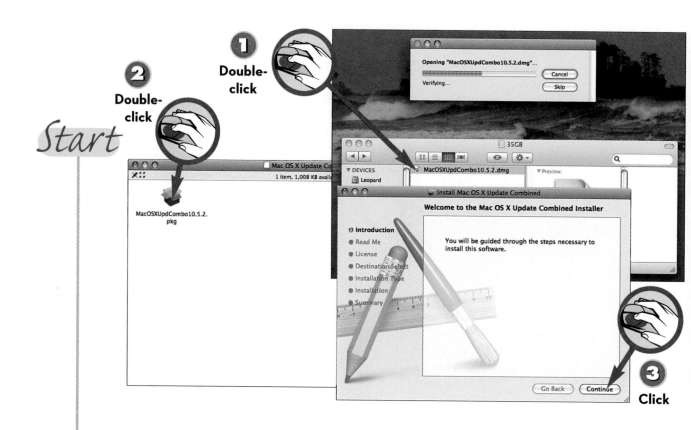

**1** Double-click the image file that contains the software update.

**2** Double-click the installer package.

**3** Click the **Continue** button. After the install completes, restart the Mac.

TIP

**Where to Find Updates**

Software updates that appear in the Software Update window are also available from Apple's website. Visit www.apple.com/support and search for the latest updates you might want to install manually.

# PARTITIONING A HARD DRIVE

Your Mac's hard drive is formatted as a single partition. If you have a means to back up your files, you can repartition your drive. When the drive is re-partitioned the drive is reformatted; all data is permanently removed from the drive. This task shows you how to view the partition information on your Mac. To reformat the internal hard drive, you must first start your Mac from an external drive or DVD.

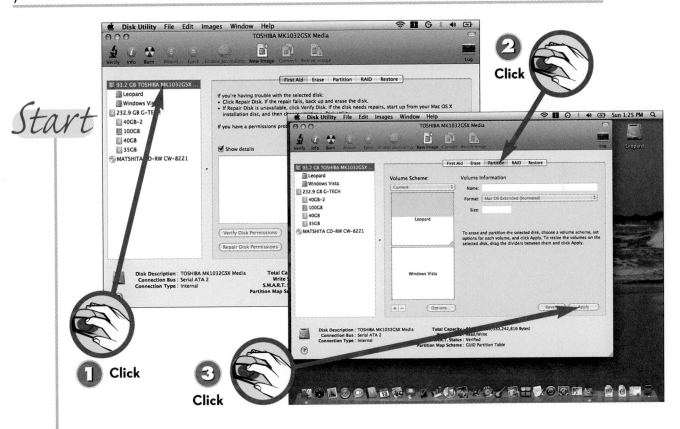

*Start*

**1** Click

**2** Click

**3** Click

**1** Select the hard drive.

**2** Click the **Partition** button. Change the number of partitions and the format for the drive.

**3** Click the **Apply** button.

*End*

**TIP**

## When to Partition

You cannot reformat the boot disk (the drive your Mac uses to run Mac OS). You must boot from a DVD or external drive in order to reformat or partition the Mac's internal drive. If you're planning to run windows with Boot Camp on your Mac, you must start with a disk with one or two partitions. If your Mac has more than two partitions Boot Camp won't work.

# SENDING CRASH REPORTS

Occasionally, an application may crash. When this happens, Mac OS X shows an alert for the application that quit unexpectedly. This task shows you how to send a crash report to Apple.

**Click** 1

*Start*

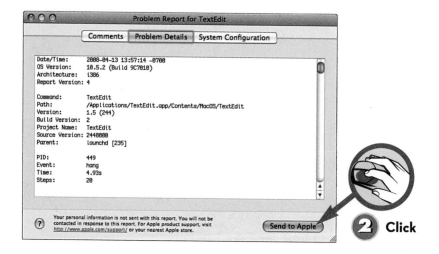

2 **Click**

1 When an application crashes, wait for the alert to appear. Click **Report** on the crash dialog.

2 Click the **Send to Apple** button.

*End*

**TIP**

### What's in a Crash?

When your Mac crashes, Mac OS X creates a crash log and displays it onscreen. The crash log contains the state of the machine when the crash occurs. When you click the Report button, the Problem Report window is created and contains the crash log. Clicking the Send to Apple button sends this information to Apple.

# RESETTING AN IPOD

Generally, iPods work pretty well. However, occasionally there is a need for a complete reset. For example, if your iPod stops responding to the click wheel, try resetting it. This task shows you how.

**①** Toggle Hold on/off

*Start*

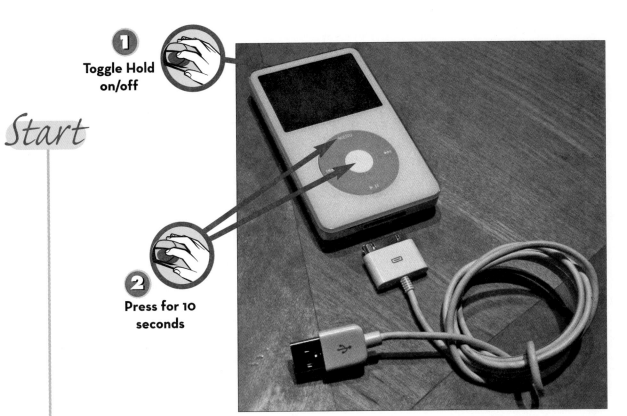

**②** Press for 10 seconds

**①** Toggle the iPod's Hold switch on and off.

**②** Hold down the center button and Menu buttons simultaneously on the click wheel for 10 seconds. Wait for the main menu to appear on the iPod.

*End*

 **TIP**
**Reset iPod contents**
For most iPods, choose **Settings** > **Reset Settings** from the iPod's menu to restore your iPod to its factory default settings. Go to support.apple.com/kb/HT1320 for a detailed list of iPods that support this.

 **TIP**
**Restore an iPod**
Click the **Restore** button in the Version section of iTunes to reset your iPod software to its factory settings.

# Index

*Index*

*Index*

*Index*

**FREE Online Edition**

Your purchase of **Easy Mac Computer Basics** includes access to a free online edition for 120 days through the Safari Books Online subscription service. Nearly every Que book is available online through Safari Books Online, along with over 5,000 other technical books and videos from publishers such as Addison-Wesley Professional, Cisco Press, Exam Cram, IBM Press, O'Reilly, Prentice Hall, and Sams.

**SAFARI BOOKS ONLINE** allows you to search for a specific answer, cut and paste code, download chapters, and stay current with emerging technologies.

## Activate your FREE Online Edition at www.informit.com/safarifree

> **STEP 1:** Enter the coupon code: ECJP-6PYK-HQ8S-3PKK-A5FL.

> **STEP 2:** New Safari users, complete the brief registration form. Safari subscribers, just log in.

If you have difficulty registering on Safari or accessing the online edition, please email customer-service@safaribooksonline.com